Cultures of Servitude

Cultures of Servitude

Modernity, Domesticity, and Class in India

Raka Ray ◆ Seemin Qayum

Stanford University Press
Stanford, California

Stanford University Press
Stanford, California

Printed in the United States of America on acid-free, archival-quality paper

Library of Congress Cataloging-in-Publication Data
Ray, Raka.
 Cultures of servitude : modernity, domesticity, and class in India / Raka Ray and Seemin Qayum.
    p. cm.
 Includes bibliographical references and index.
 ISBN 978-0-8047-6071-3 (cloth : alk. paper) -- ISBN 978-0-8047-6072-0 (pbk. : alk. paper)
 1. Domestics--India--History. 2. Master and servant--India--History. 3. Social classes--India--History. 4. India--Social conditions. I. Qayum, Seemin. II. Title.
  HD8039.D52.R39 2009
  640'.460954--dc22

                    2008046378

Typeset by Bruce Lundquist in 10/14 Minion

To our parents
Bharati and Sukhendu Ray
Ismat and Abdul Qayum
and the memories of our grandparents

Contents

Illustrations

Figures

Maps

Tables

Acknowledgments

THIS BOOK, which started as a dialogue between two friends, soon became a much larger conversation that involved virtually everyone we both know, so our gratitude to our friends, relatives, colleagues, and kind strangers is boundless and ineffable.

Above all we must acknowledge the employers and workers who so generously gave of their time and allowed us to listen to their stories, worries, and hopes. The employers often invited us into their homes and plied us with food and drink even as they submitted to our questions. The workers gave us the one thing they so lack—free time—often sacrificing their afternoon rest periods to talk to us, and generously introduced us to friends whom we could interview. This book could not have been written without the encouragement and sage counsel of Achin Kumar Pal, who not only recommended employers and servants we should interview but also enriched our daily lives in Kolkata immeasurably.

We would like to thank the following individuals for their expertise and guidance: Sukhendu Ray for his impeccable and illuminating translations; Bharati Ray for sharing with us her knowledge and wisdom about women's history in Bengal; Bela and Nripen Bandapadhay, Gautam Bhadra, Bonani Biswas, Monideep Chatterjee, Keya Dasgupta, Tanika and Sumit Sarkar, and Animesh Sen for invaluable advice and commentary on Kolkata; Ruprekha Chowdhury for photographs and translations; Professor Jyotirmoy Dasgupta for providing us with Bengali novels and short stories; Samir Dutt for locating material on colonial Calcutta; Sanjukta Ray for research documents and North Kolkata introductions; Dibyendu Law and Ramen Datta for kindly allowing us to photograph their home; Subimol Ghosh and Shakuntala Ghosh for help on urban development and land use; Anchita Ghatak and Mira Ray for information on Parichiti's work; Roya Razaghian, Nazanin Shahrokni, and Katherine Maich for research assistance; and the library staff of the Centre for Studies in Social Science Calcutta.

We are indebted to the exceptional Bela Bandapadhay who, with the help of Himangshu Chakrabarty and their team, conducted the survey and to Rama-prasad Bhattacharya for help with compiling the data.

Michael Burawoy and Sinclair Thomson have seen this manuscript develop from the very beginning and have been a constant source of guidance, criticism, and support; it is hard to put into words the extent of our gratitude to them. Barrie Thorne was kind enough to read the entire manuscript at the final stage and provide us with crucial encouragement and advice.

Many friends and colleagues have had to live with this book almost as long as we have, and we are grateful to them for engaging in multiple conversations with us, willingly reading drafts of chapters, and inviting us to share our work in various fora: Paul Willis, Fernanda Wanderley, Loïc Wacquant, Ruth Volgger, Steve Stern, Carolyn Steedman, K. Sivaramakrishnan, Rachel Sherman, Promita Sengupta, Gay Seidman, Francesca Scrinzi, Raffaella Sarti, Tanika Sarkar, Sumit Sarkar, Yasmin Saikia, Parama Roy, Ananya Roy, Amita Rodman, Silvia Rivera Cusicanqui, Rhacel Parreñas, Purnima Mankekar, Florencia Mallon, Nita Kumar, Mary John, Arlie Hochschild, Gill Hart, Olivia Harris, Akhil Gupta, Adolfo Gilly, Peter Evans, Megan Doolittle, Ineke Dibbits, Satish Deshpande, Leonore Davidoff, Bishakha Datta, Vasudha Dalmia, Nancy Chodorow, Nilanjana Chatterjee, Rossana Barragán, Ashok Bardhan, Anjali Arondekar, and Shireen Ally.

We have profited from the reception and discussion of our work presented at Bryn Mawr College, Centre for Women and Development Studies (Delhi), Claremont McKenna Colleges, Hobart and William Smith Colleges, Jawaharlal Nehru University, University of California at Berkeley, University of California at Davis, University of California at Los Angeles, University of California at Santa Barbara, University of Delaware, University of Delhi Institute of Economic Growth, University of Minnesota, University of Toronto, University of Washington, University of Wisconsin at Madison, and Yale University.

Conferences that have stimulated our thinking on this book include Feminist Interventions: Gender and History in South Asia, University of California at Santa Cruz (2001); Alternative Histories of the Family: Intimate Practices,

Subjectivities, and the State in Modern India conference, University of Michigan (2003); American Studies Association meetings in Atlanta (2004); Intimate Labors Conference, University of California at Santa Barbara (2007); ESSHC 2008 in Lisbon (2008); Waged Domestic Work and the Making of the Modern World Conference, University of Warwick (2008).

Our research was supported by funding from the Townsend Center for the Humanities, AIIS/National Endowment for the Humanities Senior Fellowship, and Faculty Research and Chancellor's Initiative Grants (University of California at Berkeley). Several chapter drafts were conceived and written during a joint residency at the Rockefeller Foundation Bellagio Center in 2006, a haven for scholarly writing and contemplation; we extend our thanks to the director, Pilar Palacia, and our fellow residents for a most enjoyable and productive stay.

We also wish to acknowledge the thoughtful and helpful reviews of our manuscript by Eileen Boris and an anonymous reader for Stanford University Press. At SUP, executive editor Kate Wahl, production editor Carolyn Brown, and copyeditor Cynthia Lindlof have seen this manuscript through expeditiously yet attentively. Jason Gordon of Berkeley's Cartography Lab produced the splendid maps. We are delighted to have one of the multitalented Naveen Kishore's Kolkata photographs on the cover.

While the two of us researched and wrote this book, we were sustained by the friendship and love of many wonderful people across four continents: in the United States and Europe, Hormuz Adrianwala and Farzine Parelwal, Kristin Barker, Godhuli Bose, Nilanjana Chatterjee and family, Ping Chong, Lisa Croen and family, Vasudha Dalmia, Shabi Farooq, Alfredo Ferrarin and Alessandra Fussi, Emily Katz and Eyad Kishawi, Shreeram Krishnaswami, Saba Mahmood and Charles Hirschkind, Marcella Marcimino, Janice Movson, Paul Rauber and Marian Mabel, Promita Sengupta, Sybil Taylor, and Vanessa Whang; in Bolivia, Rossana Barragán and family, Martha Cajías and clan, Pamela Calla and clan, Ineke Dibbits and family, Luis Gómez and Jean Friedman-Rudovsky, Jean Paul Guevara, Ana María Lema, Ximena Medinaceli, Dunia Mokrani, Silvia Rivera Cusicanqui, María Luisa Soux, Luis Tapia, the late Hernán Valencia, María Vargas, Ruth Volgger and family, Fernanda Wanderley, and Fabian Yaksic and the late Patricia Vera; and in India, Sukirat Anand and family, Lopa Banerjee and family, Madhushree Datta, Pronoti Deb, Nabaneeta Dev Sen, Anuradha Kapoor, Naveen Kishore, Dolly Narayan, Kavita Panjabi, and Nalini Swaika.

In Kolkata over many periods of research, we stayed with Raka's parents and brother, Sukhendu, Bharati, and Jishnu Ray, whose affection and concern for our well-being and research progress kept us going. They also allowed us to enter their social worlds, without which this portrait of Kolkata would not have been complete. We thank them for their extraordinary hospitality and generosity and for doing everything within their power to make our research possible.

Kabir has been a delightful presence in the last stages of writing this book, and his parents, Isha Ray and Jitendra Malik, provide a constant haven in Berkeley.

Finally, Ashok Bardhan and Sinclair Thomson for all the reasons they know.

Cultures of Servitude

1 Approaching Servitude in Kolkata

Types of work that are consumed as services and not in products separable from the worker, and not capable of existing as commodities independently of him . . . are of microscopic significance when compared with the mass of capitalist production.
They may be entirely neglected, therefore.

Karl Marx, *Capital*

IN AN ICONIC SCENE in *Aparajito*, the second film of Satyajit Ray's *Apu Trilogy*, the destitute Brahmin widow Sarbajaya watches her son being led into servitude.[1] She has recently obtained work as a cook in the household of a rich Brahmin, where her employers are both considerate and inconsiderate in the manner of feudal lords. In a previous scene, for example, the mistress of the house casually assumes that Sarbajaya should be willing to move to a different town with the household.[2] In this scene, Sarbajaya is shown observing from the top of the stairs as the master of the house sends for her son, Apu, to light his pipe and tells Apu to pluck gray hairs from his head, for which Apu receives a tip. The screenplay notes that "[s]he frowns as she slowly comes down the stairs again."[3] In the next scene, we see Sarbajaya and her son on a train, having left the job behind.

Sarbajaya's expression as she observes the master with Apu conveys that nothing could be more heart wrenching and sobering than watching one's son become a servant. We mention "son" here deliberately because it is not clear that Sarbajaya's reaction would have been quite as strong in the case of a daughter. Indeed, in the first film of the trilogy, *Pather Panchali*, the daughter, Durga (who dies at the end of the film), is shown at the service of her little brother, Apu, looking after him, feeding him, and ultimately being responsible for his well-being. Durga was born to serve in one way or another, unlike Apu, the Brahmin son, whose caste and gender combine to hold the promise of higher things. Notwithstanding the conventional correspondence between servants' work and women's work that Sarbajaya represents, in the eyes of the masters an Apu would be just as suitable as a Durga to become a servant.

We as viewers can apprehend key insights from Sarbajaya's observation of Apu. First, although certain groups may be considered more appropriately or "naturally" servants, class—poverty and inequality in this case—more than caste or gender frames the potentiality of becoming a servant or being born a servant. Second, there are demeaning behaviors and expectations associated with a relationship of servitude that Sarbajaya silently declines to accept and departs jobless rather than have her son absorb. Domestic servitude is undeniably stigmatized, as the film shows, while also a normal and ingrained element of household life.

This book began as an attempt to think about an institution that lies at the bedrock of Indian domestic middle- and upper-class existence, yet it soon became an inquiry into not only the characteristics of domestic servitude historically and culturally but also the constitution of the classes on both sides of the employer-servant relationship. Domestic servitude, principally but not exclusively paid domestic work, became a dense site for us, the examination of which could illuminate the very constitution of society. In the spirit of Tanika Sarkar's work on nineteenth-century Bengal, and Leonore Davidoff's work on Victorian England, with their insistence on seeing the public sphere as integrally related to the domestic, this book conceives of the relations within the household as a microcosm of the rules and comportment of societies, with the institution of domestic servitude providing a powerful lens through which to view social constitution and reconstitution over time.[4] Particularly in societies like that of India, with long, unbroken histories of domestic servitude, the institution can be seen as central to understanding self and society.[5] As we argue in this book, the relations of paid domestic work and servitude in India are intimately tied to the self-conscious evolution of a "modern" Indian elite. Through evolving techniques of servant and home management, employers produce themselves as the class destined to lead India to modernity, and servants as a distinct class, premodern and dependent on the middle and upper classes for their well-being. This book explores the relations of servitude in India's recent past and present, what it means to serve and to be served, and through the lens of servitude seeks to understand contemporary Indian conceptions of domesticity, class, and modernity.

Domestic servitude when considered as a historically constructed labor relation in Kolkata (formerly Calcutta), the space chosen for our exploration, requires us to look more closely at the conditions and changes in Kolkata's political economy, its history as a colonial city, rapidly transforming urban landscapes, and complex gender regimes over the past decades and generations. Yet as we foreground the home as a site where relations of class, gender, and caste/ race are produced and reproduced through the particular labor practices of domestic servitude, we find that these relations and practices are singular indeed. Home is not a jute mill, an apparel sweatshop, a company office, a rice paddy, or a street stall. We suggest that this distinction inheres in both the nature of the labor and the site of labor.

Domestic servitude confuses and complicates the conceptual divide between family and work, custom and contract, affection and duty, the home and the world precisely because the hierarchical arrangements and emotional registers of home and family must coexist with those of workplace and contract in a capitalist world.[6] This uneasy inhabitation privileges domestic servitude analytically. Because it encompasses and is realized through differences of gender, race/caste, class, and power in the home, we must consider how these differences and their attendant emotional valences dialectically produce and reproduce the relations of servitude. Examining domestic servitude enables us, following the work of Arlie Hochschild and Andrew Sayer, to address the complex emotional and moral textures of quotidian relationships of inequality.[7] Thus, we elaborate the contours of a "culture of servitude," within which and shaped by which both employers and servants, as individuals and classes, conduct daily life.

Culture of Servitude

A culture of servitude is one in which social relations of domination/subordination, dependency, and inequality are normalized and permeate both the domestic and public spheres. Our use of "culture" refers to the interconnected realms of consciousness and practice and necessarily encompasses the dimension of power. We recognize, following Raymond Williams, that while the concept of "culture" has often been used in ways that do not adequately take into account power relations and inequalities, the category of "ideology" explicitly recognizes the dynamics of class power. However, "culture" does have advantages over "ideology," where ideology is understood as a system of meanings and values that constitutes particular class interests, in that culture involves a total lived process not only of consciousness but also of experience and practice. For Williams, the Gramscian category that integrates and goes beyond these two concepts is "hegemony."

> It sees the relationship of domination and subordination, in their forms as practical consciousness, as in effect a saturation of the whole process of living—not

only of political and economic activity, nor only of manifest social activity, but of the whole substance of lived identities and relationships, to such a depth that the pressures and limits of what can ultimately be seen as a specific economic, political, and cultural system seem to most of us the pressures and limits of simple experience and common sense. . . . It is a whole body of practices and expectations, over the whole of living: our senses and assignments of energy, our shaping perceptions of ourselves and our world. It is a lived system of meanings and values—constitutive and constituting—which as they are experienced as practices appear as reciprocally confirming.[8]

The concept of culture of servitude aligns closely with hegemony because it treats the total social process of experience and consciousness in terms of power. As Williams puts it, hegemony "is in the strongest sense a 'culture,' but a culture which has also to be seen as the lived dominance and subordination of particular classes."[9]

Throughout this book we employ the concept "servitude" to capture the persistence of forms of dependency and submission in relations of what is today, for the most part, paid domestic work.[10] We treat the nexus of labor relations that is domestic servitude as an institution rather than as an occupational category, as would be implied by the terms "domestic service" or "domestic work." We use "servant" because of its popular usage in India. Even though the Bengali term *chakor* (servant) has been, by and large, replaced by the term *kajer lok* (person who works), the English words *servant* and *maidservant* have not been replaced by some equivalent of "paid domestic worker."

By "normalized" we mean, first, that these social relations are legitimized ideologically such that domination, dependency, and inequality are not only tolerated but accepted; and second, that they are reproduced through everyday social interaction and practice. Those living in a particular culture of servitude accept it as the given order of things, the way of the world and of the home. A culture of servitude is akin in some respects to Pierre Bourdieu's *habitus*, "a structuring structure, which organizes practices and the perception of practices."[11] Bourdieu suggests that not only does habitus organize practices and their perception but also converts these perceptions and practices into internalized dispositions. In a culture of servitude, servitude is normalized so that it is virtually impossible to imagine life without it, and practices, and thoughts and feelings about practices, are patterned on it.[12]

The culture of servitude is also a matter of collective patterns of subjectivity.

For a deeper understanding of such inhabitations, we have turned to Williams's notion of "structure of feeling." Williams comments, "The term is difficult, but 'feeling' is chosen to emphasize a distinction from more formal concepts of 'world-view' or 'ideology.' . . . It is that we are concerned with meanings and values as they are actively lived and felt." He elsewhere notes, "In one sense, this structure of feeling is the culture of a period: it is the particular living result of all the elements in the general organisation."[13] Thus, by culture of servitude we also mean the structure of feeling associated with the institution and relations of domestic servitude that is produced by the confluence of historical material conditions and prevailing social organization.

The structure of feeling, then, reflects the mutually dependent subjectivities of masters and servants. Ann Rubbo and Michael Taussig have noted that servanthood envelops servants "into the bosom of the employing family as part-employee and part-family, producing a dependent personality . . . and aids and abets the mystification of exploitation." However, we decline to go along with their one-sided view of the servant's dependent personality, and even less with their approval of Emily Nett's statement that "the *servant* is the genetic carrier of the colonial patron-client relationship" (emphasis added).[14] We opt for a reading of the dialectics of dependency and power in these fundamentally unequal relationships, where the subjectivity of each actor is shaped and informed by the other. Hegel's lordship-bondage/master-slave dialectic attempts to explain the unfolding of human consciousness and history, but it can also illuminate the particular mimetic relation at hand: "One is the independent consciousness whose essential nature is to be for itself, the other is the dependent consciousness whose essential nature is simply to live or to be for another. The former is lord, the other is bondsman. . . . The truth of the independent consciousness is accordingly the servile consciousness of the bondsman."[15] The slave exists to labor for the master and to affirm the master's reality and humanity. Thus, the master is perversely dependent on the slave, and the relation of domination seems to be inverted. In Alexandre Kojève's reading of Hegel, precisely because the master does not recognize the slave's human reality and dignity, the slave's recognition of the master is always insufficient for the master.[16] Frantz Fanon's engagement with the Hegelian master-slave dialectic follows Kojève in important respects, especially the absence of mutual recognition, but crucially incorporates race and the colonial condition, which paralyze reciprocal recognition. In a trenchant footnote in *Black Skin, White Masks*, Fanon categorically refutes the possibility of reciprocity across the colonial and racial divide: Within colonialism, the slave needs the master's recognition, but the master only wants labor—not recognition—from the slave and dismisses the slave's consciousness.[17] Although we would argue that labor and recognition are both in play for the master, these debates are important because they bring to the fore the relationship of domination, dependency, and inequality that lies at the heart of the culture of servitude and that complexly constitutes both servant and master.

Although the core of the culture of servitude is, of course, the employer-servant relationship, its effects are wider and diffused through both the domestic and public spheres. In this book, we explore the workings of domination, dependency, and inequality in the intimate realms of the household, the family, and subjective consciousness. Even though we privilege the site of the household and home, this is a study of class relations and their reproduction that has broader implications for the social formation. The practices, dispositions, and feelings that inhere in cultures of servitude structure the social world, and thus cultures of servitude are vital to the constitution of both self and society. Indeed, we argue, they shape the way classes come into their own. We engage with precisely the "microscopic" relations that Marx dismissed (see epigraph), and posit that the macroscopic relations of exploitation that interested Marx are rooted in the dialectics of the day-to-day and the intimacies of power that are the subject of this book.

Culture of Servitude in Kolkata

Kolkata, a major metropolis of South Asia and once the colonial capital of British India, has been an intellectual and cultural center for social reform, nationalist, and labor politics for much of the nineteenth and twentieth centuries and, as such, a fascinating case for explorations of class formation, labor relations, and discourses of modernity. Kolkata's location in the state of West Bengal (see Map 1 on page 28), which has the largest proportion of servants of any state in India according to the 1991 census (the latest census data available for this occupation), coupled with the presence of different kinds of servants and types of households, makes it a prime site for understanding domestic servitude.

Kolkata's culture of servitude exists in the interstices of two dominant social imaginaries: feudal and modern. We borrow the term "social imaginaries" from Charles Taylor to connote the ways in which ordinary people imagine their social existence and relationships with others, as well as the "deeper normative notions and images" that underlie the expectations they have from others.[18]

The social imaginary "supposes . . . a wider grasp of our whole predicament: how we stand to each other, how we got to where we are, how we relate to other groups and so on."[19] Employer social imaginaries thus encompass a social order in which classes interact in specific ways and in specific places.

We use the term "feudal" because employers and, in fact, most middle- and upper-class people in Kolkata, constantly use the term to summon up the past—in contrast to the "modern" present. As schematized in Table 1.1, the feudal imaginary refers to a lost colonial world in which employers' income was from land rents derived from rural estates, and several generations of a family lived together in one house, usually under the authority of a patriarch. Ideally, the income from the land was enough to keep the family in comfort. The servants of such a family also came from the land, that is, from villages associated with those rural estates and from tenant families who would work for the employing family for generations. The relations between employer and servant were based on loyalty and obligation, and the employer acted as patron to the servant and his family. The servant in this picture lived with the family and was typically male, the quintessential family retainer. The feudal imaginary is both an ever-present source of nostalgia and a mode of being the middle classes believe properly belongs to the past.

The modern imaginary encompasses the universe employers believe, for better or for worse, they *ought* to inhabit today—a social order still taking shape, whose contours are being uneasily but pragmatically filled—where employers no longer live off the land but are employed by the state or private enterprises and live in apartments rather than mansions. The joint families of the past are nucleated, and relationships with servants—now typically female, live-out,

Table 1.1 Elements of feudal and modern imaginaries

	Feudal	*Modern*
Home	Big house	Flat or apartment
Economy	Land based/government administration	Manufacturing based/finance
Family	Joint family	Nucleated family
Servant	Male family retainer	Female/part-time/live-out
Basis of employer-servant relationship	Loyalty, affective ties, mutual obligation	Contract

and often part-time—are based on the wage contract. As we will explicate in this book, Kolkata's culture of servitude is powerfully shaped by three premises with origins in the feudal imaginary. First, servants are essential to a well-run and well-kept household; second, servants are "part of the family" and bound to it by ties of affection, loyalty, and dependence; and third, servants constitute a class with distinctive lifestyles, desires, and habits. It is in the ideological and metaphorical interplay between the social imaginary of the feudal and modern that Kolkata's culture of servitude has developed.

Servants and Employers under Study

There is now widespread agreement that Lewis Coser was wrong when he predicted the obsolescence of the occupation of "servant" in 1973.[20] Recent studies of domestic work as an occupation around the world have made clear that domestic servitude, far from being an antiquated institution pertaining to feudal and undemocratic pasts, is an essential and thriving element of societies in the formerly colonial world of the South and has reemerged in the affluent, capitalist countries of the North. Indeed, it is increasingly recognized that domestic workers help keep the contemporary economy running.[21] The lives of the global middle and affluent classes are structured on the basis of this often invisible but ubiquitous labor.

Two intersecting themes in the literature on paid domestic work have emerged in the past decade. One highlights the effects of immigration and globalization on the structure of paid domestic work in receiving countries and the place of this institution in a newly globalized and unequal world order. The concerns that motivate this literature stem from the gendered and racialized dimensions of the migration of third world women to the first world, the effects of the care crises in global cities on the third world, the transfers of care from third world to first world, and the vulnerability of noncitizen immigrants working in private homes.[22] The second theme stems from a more domestic concern with the child-care arrangements of dual-career couples in the contemporary United States and England.[23] These researchers examine the relationships between parents, children, and child-care workers to reflect on the relationship between work and family under advanced industrialized capitalism; they study the private child-care arrangements professional women make in the absence of public policies and the concept of "care as an emotion freed from labour."[24] This literature also reflects the corresponding anxieties around the enactment of economic transactions in the intimate space of the home.[25]

This book diverges from and contributes to the literature in three significant ways. First, with a few exceptions, the literature focuses on the effects of the contemporary care "crisis" in advanced industrialized countries on global circuits of care. In other words, the literature is based on an assumption that the increased labor-force participation of middle-class and affluent women in the North has led to a care crisis and thus to the increased reliance on imported labor to perform cleaning and child-care work. The institution, relationships, and arrangements of paid domestic work are thus treated as new phenomena—or a return to old. Our study departs from this assumption of paid domestic work as a response to a new need by focusing on a country with a relatively low women's labor-force participation (11.9 percent in urban India) and in which domestic service has a very long history.[26] In other words, in India, there is no necessary relationship between the employment of domestic servants and middle-class women's labor-force participation. This difference enables us to shift the conversation from one about the *actual* needs of two-career couples to the *assumption* of household needs that underscores the hiring of domestic workers. If, as Ruth Milkman and her colleagues have so convincingly shown, the presence of domestic workers is directly correlated with inequality, and if domestic workers exist in overwhelming numbers in countries where the employing woman does not, in fact, work outside the home, then the *need* for domestic workers must be conceived of and analyzed differently.[27] What, then, is at the root of the felt need for domestic workers?

In India the hiring of domestic workers is not restricted to the affluent classes but extends to the middle and even lower-middle classes. Given this, we argue that domestic workers in India not only perform undesirable work traditionally in the purview of the women of the household, but in so doing, make it possible for employers to aspire to and maintain middle-class status. In other words, the ability to transfer reproductive work to a lower class can be seen as a hallmark of the Indian middle classes. In managing households with servants, the Indian middle classes reproduce as normal an unequal society in which groups naturally divide along class lines and in which lower classes naturally serve the higher classes. Employers act as though class divisions are immutable while striving to constantly re-create class inequality.[28] In particular, employers enact the immutability of class through discourses and labor practices at home, ordering of space, refusal to engage in manual work, assumption of control over the labor of others, and perception of servants as being distinctive, even as employers struggle to maintain such a perception. Yet, as we shall see, employers are not able to rest easy, confident in their class distinction; rather, they continually engage in acts of boundary creation and maintenance to assure their class status.[29] Sara Dickey's exploration of the mutual moral critiques offered by both servant and employer classes in the southern Indian town of Madurai is an excellent example of such boundary-maintaining work.[30] Domestic servitude, then, must be seen as an institution that produces cleanliness, meals, and child care, as well as class. Precisely because of the centrality of domestic servitude to the existence of the middle classes in India, we argue that it illuminates processes of class formation and understandings of modernity and domesticity.

Second, whereas the recent literature tends to focus on workers who have immigrated to the countries in which they now work, this book highlights the insecurity of in-country migrants, a theme that once preoccupied earlier scholars of paid domestic work in Latin America but from which the literature has turned away.[31] Most migration, in fact, takes place within a country; although there is no doubt that not having citizenship adds a layer of vulnerability, rural migrants who move to urban areas in search of better livelihoods, in contrast to the migrants who, for example, leave the Philippines for distant shores, are some of the most vulnerable populations, and their lives are precariously close to the edge. These are not transnational workers who pay others at home to look after their children. These are workers who are unable to find any other work and depend on domestic service employment to be able to feed themselves and their children.[32] In the words of one of the servants with whom we spoke, a migrant from rural West Bengal to Kolkata, they "float in a sea of nothingness." They are long-term victims of economic decline and failure of land reform who have been hurt, not helped, by present policies of liberalization. Our analysis of in-country migrant domestic servants acknowledges but sets aside the particular vulnerability to which transnational migrant workers are exposed and thereby clarifies the vulnerabilities of all domestic workers.[33]

Third, since domestic workers in much of the world today are primarily female, domestic service has appeared to be synonymous with women's work in recent research.[34] Karen Hansen's study on Zambia is among the few to discuss male servants, as servants have traditionally been men in many parts of Africa.[35] Precisely because the "domestic" is seen as a distinctively female realm, the presence of men questions the assumption of the gendered separation of spheres. Although domestic servants in India have historically been both male and female, women and children have begun to dominate their ranks over the past decades, reflecting both the secular trend toward more female labor-force employment and the worsening of economic inequality.[36] We focus on both men and women servants in India and are thus able to examine the complex, class-inflected notions of masculinity and femininity at play that might otherwise go unremarked.

Feudalism, Capitalism, and Domestic Work

The extent to which domestic service is organized within feudal or capitalist labor relations implicitly informs much of the scholarship in this field. Writing about contemporary Chile, Patricia Tomic and colleagues argue that "[d]omestic work in Chile is very much characterized by a kind of latifundia social relation—relations of subordination and reciprocity rooted in the rural hacienda system that dominated the Chilean countryside until the Agrarian Reform in the 1960s and early 1970s."[37]

In turn, Mary Romero insists that the situation differs in the United States:

> Feudal relations between master and servant no longer exist. We live in a relentlessly capitalist society, and while paternalism and maternalism may resemble feudalistic relationships, this level of analysis serves only to conceal real sources of exploitation. . . . Servitude and paternalism . . . are not a vestige of feudalistic relationships but are exploitative characteristics used within the capitalist mode of production. Domestic service must be analyzed as a sphere of capitalist production in which race and gender are played out.[38]

At issue is the relationship of the larger field of economic relations to domestic work and whether there is something distinctive about domestic work that renders it external to a capitalist work dynamic despite its existence in a capitalist society. Thus, Tomic and her colleagues argue that in Chile, domestic work is still characterized by a mode of production that began to disappear decades ago. In contrast, Romero advocates for the position that domestic work in the United States should be seen as a race- and gender-inflected capitalist relation. Romero asserts that "[a]lthough the labor process in domestic service is somewhat different from that found in other work settings, domestics are engaged in battles similar to those of other employees."[39]

The debate in India focuses on a specific form of this discussion—whether the caste model or the class model should be used to understand relations of domestic servitude. The caste model usually refers to *jajmani* relationships, where families belonging to particular castes—barbers, potters, *dhobis* (washermen)—provided their labor services in return for a fixed supply of grain or protection from other castes in the village.[40] Related to this model, Susan Bayly writes that "everyday domestic service still commonly draws on caste-defined specialisms,"[41] while V. Tellis-Nayak finds that a patron-client model is the most appropriate framework within which to understand the institution. The class model has traditionally seen the institution as one characterized by capitalist labor exploitation. Such discussions are often folded into larger concerns about the unorganized or informal sector, the most vulnerable sector within a capitalist economy with its low wages and insecure employment, and do not foreground the site or the specificity of the work that is being performed.[42]

We would contend that while different histories of agrarian relations and capitalist development must be taken into consideration, domestic work does not map easily onto conventional understandings of labor relations under either capitalism or feudalism. We thus agree with Pierrette Hondagneu-Sotelo's assessment that domestic work is not the same as other labor, even when performed in a country undoubtedly marked by high capitalism, based on her analysis of paid domestic work in the contemporary United States as governed by "parallel and interacting networks of women of different classes, ethnicities, and citizenship status who meet in multiple worksites in isolated pairs." In other words, domestic service is different from other work (such as in the service sector or in factories) because it is not formally regulated and because it takes place in private homes away from the gaze of the collectivity.[43] Writing about Zambia and colonial Bengal, respectively, Hansen and Swapna Banerjee make a similar claim.[44] Our analysis highlights both the home as a singular site of labor and the nature of the labor itself and is embedded in historically nuanced understandings of the structure of feeling of home and domesticity.

If we return to Coser's claim about the obsolescence of the occupation, we can see that he assumed an incompatibility between domestic servitude and "modernity." Much of contemporary popular literature in the North on domestic workers reflects the unease with the "return" of an occupation and social relation seemingly at odds with life in a "modern," democratic, postfeminist world, especially for the generations that came of age in the period between the 1960s and 1990s when servant-keeping had declined.[45] Some of this literature provides helpful tips to new or first-time employers on how to manage this unease—how to handle one's domestic worker, what tasks it is appropriate to ask her to perform, and what to pay her.[46] Thus, we see a veritable industry of advice books, not unlike those issued in the late nineteenth century in countries such as the United States, Britain, and India to teach women how best to manage their households and domestic help.[47] The appearance of such books and articles in twenty-first-century Britain and the United States highlights the assumed contradiction between being modern and being an employer of domestics. Nevertheless, it is abundantly clear that increasing numbers of people who can afford to do so in fact hire (cheap) labor to clean up after themselves and look after their children. The point of this advice is to assure contemporary employers that it is perfectly acceptable, indeed practical and sensible, to hire nannies or housekeepers, as long as employers are able to manage them appropriately. As the U.K. *Guardian* enthuses, "There are now more than 100,000 nannies in Britain, the highest number ever. They can be a cheap and flexible option for ordinary working parents . . . so there's no need to be embarrassed about having one."[48] Servants were once considered a luxury accessible only to the wealthy, but increasing class inequality, in part based on waves of immigrants obliged to work for low wages, has meant that middle-class Londoners and New Yorkers have access as perhaps never before to domestic workers while new discourses attempt to assuage the more problematic aspects of the incorporation of servants into the home and make it a modern necessity.

In contemporary India, keeping servants is not seen as contradictory to capitalist modernity, and no justification is needed for hiring domestic workers. Rather, in an odd reversal, the middle-class households without servants are those that feel compelled to justify their position.[49] What the middle classes debate is how to manage households and servants, and in the employer imaginary, there are two types of management practices: (more or less) feudal and (more or less) modern. Before we turn to these domestic practices, we first locate the Indian middle classes historically.

The Middle Classes of India

> And then there is the *"middle class,"* which is no more susceptible of precise definition in the Indian context than it is anywhere else in the world, but which surely includes increasing numbers of highly paid professional people, managers and executives, white collar workers, and intellectuals—and the mass of petty traders and producers, as well—and which is certainly of ever increasing significance though its actual size and precise boundaries are very hard to determine.
>
> **John Harriss, "Middle- Class Activism"**

The contradictory class location of the middle classes in general, and of the Indian middle classes in particular, has occupied considerable scholarly attention. In analyses of the Indian middle class two questions seem to excite the most attention. The first has to do with the definition of "middle class," a term that has its origins in a very different social formation, as well as its potentially mediating function in democracy. The second and more recent question has to do with what is variously called the "new" or "emerging" middle classes— in short, the middle classes of a liberalizing India. It is not our intention here to rehearse the scholarly debates but rather to understand the relation of the middle classes to notions of domesticity and modernity.

What is now called the "old middle class" in India was in essence the nationalist vanguard, which William Mazzarella aptly describes as "a Nehruvian civil service–oriented salariat, short on money but long on institutional perks."[50] The Nehruvian developmentalist state relied on planning and incremental reforms rather than on attempting to transform property relations to move toward a socialist-inflected capitalist economy. In this regime, the state and the middle-class managers of the state played a vital role. The dominant fraction of the middle classes readily took on the managerial direction of the state, as it had already occupied the colonial civil service. Moreover, its leadership in the nationalist movement secured the necessary legitimacy to continue to "represent" the nation.

In contrast to this nationalist middle class, the "new" middle class in the post-1991 liberalization period is the class about whose members business guru Gurcharan Das says admiringly that they know what they want and how to get it.[51] This is a newly aspirational middle class about which much has been written and around which election campaigns are crafted.[52] In the language of political economy, however, we can recognize that the new middle class derives its power not from the state but from the market.[53] Yet debate rages about the size and composition of the middle class—50 million or 250 million?[54] Is this class finally and truly a "middle" class?

Despite the increase in numbers, it is clear that this middle class is not technically in the middle of the class spectrum. Indeed, Satish Deshpande has effectively shown through an analysis of National Sample Survey and National Council of Applied Economic Research data that the Indian middle class may be a large class by world standards in terms of sheer numbers but is in fact a very small proportion of the Indian population. If the middle class represents, as it is popularly called, the "common man," then this common man belongs to the top 10 or 15 percent in terms of income distribution.[55]

If the middle class cannot be defined numerically and somehow falls at the elite end of the income spectrum, then what makes it such? One alternative definition Deshpande offers, following Gramsci, is that the "middle class is the class that *articulates* the hegemony of the ruling bloc; it both (a) *expresses* this hegemony by translating the relations of domination into the language of legitimation; and (b) *mediates* the relationship between classes within the ruling bloc, as well as between this bloc and other classes." Indeed, Deshpande argues, the middle classes can be differentiated into the elite fraction that produces ideologies and the mass fraction that consumes them.[56] In line with this analysis, our use of "Indian middle classes" refers to this broad understanding that covers both fractions, unless otherwise specified.

To locate the mechanisms that the middle classes use to sustain their dominance, most discussions target the institutions of the public sphere—in politics, education, and the media. John Harriss, as well as Leela Fernandes and Patrick Heller, argue that the middle classes practice certain methods of exclusion in the civil sphere and politics that reaffirm their supremacy while ensuring the boundaries separating them from the lower classes remain continually drawn.[57] Amita Baviskar's analysis of bourgeois environmentalism brilliantly articulates the new exclusionary politics of city beautification campaigns.[58] Nita Kumar's work examines exclusionary elite and middle-class modes of schooling.[59] In this book, we look closely at the household as a key institution through which these exclusionary hegemonic ideologies are produced and consumed.

The middle class sees itself as the most legitimate representative of the nation; to understand what enables it to claim this class attribute, Deshpande turns to Bourdieu. This class, he suggests, is above all dependent on possession of cultural capital for its continued existence. Cultural capital is its property, invisible though it may appear as property. These middle-class possessors of cultural and educational capital continued to expand their powers and their position through the heyday of the Nehruvian state, and, in the words of Fernandes and Heller, "From this pivotal role, the middle class developed distinctive political claims that elevated their class interests to the universal interest and laid claim to a leading role within the ruling hegemonic bloc within the newly founded Indian nation."[60]

Even as the middle classes were assumed to be speaking on behalf of the new nation, they were assiduously engaged in particular projects of modernity alongside the larger national projects of industrial and technological development. Such an engagement was pursued by many newly independent nations precisely because they had been consigned, as it were, to the "waiting room" of modernity, perhaps indefinitely.[61] But modernity, as Sudipta Kaviraj argues, was not written on a "clean slate"; thus, modernity can never be homogeneous

explore

and takes on multiple meanings in different historical spaces.[62] In the Indian context, it has its particular sources and trajectories, and an ambivalent relationship to the notions of modernity in Europe and the United States.[63] Indeed, what is thought of as traditional in the sense of predating or being antithetical to modernity can be usefully seen as one of the inventions of modernity, and the battle between tradition and modernity itself a product of modernity. To be "modern" in postcolonial India is to align oneself with projects such as development, science, progress, invention, and discovery; in turn, to be "traditional" means to react negatively to such aspirations to modernity, to perhaps reject the terms of the debate, yet often make alternative claims couched in the language of modernity.[64]

We wish to stress two points regarding the debate about modernity. First, while for the reasons highlighted previously, the aspiration to modernity is of great significance to the Indian middle classes for whom it is a self-conscious project in this globalizing age, our interest is not in the existence or nonexistence of modernity per se but in the power of the *idea* of modernity. In other words, we use "modernity"—and "feudalism"—as folk categories of considerable power. We note also that the modernity imagined and desired in India is both similar to and yet distinct from the imagined modernity of the North. Second, projects of modernity are not limited to the public sphere and to the institutions of education, politics, and the economy but, crucially, reach the home. From the late nineteenth century onward, social reform projects, initiated by both colonial authorities and Indians, targeted the "modernization" of Indian society and particularly aimed for "improvement" in the domestic sphere. Such domestic reforms, including the passage of legislation regulating marriage and allowing widows to remarry and the establishment of fields of inquiry and teaching such as "home science," attempted to introduce so-called modern principles of management to the home.[65] The home, it was asserted, was inextricably linked to the nation, and the scientific and rational management of the home was thus linked to the creation of a scientific and rational nation. Given this history, it is not surprising that today's purportedly modern practices of the home matter to the Indian middle classes.

The Middle Classes at Home

The home, household, and family are by now widely recognized for their role in the production of gender inequality, but much less so for class and other inequalities. Only in the recent studies on domestic work has the home been increasingly seen as the site of both gender inequality and class inequality.[66] Domestic servitude bridges the domestic-public divide, bringing social relations of power (class, caste, race/ethnicity, gender) into the household and mirroring and reproducing these relations within the domestic unit. Feminist theorists have firmly established the links between power, domination, and conflict in the domestic and public spheres by analyzing the relations between husband and wife, and parents and children, in the household as a means of demonstrating the structural link between capitalism and patriarchy, and as a way of problematizing "women's work"—both unpaid housework and paid employment outside the home.[67] Once the household is recognized as a site of unequal power, then it becomes possible to examine it as a site of unequal class and caste relations by bringing into the analysis relations between family members and dependent labor paid to work within the home, that is, servants.[68] As such, the labor performed by the women of the household has a very different meaning from the labor they supervise that is performed by poor and/or low-caste men and women.[69]

Debates over domesticity and the proper place of women and servants in the Indian household arose simultaneously with the middle class in the second half of the nineteenth century. Indeed, Tanika Sarkar points out that the contest over the appropriate form of domestic life was very publicly played out in colonial India. Partha Chatterjee shows how Indian middle-class men, sidelined in the public sphere by colonial rule and colonial administration, sought to control women and the domestic sphere, effectively substituting the home for the world.[70] Swapna Banerjee argues that the new Bengali middle class in the late nineteenth century articulated its class identity through a "conscious distancing from the 'other,' the lower social classes," and that, following Meredith Borthwick, the "proliferation of servants in the late colonial period was symptomatic of the desire of the Bengali middle class to acquire class status and mastery over subordinate groups."[71]

This book, in turn, examines class formation and reproduction through domestic practices a century after the emergence of the Bengali middle classes and identifies the mechanisms by which class difference is created and maintained. Just as servants are a marker of middle-class status, so is the patriarchal ability to maintain household income without women working outside the home. We have noted that India is a country with a relatively low women's labor-force participation rate. Indeed, employment of women in postcolonial India follows a classic curve with poor women and women with postgraduate degrees (obviously a tiny minority) tending to work outside the home. A sign of a family moving up the class or caste ladder is the ability to pull women back into the home, to labor within rather than outside it. Moreover, the "othering" by sexualizing women who work outside the home has been used to draw boundaries of class difference in India and is, as we shall see, an issue that resonates across class.[72]

The pioneering studies of Mary Douglas and Davidoff help clarify what makes domestic work distinctive for class constitution and class boundaries.[73] The core activities of cooking, cleaning, and child care involve managing order and disorder, dealing with hygiene and refuse, and turning the raw into the cooked. In Davidoff's words,

> In the most basic sense, housework is concerned with creating and maintaining order in the immediate environment, making meaningful patterns of activities, people and materials. The most important part in the creation of such an order is the separating out of the basic constituents and making clear the boundaries between them.[74]

The ability to be free from having to maintain these boundaries is, Davidoff argues, a sign of one's power and privilege. That is, to be middle class is to distance oneself from work on the boundaries of purity and pollution. To be middle class and male is to remove oneself even further from such boundary maintenance.

Davidoff argues that domestic service performed different functions in affluent and less affluent households in Victorian England. In affluent households, domestics performed rituals of deference because multiple layers protected the employers from the profane and the mundane. In less affluent households, on the other hand, servants performed rituals of order—the basic tasks of cleaning, cooking, and child care. In India, these rituals of order are less about disorder and cleanliness per se, and more about elimination of pollution. Whereas Swapna Banerjee primarily addresses the issue of deference in her fascinating work on Bengali domestics in the late nineteenth and early twentieth centuries, we find that the affluent and middle classes of India clearly distance themselves from the laboring classes by hiring others to perform both rituals of deference and rituals of order. In other words, the Indian middle classes distinguish themselves from the classes below them by virtue of being both actually and ceremonially removed from boundary-maintaining labor.

Finally, the spatial configuration and ordering of the middle-class home both reflects and shapes the culture of servitude. In the following chapter we map the transformation of residential urban space, from one centered on the "big house" of the feudal imaginary to one dominated by the modern flat. Analysis of the two types of employer homes provides a starting point for understanding the relations of servitude in Kolkata; certainly, the availability of different kinds of servants affects the ordering of the employer home, while the space available in the home influences servant-keeping practices.

In sum, this book departs from and contributes to the literature on paid domestic work by establishing the concept of a culture of servitude in which relations of domination/subordination, dependency, and inequality are normalized. A culture of servitude is shaped by particular historical configurations of structural economic/gender/spatial and often race/caste inequalities that traverse the domestic and public spheres and thus is a vital site for the constitution of self and society. The book examines Kolkata's culture of servitude, located in the interstices of the social imaginaries of feudalism and capitalist modernity, and traces the constitution and reproduction of the employing middle classes in dialectical relation to the serving classes. It argues that classes come into being not just through relations of production and consumption outside the household but critically through quotidian labor and intimate practices within the home.

Working with Cultures of Servitude

We have said in the previous discussion that we are interested in feudalism and modernity as social imaginaries; we do not consider this book to be about an actual transition from tradition to modernity, even though we discuss changes wrought by transformations in the political economy. In particular, we would warn against two pitfalls that commonly occur in transnational discussions of domestic service. The first is the teleological error that domestic service everywhere follows the same trajectory from a feudal to a capitalist mode, and therefore, that what happened in an earlier transition to capitalism in, for example, the United States, will naturally follow a century or more later in a country like India. This teleological error stems from the belief, as S. N. Eisenstadt puts it, that the West is the basic reference point for all others, that the trajectory of capitalism constitutes a linear development where the backward (the "less developed" or the "third world") must, usually unsuccessfully but in a similar manner, follow the advanced.[75] The second error is one of universalism so that the workings of capitalism are privileged in such a way as to assume a uniformity in their effects. This error occurs when the manifestations of neoliberalism are expected to affect domestic workers everywhere in parallel fashion, thus producing, for example, similar cultures of servitude in India, the Philippines, and Egypt.

While the study of work and labor is a classic sociological problem, we have employed an interdisciplinary approach and taken recourse to a capacious body of theory, from North and South, for this study of cultures of servitude, melding Marxist and feminist social history and tempering structural sociology with attention to culture and agency. We insist on cultural specificity even as we acknowledge the articulations of the global economy, foreground history in our sociological explanations, and reject teleological developmentalism. As such, we are committed to a historically informed sociological imagination. Thus, our aim is not simply to analyze the specific workings of Kolkata's culture of servitude so that only a sense of the uniqueness of Kolkata is conveyed. Rather, we hope to inspire a conversation about manifestations of possibly multiple cultures of servitude in which we live and a historically nuanced consideration of households as sites of particular kinds of labor.

Methods are not, of course, divorced from the repository of theory and the archive of knowledge, but the city of Kolkata as a site has shaped the project and research questions in significant ways. Against the backdrop of a developing cityscape with the rise of blocks of flats in place of spacious colonial-era homes, space became a crucial element for understanding the institution and relations of servitude over time. Thus, the scope of the research widened beyond the household to reading Kolkata's urban and architectural history and holding discussions with architects and developers who have both tracked and contributed to the changes in the urban landscape. It widened even further with an engagement with globalizing Kolkata and the decision to assess the mutability of Kolkata's culture of servitude in transnational context through the narratives of Bengali employers and domestics in New York.

Our methodological and interpretive approach is informed by questions of subjectivity and memory that are essential to grasp the structure of feeling of the relations and institution of domestic servitude. Combining participant observation from extended research trips over a period of five years (from 2000 to 2005) with fifty-two oral histories from employers and forty-four from servants in Kolkata and New York, and a survey of five hundred households in the former, the book seeks to understand how class relations are constituted in the everyday life of the home. It explores how servants and employers interpret and situate themselves in the history of their families and societies by privileging the everyday negotiations and mediations that figure prominently in their stories and focusing on the spoken and unspoken ways in which employers and their servants enact the relations of servitude. Our analysis is embedded in the historical, economic, social, and cultural forces and discourses that shape the daily performance and memory of what it has meant to be a servant and what it has meant to be served.

Researching and thinking through a book about cultures of servitude in a city in which middle-class life is predicated on servants effectively transform the entire urban landscape into an ethnographic field site. Servants walk along the streets, take children to parks, queue for milk, run errands to the market, sit together chatting outside apartment buildings, and, of course, are always present in middle-class homes. In the homes that we visited socially or for the purpose of interviewing employers, we observed servants serve their employers—and occasionally the two of us—and sweep, dust, and cook. We also watched as employers spoke with, praised, cajoled, and scolded their servants. We witnessed the servant-dependent organization of employer homes and the crises that the absence of servants occasioned. We also rode the train with servants as they commuted between work and their homes on the outer fringes of the city. Wherever we went socially, we found ourselves engaged in conversations about "the servant problem," with employers—and servants as well—often volunteering to be interviewed.

Over several research periods we became familiar with multiple households in Kolkata and visited dozens more. The employers and servants in this study were initially located through work, family, and friend networks, and those interviewed provided leads for subsequent contacts. We identified employers who represent the range of the middle classes in the city—from elite to lower-middle-class segments, owners of capital to clerks in the lower rungs of the government bureaucracy, wives of tea planters to women's organization activists—and servants born into servitude as well as those who became servants, servants with their own homes and those who live in servants' quarters, and full-time and part-time workers. In some cases we were able to observe the course of an employer-servant relationship or a servant's fortunes over a number of years; in most cases, we had an extended interview with each person. Interviews with employers were almost exclusively conducted in their homes, though we did speak to a few employers at their place of work or their social clubs. Servants chose the place where they would be able to meet us—in the homes where they work, servants' quarters in the case of live-in servants, or in their own homes in nearby *bastis* (slums). In addition to the dozens of households we observed in different parts of the city, we conducted an intensive study of the social world of servants in an upper-middle-class apartment building where it was possible to engage with servants at work and at home, with their children and their friends. All interviews were open-ended conversations, in Bengali with servants and in a combination of Bengali and English with employers.

As part of the generation that absorbed feminist and other radical critiques of ethnographic practice in our earlier scholarly work, we could not have embarked on this project without a deep realization of the chasm between those who serve and those who are served. Yet what makes ethnography rewarding, after all, is often the unexpected. Certainly, we were both identifiably of the employer class, and employers opened up to us with an assumption of shared interests to a degree that initially seemed quite startling. However, while employers' candor about their practices and opinions regarding servants did take us aback (and, often, made us flinch), so, too, did the measure of love and regret we heard employers express about the servants who brought them up. For some employers, conversations with us gave them an opportunity to discuss a source of daily frustration. For others, it was a chance to reflect on a vital aspect of life that they had hitherto simply inhabited—the lifelong relationship with those who cleaned, cooked, and helped to raise them or their children. Although we were welcomed with more immediate interest by female employers, many male employers were surprisingly ready to talk to us. If truth be told, people who heard about our project routinely offered themselves as interview subjects, and no employer we approached refused us an interview—which reflects in part the felt yet unacknowledged centrality of the master-servant relationship in contemporary India.

If we were guided by our consciousness of class differences as we sought out women servants (as part of the generation that debunked the myths of universal sisterhood), we encountered remarkably little wariness on their part. Rather, they reached out to us, sometimes physically holding us by the hand as they told us the story of their lives, as if to say, "It is about time that some of you cared to listen." They appreciated that we were not "on the side" of their employers and did not, by and large, hesitate in severely criticizing employer behaviors and attitudes. Nor were they reluctant to condemn the men they believed had failed them, sometimes explicitly assuming that as women, we would readily understand their troubles. Indeed, as scholars with histories of reading, writing, and working on gendered injustices, we were quite easily able to slip into the logic of women servants' narratives. It was in conversing with male servants that we came up against barriers. To begin with, most male servants could not instinctively produce a narrative of their lives, as if they were unaccustomed to telling stories about themselves, and even less so to women of our age and class. While younger male servants showed considerable ease once the terrain of the communication was established and were matter-of-fact about problems and obstacles, the older generation rarely made eye contact and obviously found it difficult to recount decades of hardship and life on the margins. Once they broached the topic, however, we realized how difficult and unfamiliar it was for us, in turn, to hear first-person accounts of men's suffering, their bitterness about their compromised masculinity, and their regret in failing to be the men that their families and milieu expected (see Chapter 5 for further discussion). In the pages that follow, we are circumspectly reflexive in our analysis and writing, in that we understand that we are considering particular versions of life histories told and heard in specific contexts, bringing our interactions with the subjects explicitly to the fore only to illuminate a certain point.

The narratives of servants and employers have been enriched by a reading of accounts of Kolkata's historical culture of servitude (published primary sources, newspapers, and novels), allowing us to gauge its structural inequalities, hierarchical arrangements, and emotional valences over time. The plethora of contemporary writing about what Calcuttans would call "the servant problem" has afforded invaluable insight into New York City's culture of servitude and helps situate the stories of Bengali employers and domestics in the city.

Given a dearth of large-scale studies of servants and employers in India in general and specifically in Kolkata, coupled with the inadequate census data (for example, the results of the 2001 census were not yet fully available at the time of writing), we organized a survey of five hundred households in three middle-class areas of the city—in Wards 92–93 (an area covering parts of Jodhpur Park, Jadavpur, and Dhakuria) in South Kolkata and Ward 10 (encompassing parts of Shyambazar) in North Kolkata (see Maps 3 and 4 on pages 30 and 31).[76] We chose these three neighborhoods in order to cover a range of middle-class households, apartment buildings, and single-family homes in both the older, more indigenous sections of the city (the north) and the newer areas of the city (the south). In each neighborhood, households were randomly selected from voter lists obtained from the Kolkata Municipal Corporation, and one employer and one servant were separately interviewed in each household.[77] We sought necessary basic information about servant wages, hours, tasks, castes, landholding, and place of origin, as well as employer income, occupation, household structure, and number of servants. We asked servants what they liked and did not like about the work, and employers how they responded to perceptions of servant performance. Surveys as a methodological tool are useful but limited, and certainly inadequate to address the kinds of complex and multilayered questions and themes in this book. Thus, the survey results were intended to complement the oral histories; in fact, the survey data have helped to confirm the processes and tendencies that emerged from the employer and servant narratives.

Map of the Book

We analyze Kolkata's shifting culture of servitude through the subjectivities of both servants and employers and situate it against the structural and cultural histories of Kolkata. We begin by explicating Kolkata's spatial and social formation in the following chapter. We trace the development of the city from its colonial beginnings to the present and map its residential logic, focusing on the decline of the feudal big house and the rise of modern apartment buildings. Kolkata's landscape has been significantly altered during the past decade of economic liberalization and globalization, with vast peripheral areas newly incorporated into the urban space and numerous luxury high-rise apartment complexes going up at an accelerated rate. The new globalized cityscape is associated with increasing class inequality and a growing spatial separation of rich and poor as it becomes nearly impossible for anyone of less than middle-class income to move into Kolkata proper. We argue that despite the shift to apartment living, the big house remains the defining trope for contemporary conventional and commonplace understandings of domestic servitude. The culture or ethos of the feudal household and joint families of the early to mid-twentieth century continues to resonate in the relationships and expectations of employers and servants. We next delineate the characteristics of the two generations of employers in this study (the *bhadralok*, the respectable, educated, upper-caste, middle and upper classes) and their colonial and postcolonial projects of modernity and domesticity. This brings us to the formation of Kolkata's culture of servitude, which had its origins in the social and spatial context of the colonial big house, and a discussion of its first foundational premise: the essential servant.

In each alternating chapter (Chapters 2, 4, and 6) we elaborate the premises of Kolkata's culture of servitude, examine the fault lines along which this culture has ruptured, and discuss the extent to which the premises remain largely unshaken though modified. In Chapters 3 and 5, we pay close attention to the social worlds of servants, thus interspersing the dominant logics with analyses of the myriad ways servants negotiate them.

Although the category of "servant" varies in different historical moments and places, this study concentrates on individuals who are explicitly recognized as servants in that they are not kin and are paid. In Chapter 3, we discuss four distinct categories of servants: (1) servants who as individuals or families have remained with the same family for generations, can be called "family retainers," and are usually men; (2) live-in servants who reside in the home of their employers; (3) full-time servants who work up to a twelve-hour day in the same home but live elsewhere; and (4) part-time workers who usually work for two or more hours in each of several homes per day and are almost exclusively women. The move from family retainer to part-timer constitutes a historical progression, although all four types are present in Kolkata today, which we show through a sustained analysis of the workday and lives of servants in a selected apartment building. Full-time live-in workers and part-time live-out workers inhabit different temporal and labor regimes, producing distinctive understandings of work and identity. For employers, the family retainer most closely approximates the ideal of myth and memory and embodies the standard of servitude against which servants are compared. The increasing number of live-out and part-time workers brings into question the definition of servant since they seem to have more control over their labor. Indeed, part-timers test the inherited notion of servant within Kolkata's culture of servitude because they are not constantly at the beck and call of employers. Part-timers, as freelancers, have the greatest space of autonomy and cause the employers the greatest anxiety.

Kolkata's culture of servitude is strongly marked by a familial discourse that we call the "rhetoric of love." Chapter 4 analyzes the second premise of Kolkata's culture of servitude, in which the rhetoric of love functions as a discourse that encompasses employer claims of affection and familial relationships that bind servants and employers to each other. It is a complex discourse that both masks and hides exploitation in a culture of servitude in which servants are so often depicted as "part of the family." Chapter 4 traces the divergent responses of servants to this discourse, from the family retainers who legitimate it to the part-time workers who make claims based on it, and to yet others who believe that the rhetoric of love is a ruse to make them work harder. We also examine the discomfort of the younger generation of employers, especially women, who are caught between their desire for an impersonal, contractual relationship with servants and their wish for servants to feel familial affection for their children. Although the rhetoric of love is being gradually replaced by the language of contract, this chapter posits that the contract is at best partial and contradictory. The contradictions, we argue, stem from the peculiar nature of a culture of servitude whose definition, content, and practice were scripted in a feudal/colonial past.

Kolkata's evolving culture of servitude is inserted in patriarchal hierarchies that operate on several levels within both employing and serving households. In Chapter 5, we analyze what we have come to call "the failure of patriarchy," for when women servants narrate their lives, it is inevitably the failure of fathers, husbands, and brothers to perform prescribed familial and social functions and duties that is seen to have led to these women's unfortunate circumstances. Thus, women servants assume the "patriarchal" responsibilities of supporting their households, but what they wish for their daughters is an idealized patriarchal family in which women are taken care of by their husbands and fathers. At the same time men servants are resigned to their inability to make an adequate living. Indeed, male servants think of themselves as failures and feel doubly diminished. They are full of shame that their wives must work and desire above all that their children not follow in their footsteps. This chapter testifies to the particular power of the ideological consensus criticizing women's labor outside the home.

Ideologies of family and contract, however, cannot conceal that domestic servitude is a class relation of extreme inequality. Chapter 6 articulates a necessary element to sustain a culture of servitude: the cultivation of distinction— the third foundational premise of Kolkata's culture of servitude. The operations of distinction normalize the exploitation that undergirds the institution of domestic servitude in India and elsewhere. In Kolkata's culture of servitude, distinction as manifested in physical and emotional *distance* between employers and servants is critical. In the spatiality of the big house with servants' quarters, servants were perceived to be unobtrusive. In the relatively restricted space of the flat, especially without quarters, servants are considered to be infringing on employer privacy, and thus the matter of distance becomes acutely problematic. Employers maintain distinction from servants by segregating the servant body through the politics and practices of eating, sitting, sleeping, bathing, and clothing. The difference between the bhadralok and those who are not is "naturally" reflected in a caste-inflected class distinction within the *bhadra* (civilized and respectable) home. Yet employer anxieties and servant aspirations come to the fore as distinctions begin to blur with emerging discourses of democracy and rights in the home and the city.

Chapter 7 problematizes the portrait of Kolkata's culture of servitude that has been developed in this book by placing it in comparative, transnational context. We consider the extent to which Kolkata's culture of servitude travels as seen through the lens of Bengali employers and servants in New York City. As immigrants traverse the distance between their places of origin and U.S. cities, they create new meanings around service, rights, and the nature of domestic work. As they are inserted into new urban formations and domestic circumstances, they make adjustments and compromises, bringing to bear their understandings of what it means to serve and be served. Some employers claim that the concepts of domestic servitude and servant do not apply in the contemporary United States, where a more contractual and impersonal culture of domestic work prevails and servants per se are uncommon, while others strive to re-create familiar relationships in different guises. The inclusion of New York as a site allows for a deeper examination of the concept of the culture of servitude. We conclude that many of the constitutive elements of Kolkata's culture of servitude can increasingly be found in New York—the essential servant, the servant as "part of the family," and the servant as distinctive—as a consequence of the twin forces of greater class inequality and immigration over the past two decades. We can then speculate about the lasting imprints of older cultures of servitude in the United States itself and their convergence with "imported" ones. Finally, through this comparison we are able to illuminate the characteristics of domestic servitude that vary with context and those that inhere in the work itself.

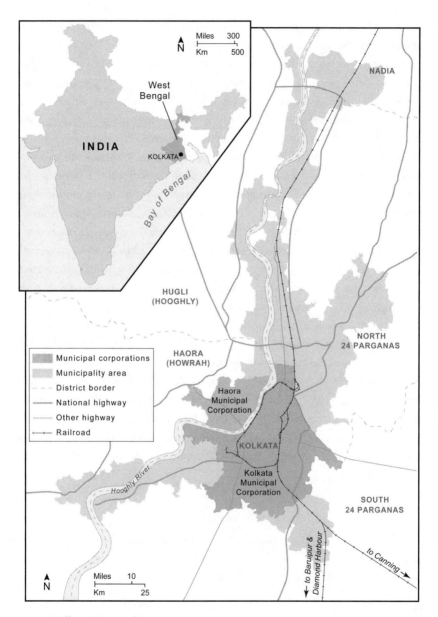

Map 1 Kolkata Metropolitan Area.

SOURCE: Data from Kolkata Metropolitan Development Authority, Base Map of Kolkata Metropolitan Area.

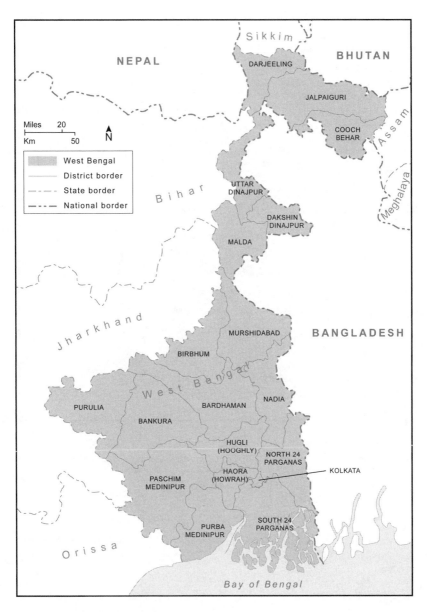

Map 2 Districts of West Bengal.

SOURCE: Data from Government of India, Ministry of Home Affairs, Thematic Maps on West Bengal Census 2001.

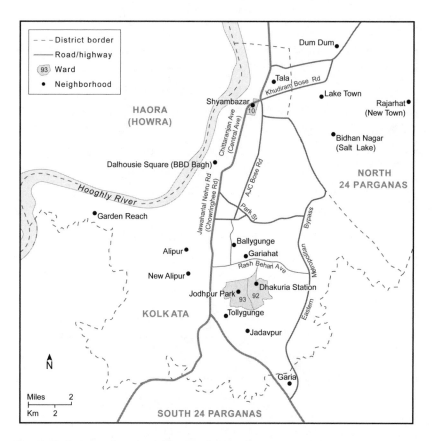

Map 3 Kolkata wards and neighborhoods in study.

SOURCE: Data from Kolkata Metropolitan Development Authority, Base Map of Kolkata Metropolitan Area; Government of India, Ministry of Home Affairs, Thematic Maps on West Bengal Census 2001.

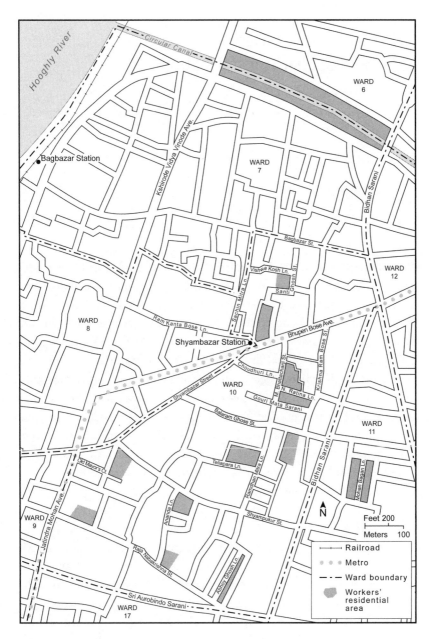

Map 4 Detail of Ward 10.

SOURCE: Data from D. R. Publication and Sales Concern, Detail Maps of 141 Wards of Kolkata.

2 Colonial Legacies and Spatial Transformations

ALTHOUGH DOMESTIC SERVITUDE has undergone many changes over the past century, the present social form of the institution is based on conceptions of the modern Indian home and life that represent not a break from but rather signify a rearticulation of ideas and practices derived from a feudal and colonial past. We use the term "feudal" because it refers to the cultural and social legacies of the *zamindari* system that formed the bedrock of agrarian structure and indirect rule in the colonial period and because employers and, in fact, most middle- and upper-class people constantly and consistently use the term to summon up the "structure of feeling" of the past. We see Kolkata's men and women, in the words of Marshall Berman, struggling "to become subjects as well as objects of modernization, to get a grip on the modern world and make themselves at home in it" through particular conceptions and constructions of domestic spatiality and sociality.[1]

Although Kolkata, one of India's premier cities, shares many characteristics with other metropolises in the South, as an urban formation and place, it has a peculiar colonial and postcolonial history and configuration of domestic servitude. In the first part of this chapter we map the history of Kolkata and in the second part its middle and upper classes, popularly called the bhadralok, who are, unsurprisingly, employers of servants.[2] In the third part, we trace the spatial, economic, and social transformations that have shaped the city's culture of servitude and analyze the increasing constraints on the premise of servant indispensability to bhadralok life and status.

Kolkata in Space and Time

In a manner reminiscent of Berman's coming to grips with the modern world, David Harvey's time-space compression refers to "processes that so revolutionize the objective qualities of space and time that we are forced to alter, sometimes in quite radical ways, how we represent the world to ourselves."[3] Doreen Massey, in turn, has criticized Harvey's assertions that this time-space compression has led to disorientation and "placelessness" (the sense of the "simultaneous presence of everywhere in the place where you are standing"). She argues instead for a geography of interconnectedness in which the "identity of place . . . is always and continuously being produced."[4] Following Massey, we highlight the "particular constellation of social relations, meeting and weaving together at a particular locus" that gives Kolkata its specificity as place.[5]

Established by the East India Company in 1690 on the banks of the Hooghly River, which flows into Bay of Bengal, with defensive fortifications at Fort William built by 1698, Calcutta was a port "created specifically for colonial extraction."[6] In 1756, the last independent nawab of Bengal, Siraj-ud-daullah of Murshidabad, attacked Calcutta and captured the fort. Company troops under Robert Clive recaptured Calcutta in 1757 in the Battle of Plassey, leading to the consolidation of British rule and the transformation of the city into a major commercial, manufacturing, and administrative center. Calcutta became the British capital in 1772 under the first governor general, Warren Hastings, and the imperial capital of all India after the pacification of the 1857 rebellion, the first major challenge to British rule; it remained so until 1912 when the capital was shifted to Delhi.

Because the British capitalist system radiated from Calcutta, the city was at the center of the orbit of production and circulation of goods and services.[7] Yet Calcutta, unlike other major Indian cities such as Bombay, has had close links with its agrarian hinterland. Its particular class structure and relationship to the rural areas may be attributed to the zamindari system of landholding established by the British. The result of Lord Cornwallis's Permanent Settlement Act of 1793, the zamindari system transformed the hereditary revenue collectors of the Mughal Empire into *zamindars* (landlords with large holdings) and reduced the peasantry to tenants in Bengal and parts of northern India. These zamindars, often absentee, held sway over lesser landlords and tenant farmers, collecting often onerous fixed annual rents for the colonial state in return for a commission and land rights. Although the zamindari system was abolished shortly after independence, Ranajit Guha describes its lasting effects on Kolkata's respectable classes:

> In his early youth the author, like many others of his generation, grew up in the shadow of the Permanent Settlement: his livelihood, like that of his family, was derived from remote estates they had never visited; his education was orientated by the needs of a colonial bureaucracy recruiting its cadre from among the scions of Lord Cornwallis's beneficiaries; his world of culture was strictly circumscribed by the values of a middle class living off the fat of the land and divorced from the indigenous culture of its peasant masses.[8]

During the colonial period, the city was effectively divided into two parts: the north inhabited by the old native elite, many of whose members derived their income from the zamindari system, and characterized as the indigenous part of the city; and the south, which was the site of the colonial state apparatus as well as the residences of the English. The city developed on the zamindari village model with great houses surrounded by bazaars and bastis whose residents provided in-house or readily available domestic service. In fact, the first rural migrants came to work as domestic servants in the homes of the English and settled in bastis within walking distance of the opulent colonial mansions.[9] Today, while North Kolkata remains more Bengali and South Kolkata is more cosmopolitan, middle-class homes of both north and south are marked by the presence of the ubiquitous domestic servant.[10]

By 1800 Calcutta was a thriving place. The British built their "spacious and imposing" houses along the Esplanade, Chowringhee, Bow Bazaar, and Circular Road as British settlement grew from the Tank Square Area to the east and south of the city during the second half of the eighteenth century (see Dalhousie Square vicinity on Map 3).[11] Architectural historian Sten Nilsson notes that the homes of the British in Calcutta were much grander than those of their counterparts in London, in part because of cheap and accessible servant labor:

> The prerequisites for these buildings were special and quite different from those in contemporary London and other English towns. It was easy and cheap to buy sites and the same was true of material and labour costs. The houses could be well designed with large dimension as there were always numerous servants available for the necessary communication between the different parts of the building. Thus the houses were large and of an external design remote from the Puritan ideals.[12]

Nineteenth-century servants with the tools of their trade.

SOURCE: J. E. Saché, Calcutta, A Group of Household Servants, Photographer's Reference 77, Albumen print, c. 1865, The Alkazi Collection of Photography.

The city expanded greatly in physical size and population in the two and a half centuries after its foundation, as the following figures reveal.[13]

Year	Area in acres
1701	1,682
1801	4,997
1901	13,237
1953	23,629

The first wave of migration to the city took place in the eighteenth century. The second wave in the mid-nineteenth century funneled workers into the jute and textile mills and transportation projects, the first jute mills having been established in 1835 and the railway hub in 1854. Jute production and manufacturing were to be driving forces of the regional economy until the mid-twentieth century. Many emerging bhadralok moved into the city during the first four decades of the nineteenth century, the elite into brick buildings

1800s–1840s

and the workers into huts. As the city became more prosperous, the former structures replaced the latter, although the city would remain one of palaces and hovels.[14] Indeed, the older slum areas of the city were settled some 150 years ago; the residents had *thika* tenancy and little fear of eviction, which led to continuous occupation by several generations.[15] The homes of the indigenous elite in Calcutta were also opulent but had features distinctive from those of the British houses previously described. The Indian homes were usually divided into several *mahals* (sections of a large compound), with small dwellings in the courtyard for employees and domestic servants.[16]

Calcutta was the center of the political and economic life of Bengal and of what would become known as the Bengal Renaissance—the nineteenth-century literary, cultural, political, and social reform and, ultimately, nationalist movements. After independence from Britain in 1947 and the partition of India and Pakistan, and of Bengal into West and East (first East Pakistan and then Bangladesh after the war of 1971), Calcutta became the capital of the state of West Bengal, by which time its population had grown to more than 4 million. The city was officially renamed Kolkata in 2001.[17] The greater metropolitan area had attained a population of over 14 million by 2005, a trend depicted in the following figures.[18]

Year	Population (thousands)
1950	4,513
1955	5,055
1960	5,652
1965	6,261
1970	6,926
1975	7,888
1980	9,030
1985	9,946
1990	10,890
1995	11,924
2000	13,058
2005	14,277
2010	15,548
2015	16,980

City of Refugees and Migrants

Although West Bengal is considered a laggard in terms of industrial growth, on the eve of independence it was the most industrialized Indian state and had a large share of foreign industrial investment. For various reasons, including the expenditure of funds to buy out foreign investors, and new private investment being channeled to other cities, industrial growth slowed in Calcutta.[19] Coupled with the extraordinary inflows of refugees and migrants, this slowdown has produced, according to economist Nirmala Banerjee, a larger than usual imbalance between capital and labor. This may in part account for the fact that there are more domestic servants in West Bengal than there are in any other state in India. According to the Government of India 1991 census (which contains the latest census figures for the occupation of domestic servant as of this writing), West Bengal has 8 percent of India's population and 20 percent of the total number of servants; Maharashtra, 9.5 percent of the population and 18 percent of the servants; and Uttar Pradesh, 16.6 percent of the population and 4 percent of the servants.[20]

Intense demographic growth and population density have characterized Kolkata and may be attributed in great part to the massive arrival of refugees after the partition of the subcontinent (into what is now India, Pakistan, and Bangladesh) following independence from English colonial rule, and to a lesser but still substantial extent, after the 1971 war and creation of Bangladesh.[21] From 1946 to the mid-1970s, 4.2 million people entered the state of West Bengal as officially registered refugees, most of whom settled around Kolkata, especially to the south of the city.[22] Another estimate raises the figure to a net inflow of 6 million refugees into West Bengal up to 1973. In either case, the refugee population constituted a determining factor in the development of the state and the city, where refugees made up more than 28 percent of the population in the Calcutta Metropolitan District (CMD, now KMD; see Map 1 on page 28).[23] The CMD was created as the regional planning and development authority and includes the rural hinterland around the urban core. The settlement of refugees in Calcutta after partition was uneven and unequal. Those with means bought properties, others encroached on vacant land and built shelter, the poor squatted on public land, and the "poorest of the poor" filled refugee camps until these overflowed and became quasi-permanent settlements.[24]

The influx of refugees has been augmented by a continuous stream of migration from the hinterland (of some 220 million people in the states of Bihar, Orissa, and Assam) as a consequence of rural economic crises, historically associated with famine and failure of the monsoon rains. As David William Martin comments, "Calcutta, as the largest business centre in the eastern region of India, automatically acts as a magnet for the prospective alleviation of fundamental distress. The slightest hiccup in living conditions in the hinterland areas sends streams of work seekers in the direction of Calcutta."[25] According to Arjaan de Haan's study of unsettled and circular jute mill migration, land scarcity, low rural wages, and repression are the basic reasons for migration, and decisions to migrate to the city are determined by the probability of finding a job and attaining a higher income.[26] Even though there have been some concerted land reform attempts over the years—especially between 1978 and 1988, the first decade of Communist Party of India (Marxist), or CPI(M), governance—the rural population remains mired in poverty. Pranab Bardhan and Dilip Mookherjee show that in 1998, over 50 percent of rural households in West Bengal were landless and an additional 39 percent owned less than 2.5 acres, which effectively means that most rural households could not be expected to live off the land and would be likely to send household members to the city in search of work.[27] This pattern of distress migration through the 1980s and 1990s has also been documented by Ananya Roy.[28]

In fact, migrants to the city outnumbered the "indigenous" population throughout much of the twentieth century, furnishing a steady supply of labor for the industrial, commercial, and service sectors, including domestic service.[29] This stands in sharp contrast, as we shall see, to employer anxieties about servant scarcity. As Satyesh C. Chakraborty explains, however,

> Calcutta did not draw people from the surrounding areas simply by offering a better quality of life. As in any other Indian city, the immigrants found in Calcutta poverty as severe and dehumanizing as in the villages. Indeed, kinship affiliations in the villages perhaps softened the harshness of poverty. The advantage that the cities offered instead was a relatively quick opportunity of new income through placement in the urban economy as handyman or casual worker in the transport, trade, manufacturing, conservancy or domestic sector.[30]

The phenomenal growth of refugee and squatter settlements forced the city to grow outward, as the lower-income north was already terrifically congested. So over the past several decades slum areas have proliferated to the south and far south of the city, along railway tracks and sewage and drainage canals. Estimates are that over 40 percent of slum dwellers are casual laborers or domestic servants or are engaged in other informal work, and that over half of women workers in the informal sector are casual and full-time domestic workers.[31]

By 2001, the population density of the Kolkata Metropolitan Area (KMA) was 44,458 people per square kilometer, and one-third of the population lived in slums; of a total of over 5,500 slums, only 2,011 were registered (that is, formally recognized and serviced by the city). Some 41 percent of the slum households have been living there for two generations or more, and a great majority earn less than the equivalent of one hundred dollars per month.[32]

The Planned City

In response to increasing population size and density and expanding city boundaries in the early part of the twentieth century, the Calcutta Improvement Trust (CIT) was established in 1911 with the objective of planning new roads and residential neighborhoods.[33] This was the first of several attempts to manage the growth of a city that, as urban geographer Keya Dasgupta frankly states, has expanded and grown largely in the absence of substantive planning.[34] The turn of the twentieth century had produced a situation in which instead of landlords seeking tenants, tenants sought land for housing. By the second decade of the new century, residential and basti areas in the center of the city had been demolished to make way for commercial buildings, and the erstwhile residents were displaced to the north and south of the city as well as to the haphazardly emerging suburbs in the inhospitable lands to the east.[35] Urban historians conclude that the spatial growth of the city did not conform to any particular pattern in the first half of the twentieth century. Rather, since at least the middle of the nineteenth century villages surrounding Calcutta received what could be called its "surplus" population—the large numbers of people who were forced out of the central areas because of planned and unplanned development and rising land prices—and at the same time villages were incorporated into the city. From the 1920s through the 1950s, the CIT acquired land from residents for development, a pattern that meant that newly developed areas remained beyond the financial reach of the working and middle classes.

After the CPI(M)-led Left Front government came to power in 1977, there was a new focus on rural development, land reform, and land redistribution. In the urban areas, initially capital flight, coupled with aging infrastructure and the need for lower- and middle-class accommodation, spurred new housing construction under government sponsorship. Much of this new development took place in wetlands or marshy areas that had to be "recovered," or in slum and squatter settlements that were "rehabilitated." The CIT had acquired extensive tracts of marshland in the years immediately following independence and developed new residential areas, for example, Jodhpur Park and Salt Lake (see Map 3). In later decades, though the Calcutta Metropolitan Development Authority (CMDA) 1980 Plan for Metropolitan Development prescribed strategies for future development targeting the urban poor as the prime beneficiaries that aimed to rectify distortion of previous development policies and programs, the large-scale development projects have ensured that "the declared 'target groups' have become the worst sufferers."[36]

Until the late 1970s or early 1980s, however, most urban development projects in the city that caused displacement were planned with some provision for resettlement/rehabilitation, but once the model of Salt Lake was established, urban sprawl has been unhindered. With the shift in priorities in the 1990s, the overall recent pattern of investment has moved further away from slum improvement to housing and then to commercial facilities. Some 35 percent of the state's small-scale investment is concentrated in the Kolkata metropolitan area, and the KMDA (formerly CMDA) has received funding to implement the Indian government's megacity program.[37]

The Salt Lake development in the 1970s was designed as middle- to upper-middle-class housing, "with signs of visible poverty removed" so there were no bastis—and few accessible servants, creating a "servant problem" for the newly suburban elite.[38] In common with much of the rest of India, "cities have been developed with no land earmarked for the poor, although cities cannot exist without the labour of the poor."[39] Now, however, with the rapid development of New Town (also called Rajarhat), seven thousand housing units, called service villages (to house the displaced people), have been incorporated. In the view of some observers, these are in fact mini-slums, planned to avoid the servant problem of Salt Lake.[40] Similar enclaves have been developed throughout eastern and southeastern Kolkata for the new globalized elite involved in the high-technology and financial sectors.

The surge of development projects that entail displacements of communities, habitats, and livelihoods is a comparatively recent phenomenon in Kolkata, compared to other Indian metropolitan areas, and has been largely prompted by the recent massive flow of funds from the multilateral development banks and private capital, both local and national. Implementers of development projects—with the support of state administration/planning bodies on their own or in conjunction with external funding agencies—constitute "a burgeoning private sector [that] operates as part of a globally networked economy."[41]

Kolkata has traditionally accommodated a wide range of communities from diverse sources and classes; yet as Dasgupta argues,

> The present urban restructuring is marked by an exclusionist agenda whereby an already marginalized yet integral segment of city's populace is gradually being wiped out to make way for the forthcoming spaces of 'modernity'. . . amusement parks, multiplexes, high-class residences, techno-parks. . . . An accommodative agenda has given way to an exclusionist one, where a new upper-class transnational cultural mind is being catered to, at the cost of erasing away the identities of an underprivileged labouring society from the urban fabric of Calcutta.[42]

As of January 2006, nearly sixty large building projects and one thousand medium-sized projects, mostly five-storied apartment buildings with a car park on the ground floor, were under way in Kolkata. This means nearly twenty million square feet of both commercial and residential space are being developed, up from under five million in 2001.[43] Much of the new construction is around the new Eastern Metropolitan Bypass (see Map 3 on page 30), a highway that, as Dasgupta emphasizes, "violated all ethical and civil rights norms by displacing the life and livelihood of the farmers and fishermen inhabiting the region, as well as all norms of environmental protection."[44] Even as the poor get pushed out of the fringes of the city, real estate developers bemoan the political influence of bastis and squatter settlements that resisted the sure destruction of their homes and prevented the bypass from becoming the efficient eight-lane highway that "it should have been." Such have been the battles over development in Kolkata over the past twenty-five years.

In a special supplement of the Kolkata edition of the leading English language daily, *The Times of India*, real estate developers and government officials highlight the marvel of Kolkata's expansion. Developer Rahul Todi extols the public-private partnership model adopted by the West Bengal government that supports joint ventures between public agencies and the private sector to develop land.[45] And Gautam Deb, minister for housing and public health engineering, lauds the fact that the expansion of the city has never been more rapid but cautions against the mistakes Mumbai (formerly Bombay) made in its real estate boom where skyrocketing property prices resulted in one of the costliest cities in the country. Thus, in Kolkata, a cross-subsidy model has been established as an integral part of new residential development. A percentage of the apartments are designated for poor or economically weaker sectors and are made available at a price fixed by the government. "That is exactly why the state government has decided to be a player in the market. . . . You can get an apart-ment of your own no matter what your budget is."[46]

Nevertheless, land prices have doubled in the new century, and the prices of flats have increased 20 to 30 percent. In 2001, flats in the new suburban development of New Town sold for Rs 1,000 per square foot, but by 2006 had risen to Rs 1,500–1,600 per square foot. In the upscale neighborhoods of New Alipur and Ballygunge in Kolkata proper, flats are priced at Rs 3,300–3,500 per square foot, up from Rs 2,500–2,700 in 2001.[47] Property developer Animesh Sen adds a sobering note: "You would need at least Rs 10,000 monthly income to be able to live in Kolkata, assuming a family of four plus parents. People who earn less than Rs 10,000 cannot live in Kolkata proper and must go out to the suburbs. These people are culturally middle class but financially lower middle class."[48]

What we see in the beginning of the twenty-first century, therefore, is a highly unequal spatial configuration in which elite reappropriation and trans-formation of urban space are enabled by a "public-private partnership" that consigns the lower middle classes to new developments outside the city proper and new poorer migrants to "unrehabilitated" slums and squatter settlements. In other words, globalizing Kolkata is superimposed upon a colonial city of palaces and hovels.

New high-rise apartment development on Eastern Metropolitan Bypass.
SOURCE: Photograph by Partha Pratim Sinha.

From Big House to Flat

With skyrocketing land prices and increasing population density over the past decades, a conspicuous element of the city's spatial transformation has been the demolition of detached family homes in favor of multistoried apartment buildings. Although this change has taken place in many of the world's major cities, the advent of towers of flats has been relatively recent in Kolkata, and certainly within the lifetime of many of its middle- and upper-class residents.

While old colonial apartment buildings with gracious interiors had existed—and some on a grand scale, such as the Queen's Mansion on Park Street—the first mass-scale apartment buildings began to appear in the 1960s. Tivoli Court, for example, with 180 flats on nine floors, was erected in 1964 on the site of a sprawling bungalow belonging to erstwhile zamindars in Ballygunge in South Kolkata. The erasure of the colonial landscape of big houses to make way for modern residential high rises intensified in the 1980s and 1990s in much of the southern and eastern areas of the city. In the early stages of this process, descendants of North Kolkata zamindars who had *bagan baris* (the equivalent of weekend country homes) and other properties in the south begin to sell them off as their incomes declined, thereby stimulating the land and property market. In other cases civil servants, who perhaps lived and worked outside Kolkata, bought large plots of land as an investment for retirement, building their homes on half the plot and—responding to the burgeoning interest of property developers—selling the other half to be developed as an apartment building. As South Kolkata developed, the dramatic increase in land prices prompted established families to accede to the urgings of property developers to sell their homes.

The story of the shift from the big house to the flat is incomplete without reference to concomitant changes in family structure; as the old joint families declined in South Kolkata, the urban formation altered irrevocably. Daughters left their natal homes upon marriage following the principle of patrilocality, but sons typically remained and their brides came to live with them. As sons began to leave Kolkata for jobs elsewhere, their aging parents, often left alone with a few family retainers, found the family home increasingly difficult to manage and expensive to maintain. In some cases the house was sold, and the parents settled into a more manageable flat. In others, when the parents passed away, the children sold the house and land to a property developer. Evolving conceptions of household resources and necessities also contributed to the disintegration of the joint family lifestyle and, therefore, of the big house. Certainly through the mid-twentieth century but less so since then, joint households pooled members' resources and income and the extended family was sustained from common funds. The growth of the middle classes and middle-class ideologies from the 1960s onward, combined with the increasing accessibility of consumer goods and aspirations, compromised the ethos of the joint family. For example, as the comforts, needs, and wants of individual members became more important and expensive, these were privileged over contributing to the family as a whole. Abhijit, a scion of a joint family, told his story:[49]

> Everyone crowded around one radio during the England/India test matches of 1951. Now every room has a television. Earlier, we had twenty rooms with three toilets for fifty or sixty people [in the family home in North Kolkata]; now there is one toilet for every person or couple. Even a one-bedroom flat needs two toilets. . . . We tried our utmost to keep the house going. Our mothers, who had married into the family and had lived in that house for sixty years, could not conceive of living outside of a joint family arrangement.

It is when households reach such social junctures, between a collective past and an individualized present, that they become the prime targets for property developers, inexorably leading to the conversion of old houses to apartment buildings.

Even as the skyline of South and now East Kolkata has changed dramatically, a similar transformation has not taken place in North Kolkata for both historical and cultural reasons. Abhijit, who now lives in South Kolkata, explained:

> North Kolkata is biased against it. People there are still not attuned to "community living" in these flats. So they won't convert their houses. They [the men] are used to a certain life: Go out in the morning, buy fish, give it to their wives, go to work, come back and do *ro'akey adda* [street conversation and discussion],[50] then go to the cinema, come back at night and eat dinner. They don't want to change it. In terms of development, too, it's difficult because now by law they can only build on fifty percent of a plot and the North Kolkata plots are small and the streets narrow.

Thus, the legacies of zamindari culture and questions of technical feasibility conspire to inhibit residential property conversion in North Kolkata.

Servants and the New Flats

Most of the apartment buildings built since the 1960s in Kolkata are seven to ten stories high, with two or three units per floor, but many of the complexes going up to the east and southeast of the city since the turn of the millennium are considerably higher and have many more flats—up to thirty stories with hundreds of units—along with a plethora of amenities and leisure facilities. According to architect and property developer Sen, three categories of apartment buildings, distinguished by square footage and the presence or absence of servants' quarters, can be identified:

1. Flats up to eight hundred square feet with no servants' quarters (in the southeastern areas of the city, such as Garia)   *p t*

2. Flats under two thousand square feet with servants' quarters on the ground floor or none at all (in the southern parts of the city, such as Gariahat)   *live in or ft*

3. Flats of twenty-five hundred to three thousand square feet or more with attached servants' quarters (originally in central Kolkata, now in the elite residential areas of Alipur and Ballygunge); normally four-bedroom flats with a room and toilet for servants   *live in or ft*

As we will analyze in detail in the following chapters, households in the first category typically have part-time servants, whereas the second and third may have live-in servants or full-time servants who live nearby or commute—but all have servants. Sen confirmed one of the major arguments of this book, that while the big house determined the culture of servitude, and servants have most definitely accompanied the transition from the big house to the flat, servant keeping has been transformed: "Previously, domestic help was a must because of the structure of the old houses. It was impossible to clean,

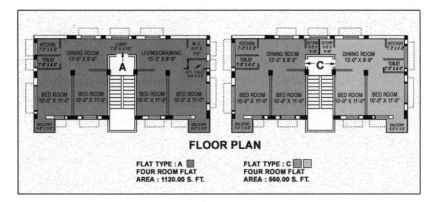

Floor plan of contemporary flats in Kolkata.

dust, sweep, and swab without help. You certainly need domestic help today, too, but they can be part-time or full-time."

"In Ballygunge Park," another developer told us, "you cannot sell a flat without [servants' quarters]." This developer once experimented with not including servants' quarters or parking spaces in a new flat development because the costs would have been too high. He was later obliged to add a few quarters on the ground floor of the complex because it was customary and expected by residents. Nonetheless, some of the newest apartment complexes on the Eastern Metropolitan Bypass are built without servants' quarters and tend to house younger couples, both of whom work outside the home and rely almost exclusively on part-time domestic workers.

Architects, property developers, real estate tycoons, and the middle and upper classes who are their clients seem to be convinced that apartment living is the present and the future in Kolkata, for reasons of security, easy maintenance, convenience, and cost. Said one architect we interviewed, "Who builds separate houses these days? Either the very rich or the very poor who just need a roof over their heads"—invoking once again the unequal landscape of palaces and hovels.

Kolkata's Employing Classes

The employers whose families once occupied feudal mansions and spacious bungalows, and now increasingly reside in multistoried apartment buildings, belong to the social group called the bhadralok. The bhadralok came into being in the mid-nineteenth century and have dominated the social world of Bengal ever since. Today's bhadralok include the middle- to upper-class white-collar workers, professionals, managers, and capitalists that form Kolkata's servant-employing classes.[51]

Yet there is considerable debate in the historiography on nineteenth-century Bengal about whether the bhadralok formed an actual class or were so wide ranging as to encompass several classes or groups marked by a combination of class, education, and lifestyle. In historian Sumit Sarkar's famous phrase, the bhadralok include everyone from the maharaja of Mymensingh to the railway clerk.[52] A consensus is emerging, however, on four issues regarding the early bhadralok. First, they located themselves beneath "the aristocracy of dewans and banians" and above the working classes and lower castes.[53] Second, what united them was not so much common material interest but an ideology of respectability not unlike the ideology of the "gentleman" in Britain. Third, the bhadralok were heterogeneous in origin; and fourth, membership in the group was not ascriptive but had to be achieved.[54]

Tithi Bhattacharya divides the bhadralok into two classes, the first of which derived from a landed rentier class and the second from what may be called the petty bourgeoisie. She argues that the families of the first group "had made their fortunes as dewans and banians to the [East India] company" and eventually invested in rural and urban land.[55] As members of a rentier class they were free to pursue and cultivate arts and culture, and some would eventually become great patrons of the arts. The second class comprised the civil servants. Given Calcutta's increasing importance as the commercial capital of the British Empire, it rapidly became a vital administrative center; as early as 1851 well over one hundred thousand Indians were employed in the government service in Bengal. Even those who may have worked as clerks in Calcutta were not poor migrants, as might be imagined, but came from propertied homes in villages or outlying areas of the city and for whom an English education was the key to upward mobility.

Yet both classes were considered bhadralok—the richer called *abhijat* and the poorer *grihasthya*—separated as they were from those above and those below. The British predictably classified them together as "the educated natives" to distinguish them from the old nobility and the masses.[56] By the end of the nineteenth century, the bhadralok were clearly a "social category embracing different strata of upper and middle income groups, landed interests as well as administrative employees and professionals."[57] It is significant, however, that the bhadralok maintained a strong interest in property. Nineteenth-century Bengali landowners with surplus capital tended to plow their profits back into land for a number of reasons. Foreign trade was virtually closed to them because of a "combination of powerful European mercantile organizations and governmental discriminatory policies."[58] The major banks were in European hands, so it proved difficult to borrow capital for industrial ventures. Moreover, financial crises in the 1840s and 1870s confirmed the dependence on property as the only safe form of investment.[59] Bengali capital was thus tied up in urban real estate and rural landholding, as well as in local trade, with little potential for growth. By the late nineteenth century the top rung of commerce was already in the hands of the British, and the next rung in the hands of the Marwaris (a business and trading community from Rajasthan who settled in Bengal). Bengali bhadralok were thus squeezed into the administrative sector—which they came to dominate from the lowliest clerical workers to the highest-level government bureaucrats and civil servants—and constituted, in the words of historian Rajat Ray, "a landed literati far more numerous than similar groups in other parts of the country."[60]

As the primary seat of the British Empire in India, Calcutta was the site of the earliest colonial social and cultural experiments. The Charter Act of 1813 encouraged British missionaries to establish educational institutions in India, the first of which were founded in Calcutta—initially schools where English was the medium of instruction and, later, vernacular schools. Following William Babington Macaulay's now infamous "Minute on Indian Education," a system was created whereby "the task of producing knowledge was assigned to the metropolitan country, while its reproduction, replication and dissemination were left for the colonized people."[61] The bhadralok were among the first to partake of this educational project, and the first to ascend the lower rungs of the British administrative system armed with that education. Active participants in colonial projects, certain of the bhadralok embraced a post-Enlightenment rationalism and fascination with modernity that unleashed a desire to reform Indian society from within to match the vaunted progress of imperial England. Indian reformers struggled with making social reform and modernization projects somehow compatible with Indian tradition, especially given their sustained engagement with "the woman question" that we examine later. Raja Rammohan Roy, one of the central political and cultural figures in nineteenth-century Bengal and representative of bhadralok reformers, belonged to the "upper caste gentry whose power was enhanced by the Permanent Settlement and other opportunities opened up by colonial rule."[62]

Segments of the bhadralok, at a crucial juncture, also formed a nationalist movement, and their history thus came to be joined with the history of Indian nationalism. It is not surprising that some of the first stirrings against British rule came from the very class that had been trained by it but found that the colonial state apparatus prevented the exercise of the rights that a colonial education promised. Rammohan Roy, later to be called the "father of modern India," pressed the British on the separation of powers, freedom of the press, and trial by jury. Indeed, the bhadralok came to see the political modernity that they were denied as a goal worth fighting for.[63]

Bhadralok Patriarchy and the Domestic World

It was at this time that the ideal of the middle-class Bengali woman was imagined out of intertwined impulses of colonialism, social reform, and nationalism. British political and economic domination of Bengali society entailed a civilizational critique that rested at least in part on strategic deployment of "the woman question."[64] As Tanika Sarkar and others have shown, out of contending interests and discourses, some of which called upon a glorious Indian past and some of which looked for inspiration from social reform in England, was created a new domestic ideal. The masculinity of the newly English-educated bhadralok, who were deemed effete and unfit to rule by the colonial powers, could be reclaimed through a project of social advancement, in which a crucial role was to be assigned to women.[65]

While men's education had economic and cultural value, that of women lay in the value it could add to men and to their households: "If we can educate women, it will be of immense benefit to us [men]."[66] As they entered the colonial administration, men found themselves grappling with new forms of discipline and time regimentation, which were the source of much distress.[67]

> Every *babu* [originally a title like Mr. or Esq., also clerk or bureaucrat], whether a *munsiff* [lower-level judge], or a Deputy Magistrate, or a physician, has to suffer the same fate. He has to work hard at the office, do office work even at home, study the rules of law, write judgments, and think of the next day's work.[68]

While enduring the rigors of the new order, Bengali men in the late nineteenth century simultaneously argued that the new time demands absolved them from responsibility for doing housework, nurturing children, and looking after all the members of the family.

By the late nineteenth century, the bhadralok found that the higher reaches of the new liberal professions were racially structured and congested, and increasingly men found employment only as petty clerks. Tanika Sarkar convincingly argues that since "[i]n the discourse of the master race, manhood was defined not just through financial solvency but by the nature of relationship to property . . . [a] passive and subordinate working life produced, therefore, a deep sense of emasculation."[69] The one place in which the clerical worker could be king was home. Having no sense of efficacy in the economic and political world, the bhadralok tried to stake a claim for a share of power in the world through re-creating and remaking his home: "The karta [head of the household] therefore, becomes within the home what he can never aspire to be outside of it—a ruler, an administrator, a legislator or a chief judge, a general marshalling his troops."[70] Although the historiography has dealt extensively with the reimagining of women and domesticity through the many domestic manuals that men in fact wrote, men sought to control not only their wives but, through them, the servants who were rapidly becoming indispensable to bhadralok status.[71]

Contemporary didactic literature consistently advised women on how to become competent housewives, intelligent companions, and good mothers to children, with particular attention paid to the mistress-servant relationship.[72] However, the prospect of women's education also generated fear that education would make women *bibis*—westernized women with no sense of duty— who relied on servants to run their households and raise their children. Anxiety revolved especially around the education of children, for how, the argument went, could children left with servants develop a proper moral and civilized character? When it became clear that no middle-class home was without servants, women were advised on how to behave with servants and ensure through supervision and surveillance that the home was run according to appropriate standards. As Kumkum Sangari astutely points out, supervision of servants was "presented as *work* and designed to ensure that hiring servants would neither release housewives from domestic labour nor prevent any abdication of household chores."[73] Whether they had a staff of servants to help with the household chores depended on the family's economic capacity, but even with the assistance of servants, "the amount of work was so great that she [mistress of the house] worked ceaselessly from dawn until late at night."[74]

The respectable *bhadramahila* (women of the bhadralok) came to be defined by her active and cultivated *presence* in the home. She was to be culturally refined and responsible for the inner life of the family, and protected by her kinsmen.[75] She was to have *lajja* (shame and modesty), which embodied attributes closely connected with virtue and respectability. "To be civilized," as Himani Banerjee reminds us, was "to have a sense of shame."[76] Civilized protection for women was to be found within the confines of the home and family; therefore, unprotected women—those who were exposed to the moral and social opprobrium of the public gaze—were by definition uncivilized and shameless. For the poor woman or the low-caste woman who was obliged to work outside the home, the street was unavoidable; thus, she was inevitably classed with "women of the street," or prostitutes. The assumption of sexual misconduct on the part of domestic servants and other women workers stemmed, therefore, from crossing the line between the home and the street, lajja and shamelessness, respectability and promiscuity.[77]

The bhadralok created a world in which educated middle- and upper-middle-class women were relegated to the domestic sphere, materially and ritually, and had the overall responsibility for managing the typically joint family *sansar* (households) while deferring to their husband's ultimate authority. A potent and pervasive domestic ideology and practice (*grihadharm*) was constructed whereby dutiful and pious women attended to the needs of their husbands and children in the home. This hegemonic ideology was carefully nurtured as the bhadralok class consolidated itself in the late nineteenth century. As the maximum domestic cultural expression of the dominant class, this had widespread influence across social classes and castes, yielding what Sangari has called an "astonishing consensus" around domestic labor, domesticity, and the domestic sphere.[78] The losers in this consensus were those without protection and those who could not afford to stay at home—women who were thereby excluded from the domestic sphere and proper domesticity and, we would add, those men who were unable to provide protection—themes we explore more fully in Chapter 5.[79]

The domestic arrangements of the bhadralok, and perhaps more centrally, the ideology that undergirded these arrangements, were thus firmly in place by the 1920s, when the older generation of employers in this study were born.

Bhadralok Employers Then and Now

Two generations of bhadralok employers are presented in this book. While the older generation of bhadralok employers (58 percent of our sample of employers), businesspeople and professionals who today range in age from sixty to over eighty, are still imbricated in an ideology of reform, nationalism, and progress that has at its center a particular notion of domesticity, we also focus on a younger generation in their thirties and forties (42 percent) who may be considered to be part of India's cosmopolitan elite.

Although varying by class fraction and wealth (59 percent were upper-middle to upper class, and 41 percent, lower-middle to middle class), the older generation of employers had vivid memories of the household arrangements of their youth and of the servants with whom they grew up, many before Indian independence in 1947. The most well-off employers were children of the owners of tea estates, collieries, and indigo plantations or of senior civil servants. Several grew up on large estates or in city mansions, some with as many as forty servants to look after the family. The servants came either from the employers' own estates or from neighboring villages, and even today ties are maintained between employer and servant families from the same ancestral property. As one seventy-year-old employer who grew up on an estate in northern Bengal recalled, his family had twenty to thirty servants, both inside and outside the house, under the supervision of his mother:

> We had a cook, cook's helper, bearer (who doubled as peon), duster, drivers, *durwans* [gatekeepers] who were all Muslim . . . maids or *jhis* who did child care, washed clothes, and were my companions. And there were cowherds and *chowkidars* [watchmen]. Servants lived on the periphery of the compound—they were always there—except at night, when only the durwans were around.[80]

A second category of employers belonged to the urban professional middle to upper-middle classes. They often lived in large joint families, pooled resources, and shared servants. Their servants tended to come from the neighborhood rather than primarily from ancestral properties. Another employer in his seventies described the joint family home of his youth in South Kolkata:

> We had ten servants who looked after about sixty people; the older women of the house were in charge. There was a low-caste maidservant who washed dirty dishes two or three times a day. Each meal had five sittings, and there weren't enough plates and glasses to go around. She also washed and cut the fish, cleaned the kitchen and pantry, and cleaned the eating area. We had two additional maids who were attached to the aunts, and who looked after the children, massaged oil in hair, washed children's clothes and saris. A fourth maid ground spices and helped the cook. Three out of six menservants were assigned to uncles and did office and clothes work. Two others washed clothes, made beds with mosquito nets, brought morning and afternoon tea. Then there was a [male] cook—always Brahmin. All the aunts and older [female] cousins helped in the kitchen with the chopping, but only the cook cooked.

The third and least well-off category of employers was composed of children of provincial government employees or school or college teachers, such as the household in which Mala, now in her late sixties, grew up:

> We had one part-timer who was paid five rupees a month—she did cleaning but not cooking. She received no food but was given *tiffin* [a snack] in the morning. We had a Brahmin cook after my mother fell ill. But he would refuse to wash dirty *jhuta* dishes,[81] so if the maidservant was absent, we would have to wash dishes ourselves. Until 1956, we had an eight-anna [less than Rs 1] person who came to clean toilets and take away "night soil" on his head—this happened even in Calcutta.

The younger generation of employers are children of businesspeople, professionals, and government employees. They are themselves corporate executives, professionals, nongovernmental workers, and teachers. Now in their thirties and forties, this generation is immersed in a world economy and is, to varying degrees, participant in global cultural and consumption practices. An educated, world-traveling class, created by and invested in the Indian nationalist project of modernity, it situates itself complexly as simultaneously national and transnational.

Those of the younger generation whose parents owned their own businesses or were successful professionals described their servant arrangements the following way: "We had one cook [a man], one servant for cleaning and washing and odd jobs, one *ayah* [nursemaid] per child. We also had a sweeper, a driver, and a gardener, as well as the *jamadar* who cleaned the bathrooms." The younger generation for the most part grew up in houses rather than flats, with staffs of between one and ten servants. Some of these servants came from their grandparents' estates; others were recruited from the neighborhood. A more classic middle- to upper-middle-class arrangement was one full-time servant (often a man) with two part-time servants helping out (usually women), while those from the lower middle class, whose fathers may have been low-level government clerks, report growing up in a household with one part-time maidservant.[82]

Despite the generational differences, the two groups of employers have more in common than not. Both older and younger employers consciously compare the past life of families and households to present circumstances and attempt, variously invoking sentiment and expedience, to retain aspects of Kolkata's culture of servitude rooted in the feudal past while viewing themselves as the vanguard of an Indian modernity. As we will see throughout the book, today's bhadralok have a complex relationship to their ideas of modernity, both ruing the demise of things as they were (in an idealized past)—holding fast to elements that seem to have withstood the passage of time—and eagerly embracing modernity as social and economic progress in a globalizing age. Most significantly for our purposes, Indian middle- and upper-class elites engage with modernity as a self-conscious domestic project through which the sociality and spatiality of the intimate sphere of the home may be reconceived. Yet neither younger nor older employers can quite imagine domestic life without the essential servant, even though that servant may now be a stranger and part-time worker rather than belong to a family or village that has served the household for generations. As Table 2.1 shows, the proportion of domestic servants per capita is significantly higher in West Bengal than in other comparable states

Table 2.1 Population of key Indian states and number of servants

States	Population	Number of servants Total	Male	Female	Proportion servant : population
Tamil Nadu					
1981	48,408,077	31,309	7,421	23,888	1:1546
1991	55,858,946	30,612	6,102	24,510	1:1825
Maharashtra					
1981	62,784,171	116,778	43,112	73,666	1:538
1991	79,937,187	139,043	31,792	107,251	1:575
Uttar Pradesh					
1981	110,862,013	35,405	27,770	7,635	1:3131
1991	139,112,287	32,205	23,082	9,123	1:4320
West Bengal					
1981	54,580,647	149,100	74,152	74,948	1:366
1991	68,077,965	146,621	47,832	98,789	1:464

SOURCE: Figures from *Census of India 1981*: Tamil Nadu, Series 20, part III A&B[ii]; Maharashtra, Series 12, part III A&B[iii]; Uttar Pradesh, Series 22, part III A&B[v]; West Bengal, Series 23, part III A&B[ii]; 1991 population figures from *Census of India 1991* Final Population Totals, paper 2 of 1992, Brief Analysis of Primary Census Abstract and *Census of India 1991*, Part IIIB series, Economic Tables, Vol. 8, Table B-19 F, Category 531, domestic servants.

in India. Indeed, through all of our in-depth interviews and our survey of five hundred households, we came across only one couple that had deliberately decided not to keep a servant. Our interest, then, is in the power of the idea of modernity and the ambivalence with which it is deployed, rather than in tracking in teleological fashion movement from one condition to another.

In the remainder of this chapter we explicate the foundational premise of Kolkata's culture of servitude—the indispensability of servants to the functioning of middle- and upper-class households—and address the tensions engendered by the move from the joint families and feudal structures associated with the big house to the more streamlined flat-living of twenty-first-century Kolkata.

The Essential Servant

> Servants are the privileged witnesses to private life. People are as little embarrassed in a servant's presence as they are in the presence of an ass, and at the same time the servant is called upon to participate in all intimate aspects of personal life.
>
> **Mikhail Bakhtin, *The Dialogic Imagination***

◆

Bikram spent part of his childhood on his father's tea estate and part in Calcutta. On the tea estate, the "house and atmosphere was very British. We had a governess for my sisters. I ran wild but had a Bengali teacher." The servants on his father's estate were local or migrants from Nepal, but since the main employer in the area was the tea estate, most local people worked either in the house or for the estate. Bikram's family had cooks, bearers, gardeners, watchmen, and maids, as well as a caretaker who was a distant relation but had a separate residence. The servants for their Calcutta residence were recruited either from the tea estate or another landed estate in Medinipur. Servants were both everywhere and nowhere in the descriptions of the old order. In these reminiscences, servants were always available, albeit not always physically present, marking a fundamental characteristic of the ideal servant.

His wife, Rani, who came from a family with many fewer servants (one cook, two bearers, and a sweeper), found it difficult to adjust to the size of servant staff to which her husband was accustomed. In their household in South Kolkata today, the two of them, now in their seventies and their children grown and gone to homes of their own, have a cook whose father, uncle, and grandfather had all worked for Bikram's family. In addition to the cook, they have a part-time woman to clean and two live-in men who do cleaning and washing. Of the three drivers, one lives in, another nearby, and a third at some distance. They have a gardener and several watchmen and gatekeepers whose families have worked for them for four generations. The traditional supply of servants from Bikram's estates in Medinipur has now dried up because horticulture and floriculture have made Medinipur relatively prosperous and provided job opportunities. As their servants age, therefore, Bikram and Rani face the prospect of eventually having to rely on the domestic workers from the South 24 Parganas and Canning villages who commute daily by train to Kolkata.

◆

A staff of well-trained residential servants was considered essential to run the big house in the past and the remaining such establishments in the present. Rani stresses, "We need servants to run such a large house, though I wish I had one very efficient person." The staff of ten servants split between indoor and outdoor duties in her spacious South Kolkata home and garden are considered not so much her personal requirement but a requirement emanating from the space of the big house. Factory owner Bankim, who lives in a palatial North Kolkata house, employs fifteen servants, including six inside servants—a cook and a special Brahmin deity cook (who cooks for the household gods), an ayah (in this case, a lady's maid), and three live-out housecleaners—although

Bankim and his wife insist that "to maintain the house properly, we need many more." In addition, nine outside servants are employed: three gardeners, three watchmen, two drivers, and a live-out groundskeeper. Almost all of the servants live on the premises in separate servants' quarters, as they would have several generations ago.[83] In both of these cases, the current setup is very much in the tradition of the feudal big house, with numerous residential servants with different duties covering the gamut of tasks perceived as required to maintain the home, the garden, and the car.

On a much less lavish scale, Jyotsna, living with elderly relatives in the ruins of a grand old North Kolkata house, is able to manage the family home without many resources by lodging a crew of quasi servants. A retired librarian, she is well aware that it would be impossible for her to keep up the house in the absence of the staff of servants that it took to run it in her parents' time. Since she does not have the means to employ numerous servants, in a rather unusual arrangement, she pays for some while providing food and lodging in exchange

North Kolkata mansion.
SOURCE: Photograph by Seemin Qayum.

Servants' quarters of North Kolkata mansion.
SOURCE: Photograph by Seemin Qayum.

for the services of many others. Some of the men who have domestic duties in this house also work in a variety of semiskilled jobs outside the home. For these workers, Jyotsna provides a place to live in an otherwise unaffordable city, and thus the possibility of a foothold in the vast informal economy. In this case, the "structure of feeling" associated with the big house produces a social adaptation in economic circumstances that would otherwise not permit occupation of such a space. In other similarly downwardly mobile situations, the burden of the upkeep of the big house is borne not by several but by one or two overworked servants.

Those who now live in flats have had to make at least three adjustments in order to retain the essential servant: first, the acceptance of primarily female rather than the traditionally preferred male servants; second, the replacement of live-in with live-out and full-time with part-time servants; and third, the adaptation to the servant body and new spatial management in the restricted space of the flat.

From Male to Female Servants

> *I prefer male servants. But it's difficult to get them nowadays because they can get jobs elsewhere. You see, men, if they work for eight hours in a factory, they are free after that. If they work for me, they are not free. They are, after all, always at my beck and call.*
>
> Mala, age sixty-eight

The ideal servant of Kolkata's feudal past—typically a male, live-in, family retainer who stayed in service for his life—has been increasingly replaced by a female, live-out, part-time domestic worker. While many employers, both old and young, have elaborate memories of male family retainers who were also often the companions of their youth, the increasing visibility of female servants has accompanied the breakdown of the joint family household and the move to apartment buildings. Indeed, many employers express an unwavering preference for male servants despite their declining numbers.[84] Thirty-year-old Vijay rationalized this preference in the language of skills and psychology: "If you look at the skill content required in cooking—it is much higher than in, say, washing the dishes. Any old person can wash the dishes. The male psyche calls for a more skilled job." Clearly, even though both men and women work as domestic servants, they are not interchangeable in the eyes of employers. Furthermore, employers and servants alike recognize a gender division of labor in which certain domestic chores and duties are considered more suitable for women than men, and servitude as such—being at the beck and call—"unmanly." We discuss the implications of these gender ideologies in detail in Chapter 5.

Although domestic servants in India have historically been both male and female, women and children have come to dominate the ranks of this occupation, which reflects the secular trend toward more female labor-force employment coupled with worsening economic inequality. The 1971 Census of India showed that there were 675,878 domestic servants in India, of whom only 251,479 were women. A decade later the picture was quite different, with the 1981 national census reporting that there were 807,410 people who worked as domestic workers in India, evenly divided between 402,387 men and 405,023 women. By 1991, the census reported 270,835 men and 460,279 women working as servants.[85] The transition from primarily male to primarily female domestic workers has happened relatively recently in Kolkata, rendering the issue more salient than in other cities where male servants are ever more invisible (see Table 2.1).

The increasing number of female servants in Calcutta over the past fifty years is due in large part to their gradual exclusion from agriculture and industrial employment; as employment alternatives closed for women, they expanded for men, so the number of women domestic workers slowly increased, while the number of men servants decreased.[86] In the aftermath of the partition of Bengal that occurred with Indian independence, scores of women refugees from what was East Bengal (now Bangladesh) who had previously not worked outside the home had no recourse but to go out to work as servants. With the move to the more restricted and isolated space of the flat, employers also began to consider questions of servants and security in new ways. Many flat-dwelling employers came to terms with keeping servants in these more confined spaces by hiring female rather than male servants—despite the persistent belief that men make better servants—in part because women are considered less threatening, especially when there are daughters in the house and no adult family members to ensure their safety.[87] Previously, as one young employer told us, referring to her childhood, "there was no question of being left alone with servants. I have no memory of being left alone. There were always grandparents or aunts and uncles."

From Live-in to Part-Time but No Less Essential

> My mother-in-law loved having live-in men "at her call"—she had a colonial lifestyle. But we, the daughters-in-law, didn't like having men around. We felt that live-ins were cumbersome because of space, cost, risk, and responsibilities around sexuality [of young women servants]. We did need someone, but not all the time. Our mother-in-law wanted servants to do everything, but the rest of the family wanted less dependence on servants. So a combination of attitudes and economics has led us to have two part-timers for the past ten years who wash pots and pans and do floors.
>
> **Kavita, age forty-eight**

Not only the wealthy have servants. In our survey, each and every one of the five hundred households employed at least one servant, including the 38 percent of our respondents who earned less than Rs 10,000 per month. In ordinary middle- or lower-middle-class homes that can afford only one part-time servant, she—usually she—will not be assigned child-care or cooking responsibilities. The widespread sentiment, harking back to the ideologies about the duties and responsibilities of middle-class mothers and wives, is encapsulated in the aphorism that "you can only eat food prepared by your mother's caring hands." In these homes part-timers are hired to take over the least desirable everyday jobs, such as washing the dishes or cleaning the floors. Time and time again, employers pointed to washing dirty dishes and pots as the most menial and lowly of household tasks, identified as this chore is with ritual pollution,

Lower-middle-class flats in North Kolkata.

SOURCE: Photograph by Ruprekha Chowdhury.

and this was overwhelmingly borne out by the survey in which 75 percent of the servants perform this function. Sanjay, a young man from a lower-middle-class background, said every family he knew hired a part-time worker for two daily chores: the floors and the dishes—as does Kavita, who is quoted earlier. Indeed, he argued, "however poor the family—and I know several very poor ones in my neighborhood—they'll cut back on the number of times cooking vessels need to be cleaned; that is, they'll have them washed once instead of twice a day, to cut back on costs, but they will hire someone to do it."

Making do with a combination of one or two full-time or part-time servants is the norm for most upper-middle- and middle-class families today, especially those who live in flats. Changing economic fortunes could certainly contribute to making the staff of servants once associated with the big house a financial impossibility for most employers. In fact, space and servants' changed expectations and desires are the two factors most often cited by employers for the change from a retinue of old family retainers in the past to today's pared-down staff. Servants' quarters, once a separate block behind the big house or on its roof, are now at best just one room or a cubicle in most apartment complexes. Although these apartment servants' quarters are generally intended to lodge only the servant, spouses and children often end up living in them, given the scarcity of land and shelter for the urban poor. Servants in many middle-class homes sleep on the floor of the kitchen, child's room, or wherever there is some space available.[88] As noted, servants increasingly tend to live elsewhere—in near-by bastis and squatter settlements or outlying villages a train commute away—and come in for the workday, often working part-time in several different houses. If one striking characteristic of domestic arrangements of the big house was that servants were always, as one employer put it, "at the beck and call" of the employer, the new temporality associated with flat-living without servants' quarters has meant that servants are now on a schedule, and employers find themselves with less control over servants in both spatial and temporal terms.

Even though employers have to adjust their behavior with and expectations of servants in the modern flat, the habit of having an ever-present servant is difficult to give up. Bhagat Singh, a well-off, retired bachelor of seventy, who now lives in a flat with separate servants' quarters and who briefly experimented with having just a part-time cleaner with meals catered, is very much aware of his class origins as the son of a tea plantation owner. He commented, "After living for fifty-five years in feudal splendor, it was a hardship to wash dishes and so on. Since I could afford it, I [went back to] a full-time servant."[89] Bhagat Singh's wealth makes it possible for him to buy not just labor but also the constant availability of another human being. This he recognizes as a sign of "feudal splendor," and it is what demarcates his current upper-middle-class status. His lifetime class and gender position exempt him from household labor and allow him to purchase the comfort of an ever-present source of domestic labor.

Servant and Space Management

"On the one hand, we have to have servants; and on the other hand, we have neither the space nor the money to house them. So you tell me, what does one do?" asks the employer in Mrinal Sen's film *Kharij*.[90] Servant management in the flat has to be reengineered relative to that of the big house. Rani, the wife of the tea planter introduced in the beginning of this section, contrasts her daughter-in-law's situation with her own. The daughter-in-law, according to Rani, manages to keep "everything under control in a flat with two live-in women who sleep in the living room." For Rani, servants are indeed essential to the big house as well as to apartment living, but the conditions of the latter require the employer to deploy different management skills—such as the exercise of strict supervision over both the servants' work and the servants themselves. Here we may recall Lefebvre's insistence that the command over space is a key source of social power in everyday life.[91]

The challenges for the employer-servant dynamic go much beyond just the physical and spatial. Mrinalini, an artist in her sixties, reflects on the problems of having a live-in servant in a small flat:

> In this new social milieu there is no place for a person living in your house who is not a relative or a friend. In those days, when you had servants living in the house, there was space; they weren't mingling with you all the time. In a flat you don't have that—your own space. You don't have physical space, so you have to create your distance. They are physically always there; you cannot move them out of sight. If you become too close in a flat, you don't have any privacy.

If servants were both everywhere and nowhere in the descriptions of the old order, the new order produces a spatial conundrum since the servant is never invisible. Servants may have quarters that they occupy during their periods of rest, but when they are "on duty," they share the intimate space of a two- or three-bedroom flat with employers.

Interior of middle-class flat in Kolkata.
SOURCE: Photograph by Ruprekha Chowdhury.

The modern flat was not designed for the extended family, or the multigenerational joint family, but rather for the capitalist nuclear family. Middle- and upper-middle-class dual-income couples today feel acutely the need for servants, especially in the absence of extended-family members who contributed to child care. In most cases, however, changed spatial and social circumstances have made the residential ayah a thing of the past, and families often rely on part-timers or daily live-out workers for child care. Some young couples actively try to create an ideal nuclear family with its corresponding emotional space. A servant has no place in the ideology of this nuclear family, yet those who are fashioning such families carry with them the assumption, originating in the big house, that households cannot be run without servants. These new nuclear families—typically a married couple, both working outside the home, with one or more children—thus make their own compromises. Some couples do not want a servant in the house in the evenings and weekends when they are home from work; they want to benefit from the housework and child care performed by a servant in their absence without having to deal with the physical and emotional proximity of a "nonfamily member."

Conclusion

From its colonial origins, the sprawling metropolis of Kolkata was built around the assumption of a service class for the affluent. For the bhadralok, created out of the crucible of colonial agrarian, educational, and administrative experiments, domestic work is to be managed, but not performed. In recent times, the transformation of Kolkata's large houses into soaring apartment buildings has meant less space for servants, obliging Kolkata's employing classes to accommodate the alternative rhythms of part-time and live-out servants.

The attribution of indispensability to servants has been a constant during the transition from the feudal big house to the modern flat, crossing class lines from middle-class to elite sectors. Employers cannot imagine a domestic arrangement without servants, though, as we have seen, they uneasily make compromises with the servant body. The smaller space of the flat obliges employers to make exertions in the interests of their "privacy" or "personal space." At the same time, the new temporal rhythms of part-time work have forced them to accept that servants are no longer always physically present to be called upon. Employers and servants struggle to come to terms with the implications of these temporal and spatial transformations for Kolkata's culture of servitude, as we will examine in subsequent chapters.

3 Between Family Retainer and Freelancer

IN THE 1970s, a large colonial mansion in South Calcutta was demolished, like so many others, to make way for a multistoried building of individually owned flats. Gitanjali Building is located in an affluent area of the city, and although quite upper middle class in its residential composition, it is by no means the most luxurious building in that area. An L-shaped seven-story structure consisting of two wings with several apartments on a floor, the Gitanjali flats range from twelve hundred to seventeen hundred square feet and most have two or three bedrooms. Gitanjali can be viewed as representative of the first stage of the transition from the big house to the flat since it was designed to accommodate families with live-in servants housed in attached quarters. As discussed in the previous chapter, newer apartment buildings or complexes may have servants' quarters only on the ground floor or none at all, but in the area where Gitanjali is located—one of the city's prime residential areas—live-in servants are still assumed. Gitanjali residents include corporate executives (ranging from young to retired), businesspeople, professionals, and artists, whose family structure varies among nuclear, extended nuclear, and joint families. There is also a sprinkling of single men (bachelors) and women (widows). Gitanjali residents are thus in many ways typical of the servant-employing Kolkata upper-middle class.[1]

Servants' quarters, located in a clearly demarcated section at the corner of the L where the two wings of the Gitanjali building meet, are occupied by the servants who work on each floor and, frequently, their families. Each wing has its own set of lifts used by apartment dwellers, servants, and visitors; there is no separate service lift, although servants often use the stairs. Gitanjali residents almost always use the lifts to move about between the ground floor and the flats and will rarely traverse the section with servants' quarters to reach the adjoining wing to visit neighbors. Employers are, in fact, rarely seen in the corner of the L—the servants' separate space—yet servants are silently visible everywhere: in the flats, corridors, lifts, and stairwells, and in the courtyard outside, going about their daily tasks. The flats could be considered the space of the employers, but their upkeep and functioning are almost entirely dependent on the labor and presence of servants. By the same token, servants' livelihood and living space are entirely dependent on the residents' continued need for servants.

Domestic work in apartment buildings like Gitanjali thus constitutes a kind of Maussian "total social fact," the analysis of which reveals sociologically, psychologically, and physiologically the characteristics of a particular social formation.[2] As such, it is an entry point into the world of servants and employers and the culture of servitude in wider Kolkata.

Gitanjali employers for the most part grew up in families in big houses with staffs of servants, as described in the previous chapter. In the past of these families, women of the household (wives, daughters, mothers, daughters-in-law), as well as "poor relations" dependent on the household for food and shelter, may have actively participated in housework and child care. Indeed, there may have been a continuum between women of the household, poor relations dependent on the household, and servants employed by the household in terms of who was responsible for domestic work and reproduction. We will explore these patriarchal domestic arrangements further in Chapter 5.

Today, it is safe to say that no Gitanjali resident is engaged in a meaningful way in domestic work. While in our study at large, we did come across one middle-class family that did not have servants, in Gitanjali—and in this it definitely serves as a microcosm—no resident is without a servant. The division between employer and servant is clear, in that servants in Gitanjali are not kin and are all employed to perform domestic work for a wage. In this chapter we concentrate on the world of servants in Gitanjali, distinguishing the different kinds of servants and the domestic work they do. To contextualize Gitanjali's servant world, we turn first to our survey, which provides a map of the state of domestic servitude in the city, covering five hundred households in three wards in North and South Kolkata (see Maps 3 and 4 on pages 30 and 31). We then examine the ways in which servants and employers differently understand the relevant terms of Kolkata's evolving culture of servitude.

Servants in Kolkata at the turn of the twenty-first century can be differentiated into four groups, defined fundamentally by residence, work schedule, and length of service. The first group, which is also the oldest and numerically the fewest, are family retainers, usually men, who have served several generations of the same family. The second group consists of live-in, full-time servants who live and work in the homes of their employers. The third group are live-out, full-time servants who work for one employer every day but who return to their own homes at the end of the day. The fourth, and today the most prevalent group in the city (74.2 percent in our survey), are the part-time domestic workers who work for several employers every day, spending a couple of hours on particular chores in each household. These part-timers, too, return to their homes each day. Table 3.1 provides some background information about domestic servants in Kolkata based on our survey.

Part-timers now constitute the clear majority of Kolkata's servants and are helping to redefine Kolkata's culture of servitude in that, as freelancers, they do not necessarily have a long-term arrangement in any one household.[3] They travel to work by foot or by train and do short stints of work (typically two hours) for multiple houses. Of course, as reflected in the survey, the power of that culture of servitude is such that part-timers often end up working in the same household for several years.[4] Nevertheless, because part-timers tend to have a home of their own and more flexibility to choose among employers, they may have a greater degree of autonomy. Although both men and women work as servants in Kolkata, most part-time servants are women. Some of the workers in the last two categories of live-out and part-time servants live in bastis and squatter settlements, while others live in outlying villages and commute to work by train (32 percent in our survey).

Gitanjali presents a cross section of the four groups, though it deviates from the survey in two significant ways. First, unlike the numbers in the survey, there is a preponderance of live-in, full-time servants, which is to be expected given that the building was designed to accommodate them. Second, wages in Gitanjali are relatively higher given its location in one of Kolkata's most affluent neighborhoods. All full-time servants working in Gitanjali flats live in the building, as do a few part-time servants, mostly women whose husbands are employed (in the building) full-time. In some cases, the children of these couples also live with them in the servants' quarters. Indeed, one of the attractions of working as a servant in Gitanjali is precisely that it offers a place to live in a city known for acute housing shortages for the poor. Other part-time

Table 3.1 Survey of Kolkata servants

	(%)
Number of servants per household	
1	62.4 (N = 59.3, S = 64.3)
2	28.4 (N = 28.6, S = 28.3)
>2	9.2 (N = 12.0, S = 7.3)*
Servant type	
Households with live-in servants	25.0
Households with live-out servants	75.0
Home of live-out workers	
Bastis in Kolkata	62.8
Outside Kolkata	30.0
Age of worker	
Under 15 years	4.4
15–20	8.2
21–30	22.8
31–40	34.6
Over 40	30.0
Family status of workers	
Single	11.0
Married	70.0
Divorced/widowed	19.0
Landownership of worker	
No land	53.6
Only homestead (without arable land)	17.0
Some land	29.4
Mode of travel to work if live-out	
By foot	66.0
By train	32.0
Tasks done*	
Wash dishes	73.8
Clean house	72.6
Cook	26.4
Provide child care/elder care	9.8
Run errands	43.4
Number of homes worked in	
1	27.8
>1	72.2
Total monthly wage**	
<Rs 500	21.4
Rs 501–1,000	53.2
>Rs 1,000	23.2
(Mean monthly wage from one house: Rs 201– 500)	
Number of years as domestic worker	
1–5	20.8
5–10	22.8
10–20	32.0
20+	24.4

SOURCE: Survey of 500 households, Kolkata 2001.

NOTE: N = North Kolkata; S = South Kolkata.

* Percentages do not total 100 because workers may perform multiple tasks.

** Percentages do not total 100 because seven workers did not receive any wages.

servants, working for several households following the general Kolkata pattern, live and walk to work from a neighboring basti. Arun, the oldest live-in servant in Gitanjali, has worked for his employers for almost thirty years, other servants have been working in the building for several years, and yet others have just begun working for one or more families. Thus, in Gitanjali, there exists simultaneously a continuum from family retainer to freelancer. While it may seem that the family retainer is a vestigial figure from the past, and part-time workers represent the present and future, in fact, at this moment, Kolkata's social formation sustains both ends of the spectrum of the culture of servitude.

The quarters are home for many of the servants of Gitanjali, and it is in the confined spaces of these rooms and corridors, the stairs, and the courtyard, that they carry out their daily lives when they are not "at work" in the apartments. The living space in a "quarter" consists of one narrow room with a window, with barely enough space for a single bed and a table. There is one bathroom for every six quarters. Servants keep their clothes and other possessions under their beds or in trunks squeezed in next to them. Many also store kerosene stoves to cook meals for their families. Saris, school uniforms, and other clothes are hung on ropes strung across the walls from corner to corner. The bits of wall that can be seen are covered with brightly colored posters of gods and goddesses. Crammed into these rooms, along with their clothes, provisions, rolled-up *madur* (sleeping mats), and children's schoolbooks, are little knick-knacks cast off by the employers—some beads, a puppet, a tarnished brass statue of the goddess Kali, a toy dog whose clockwork mechanism no longer works. In some rooms, small televisions perch precariously on a pile of battered trunks.

Those part-time servants who do not have access to Gitanjali servants' quarters, such as Ganga, an elderly widow who sweeps and mops floors in several flats, live in a basti about a ten-minute walk away. This is a relatively well-kept and clean basti with *pukka* (constructed of brick or other durable material) one-room houses, as opposed to *kacha* structures (made of mud and thatch). Some of the homes have tiny sheltered courtyards in which the residents can bathe and change their clothes. There is a tubewell in the basti from which its residents draw buckets of water for their daily use, and despite clear efforts to keep the area clean, an open drain runs along the alleys between the houses. In these one-room homes, as in the servants' quarters, the bed dominates the space, serving as seating during the day and for sleeping at night. Usually these beds are built to be quite high to maximize storage space underneath. Where there is a courtyard, men often sleep outside during the summer.

Most Gitanjali servants are migrants to the city or children of migrants, as discussed in the previous chapter. The average worker in our larger survey came from different parts of West Bengal (see Map 2 on page 29), such as Medinipur (southwest of Haora district), Murshidabad (north of Nadia district), and the Sundarbans (South 24 Parganas).[5] Many were part of the massive refugee migration between 1946 and 1971—estimated to be about four million—from what is now Bangladesh to West Bengal. Indeed, when asked where their natal home was, several Gitanjali servants named refugee camps and resettlement colonies around Kolkata.[6]

The swelling ranks of the rural dispossessed, the landless, or those who have come to be viewed as the "nearly landless," form the bulk of the migrants to the city. Our survey confirmed that the origins of Kolkata's servants are overwhelmingly in the rural areas around the city (85 percent). They or their parents left their natal villages primarily because the land could not sustain them. Over half have no land at all, and another 17 percent have only a homestead but no cultivable land.[7] In most cases, work as a domestic servant was the only source of employment available upon arrival in the city, and for many servants and their children it remains so in a context of steadily declining opportunities in the industrial and public sectors.

The fact of domestic servitude as a "permanent" occupation was borne out by our survey, in which over 75 percent of domestic workers had worked as such for more than five years, and a quarter had worked for more than twenty years. Gitanjali servants, with a few exceptions, tend to have been engaged in domestic service for many years, despite low wages, for lack of any viable alternative to the combination of work and shelter that their present situation provides. The live-in full-timers earn between Rs 500 and 2,000 per month; live-in part-timers earn less. The live-out part-time workers earn at least Rs 1,000, depending upon the number of houses in which they work.[8] Kolkata servants in general, and those in Gitanjali in particular, are clearly servants for life. Domestic service is rarely a stepping-stone to better work in the tertiary sectors, or to marriage in the case of young female migrants, as may be the case in some Latin American countries. As the survey shows, most servants are married or have been married. Nor is it a matter of apprenticing with a master until one learns appropriate skills or of being a servant until able to set up one's own home, as is the commonly told story of servants in early modern Europe.[9] Nevertheless, many of the male servants came to Kolkata with the expectation of finding office or factory work and continue to nurture such hopes, a subject we will address more fully in Chapter 5.

Tasks and Castes

> Mamata: *He'll fetch the coal, light the stove, make the tea . . . wash the tea things.*
>
> Anjan *(off-screen): Fetch cigarettes and matches.*
>
> Mamata: *Yes, and run small errands, do the dusting, go to the shops, queue for the kerosene, go to the washerman . . . look after the house whilst we're at work . . . play with Pupai. . . . And what else will he do for my darling Pupai? He'll take him to school.*
>
> Pupai: *And bring me back . . . ?*
>
> **Mrinal Sen,** *Kharij* **from** *The Absence Trilogy*

In this scene from the film *Kharij*, a young, newly middle-class couple discusses hiring a servant for the first time. As detailed in Chapter 2, a defining feature of Kolkata's culture of servitude is that servants are essential to a well-run household, and Gitanjali certainly exemplifies this premise. Gitanjali residents usually have one full-time and perhaps two part-time servants, in addition to a driver. A male live-in servant may cook and serve as a sort of "man Friday" (combination valet, butler, and runner of errands), a female part-timer may come in for two hours daily to sweep and mop the floors and wash the dishes, another may wash clothes by hand for an hour, and a jamadar may come to the flat for half an hour to clean the bathrooms and remove the garbage. Another worker washes the car daily and brings in the newspaper and the milk. A dhobi may come by every week to pick up the week's heavy laundry (sheets, towels, clothes that require starch), and yet another man sets up an ironing booth within the courtyard downstairs for the daily ironing of clothes, a chore that has recently been outsourced.

Table 3.2 shows the breakdown of tasks performed by twelve Gitanjali servants whom we interviewed about their work routines. Most of the tasks are done on a daily basis because this is considered necessary by the employing households; some tasks, however, such as polishing brass and silver, may be done less frequently.[10] In Kolkata, servants' domestic responsibilities vary within the broad parameters presented in the following discussion. As servants attest, each employer has peculiarities, and the servants' task is to familiarize themselves with their employer's particular demands.

All the servants in this table are full-time live-in servants, with the exception of part-timer Aparna, who shares the Gitanjali quarter assigned to her husband, Kamal; Guru, who, as a bathroom sweeper in the building (part-time for each flat), lives separately in quarters on the lower level; and part-timer Ganga, who lives in a nearby basti. Cleaning, cooking, and washing dishes are

Table 3.2 Domestic tasks performed by selected Gitanjali servants

Tasks	Aparna (F)	Sonali (F)	Durga (F)	Ganga (F)	Shyamali (F)	Shibani (F)	Arun (M)	Sunil (M)	Raghu (M)	Balai (M)	Kamal (M)	Guru (M)	Total
Housekeeper								x	x				2
Cleaning	x									x	x		3
dusting	x		x		x					x	x	x	6
sweeping	x			x								x	3
mopping	x			x									2
polishing					x					x			2
making bed					x					x	x		3
Bathroom												x	1
Laundry													
washing	x			x	x					x			4
ironing					x					x	x		3
Dishes				x	x	x		x	x	x	x		7
pots and pans										x			1
Bazaar													
food								x	x	x	x		4
errands										x	x		2
Cooking		x	x	x		x	x	x		x			7
grinding masala				x	x					x			3
chopping vegetables					x					x			2
serving meals										x	x		2
Child care			x		x								2
Patient care	x												1
massage					x								1
Gardening											x		1
Number of tasks	6	1	3	6	10	2	1	4	3	14	9	3	

NOTE: F = female; M = male.

the predominant tasks (which corresponds to the results from the survey presented in Table 3.1), with most servants assigned a handful of specific tasks. Two of the men, Balai and Kamal, who have the overall charge of a household, perform the most tasks, along with Shyamali, who is burdened with tasks that would be allocated to additional part-timers in most other Gitanjali households. We observe here that the task categorization and boundaries are such that sweeping and cooking are never done by the same servant (Aparna, the exception, sweeps in one house and cooks in another). The worker who takes out the garbage and cleans the bathrooms does only that. We also note that, as in the survey, very few servants are dedicated to child care. We speculate that this may be an artifact of the families we happened to interview, whose children were either school age or older, or could reflect the fact that few of the women employers work outside the home, or indeed that there are still viable joint families or joint family sensibilities such that female relatives take responsibility for child care. In other words, cooks, maids, and part-time workers may in fact assist in getting children ready for school (packing lunch boxes, ironing school clothes) and look after children while performing other duties, but they are not considered child minders.

Keeping the upper-middle-class home functioning smoothly seems to require constant vigilance and care. Sounds of servant activity can be heard as early as six in the morning in Gitanjali as servants arrive in the flats, bring in the milk, and begin making the morning tea for the employing households. At 7:00 A.M., the doorbell starts ringing as the liftman (elevator operator), who earns extra money delivering newspapers, drops off each apartment's selection of newspapers, followed by another worker who comes to the flats to pick up car keys in order to wash and clean the residents' vehicles, and later drops the keys off. In the meantime, usually the cook or other full-time servant makes breakfast (often a cooked meal), lays the table, and clears once the household has eaten. Once breakfast is over, beds are made, often by the same servant, and a part-timer arrives to help with the daily dusting, sweeping, and mopping. The employers' children get ready (their clothes have been washed and ironed by part-timers and are ready to wear, and lunches are packed in lunch boxes, thanks to the cook) and are taken to school by a driver. The employers leave for work (usually only the man but sometimes the woman as well), and the servants continue cleaning the house and start preparing lunch.

Lunch is always a cooked meal and requires the fresh grinding of spices every day. Food preparation and consumption are a central organizing principle of Bengali middle-class life, and few shortcuts are permitted. Durga, who does the cooking for a multigenerational joint family, describes a work schedule that seems almost impossible to sustain. Her employers like variety in the meals, so in addition to preparing a cooked breakfast and a midmorning snack, Durga must make several different vegetable preparations for lunch, as well as packed lunches for the children and their working father. In addition, she prepares fried snacks at teatime, followed by a multicourse dinner.

At any time during the morning, one hears the rhythmic sounds of carpets being beaten, the clang of pots and pans being washed, crying children being comforted, food sizzling as it fries, garbage being emptied, and the raised voices of women employers giving instructions to the servants and berating them for a job done sloppily or slowly or incorrectly. The doorbell rings incessantly as part-time servants, deliverymen, repairmen, and vendors of food and snacks arrive. The two or three hours following lunch are the only quiet period in the building; then with afternoon tea at five begins the evening routine, which persists until at least ten o'clock at night when the dinner has been eaten and cleared away and the beds prepared for sleep. Hence the workday for most full-time servants in Gitanjali is 6:00 A.M. to 2:00 P.M. and 5:00 P.M. to 10:00 P.M.—typically more than a twelve-hour working day.

Gitanjali forms a social world for the live-in and longtime live-out servants. There are close friendships and enmities, rivalries and alliances, that flourish in the corridors and in the courtyard. Most live-in servants in Gitanjali are allowed a rest period in the afternoon. The women tend to cook for their own families, wash clothes, and rest for an hour or so, while the male servants get together to play cards, smoke, and chat. In these periods, stories are exchanged about home, daily problems, and troublesome employers. The servants (with the exception of Guru, the jamadar, who is an employee of the building association) do not belong to a union, but certain servants are informally recognized as leaders or brokers, even by the employers. These leaders play an important role when it comes to blacklisting bad employers, obtaining employer help for particular servants in need, or, indeed, withdrawing support from a particular servant after a falling-out or because that person has come to be considered problematic by the group. The children of Gitanjali servants play in the courtyard downstairs, occasionally with the children of the employers but usually only with one another.

Whether servant occupations or tasks are related to their caste is a complex issue. The question of servant caste has indeed depended historically on occu-

pation and task, though in Bengal, castes have been less associated with hereditary occupation groups than in other parts of India. Although one would expect
servants to be lower caste precisely because they are lower in the class and race
hierarchy in the same way that African Americans in the past and Mexicans
today form the bulk of domestic workers in the United States, or indigenous
women in Latin America, this is only partially true in Bengal. S. N. Mukherjee
has argued that three-fourths of Calcutta's Brahmins in the nineteenth century
were domestic servants.[11] Indeed, cooks in traditional Bengali Hindu households were almost exclusively Brahmin through the mid-twentieth century.
The main caste distinction in nineteenth-century Bengal appears to be between
those servants from whose hand upper-caste Hindu employers could accept
water (*jalchal*) and those from whom they could not (*ajalchal*).[12] The ajalchal
belonged to low castes and tended to be those servants who performed ritually impure tasks such as cleaning bathrooms and, especially, washing dishes.
In the past, therefore, servants could be upper or lower caste, according to the
nature of the task. Today, by and large, servants are lower caste; our survey,
for example, shows that more than half of the servants are scheduled caste.[13]
Gitanjali servants include Brahmins, scheduled castes, other backward classes
(OBCs), and Christians.

In Gitanjali there are no Muslim servants—quite possibly because of the
absence of Muslim employers—although there are Muslim drivers (chauf-
feurs). During the colonial period, in the nineteenth and into the twentieth
centuries, some rich and westernized Hindu households distinguished themselves by keeping Muslim cooks; otherwise, those Muslim servants employed
by Hindu families did outdoor jobs. Today, wealthy and westernized Hindu
families continue to hire Muslim servants for defined jobs, principally as drivers and perhaps as bearers (butlers). In parallel fashion, Muslim families in
general have Muslim servants. Yet, as we have seen, most middle-class families
tend to acquire servants from the surrounding area. Middle-class Hindu families who live in areas adjacent to Muslim slums have access primarily to Muslim
maids. In these circumstances a mutually satisfactory fiction is created such
that a woman whose name may be Rehana will find work with a Hindu family
by presenting herself as Lakshmi. The only discrepancy in this fiction is that
Hindu Lakshmi fasts during the Muslim fasting month of Ramzan (Ramadan),
a fact about which no one chooses to comment. Servants from other minority
communities also take care not to offend or draw the attention of the dominant
religion. In Gitanjali, Balai, who is Christian, refuses to cook beef for his secular

Hindu employers and declines to eat beef himself, in order not to be perceived as an outsider by the Hindu servants with whom he lives.

An unmistakable task- and caste-driven division of labor is evident in most Kolkata households, exemplified by the fact that the bathroom cleaner is almost always exclusively that, and always belongs to the lowest castes. In all houses servants eat separately, often in the kitchen, from plates and glasses specially kept aside for them. They generally sit on the floor or on low stools and have separate toilet and washing facilities. Employers may speak easily of discarding old caste habits, but these habits have peculiar resilience. Within the social world of servants, too, we noticed that many of the live-in servants of Gitanjali were unwilling to introduce us to Guru, the scheduled caste jamadar. Nonetheless, we could not make the easy assumption that his caste set him apart since several Gitanjali servants are also scheduled caste. It may be both his inferior status as one who cleans bathrooms and his outsider status as a Bihari that set him apart in the other servants' eyes.[14]

Yet Guru's life story reveals just how entrenched caste-based servitude can be. He comes from a line of men who have worked as jamadars, or sweepers, as they are also called in local parlance. He works for the Gitanjali Building Association as a sweeper, his father was a sweeper for the Calcutta Corporation (municipality), and his grandfather before that. Born in the state of Bihar in 1956 to an impoverished family (his father, like many, had migrated to the big city, leaving his family behind), Guru worked from the age of four as a domestic servant, for which he received food and Rs 10 per month and was also allowed to study. In 1962, he came to Calcutta, and since his father was earning only about Rs 30 a month, as the eldest son (with three brothers and a sister who died) Guru had to quit school; from around the age of ten or twelve, he worked as a coolie carrying loads. In the 1970s Guru started working as a sweeper, first for a printing press and then in 1978, through his maternal uncle, who was the sweeper for the assistant commissioner of police, he found his present job at Gitanjali.

Guru also married in 1978 when he started working at Gitanjali and now has three daughters and a son. He lives in Gitanjali servants' quarters, but like many servants who migrated from the countryside and cannot afford to keep their families in Kolkata, including his father before him, Guru's wife and children live in a village in Bihar. He sees his family every six months for two weeks (which corresponds to the twenty-eight vacation days allowed by the Gitanjali Building Association). As landless laborers, the members of his caste community work in the homes or fields of peasant families in the village. Guru's wife does casual farm labor when there is work available.

Guru works from 6:00 A.M. to 8:00 P.M. six days a week, with an hour for lunch. He augments his income from Gitanjali with jobs in other houses in the area, for which the wage is negotiated separately depending on the kind of tasks performed (sweeping, mopping, dusting, and/or cleaning bathrooms). Guru indicated that basically he takes whatever wage is offered; his circumstances do not allow him to pick and choose. In general, he has no complaints about his employers, displaying a rather stoic indifference to being on the receiving end of "rough" language.

While there have been some attempts to organize domestic workers in Kolkata, both by organizations linked to the ruling Communist Party of India (Marxist), as well as by independent women's groups, these efforts have had minimal success (a topic addressed in Chapter 8). Guru is one of the very few who actually belong to a union, quite possibly because his is a relatively unique case in that he works primarily for a building association that includes all the households in the Gitanjali flats, rather than for numerous individual and unrelated households, as is the situation of most part-timers.[15] He joined the union in 1981 when, he says, his salary was very low. The union was able to negotiate a higher salary as well as a uniform (which not only saves on expenses for work clothes but also confers a certain measure of status). However, Guru does not see much benefit in turning to the union; if he is let go by a particular house, he loses money while the union tries to rectify the situation. Moreover, if too many union-backed demands are made on employers, he believes he will be fired and will be the one to suffer. Although he views the union as being of greater utility in factories than in houses, the union succeeded in negotiating, for him and the other workers employed by the building association, a three-year agreement with Gitanjali that covers salaries, vacations, and bonuses. A bonus often takes the form of one month's salary during the main Bengali Hindu festival season known as the *puja* holidays. Notwithstanding, Guru only laughs when asked whether he will eventually receive a pension when he retires.

Although he would rather not be a sweeper, Guru sees no way out. Given his scheduled caste origins, his life as a sweeper in the city is better than what it would be in the village in Bihar:

> I would certainly do something else if I could get it. But I never did get any other kind of work [repeated]. Now where will I get other work? . . . I'm older; my

family has increased. If I don't work, I can't feed them. . . . Of course I would rather be in the village with my children and family, but I have to work here. If I had found work in the village, of course I would be there; why would I leave? But there are no jobs in the village. The only jobs available are pulling rickshaws or *thelas* [carts]. In the village, we can't sit in front of the *baniyas* [trading castes]. They would not like us to sit on this cot that I am sitting on in front of them, and they would want us to stand when we are talking to them. We work as laborers in their homes. The upper castes run the *panchayat* [village council] and have to be bribed if we want anything like tubewells. . . . Things will get better if we have a better leader; someday there has to be one.

Guru's trajectory is in line with an already charted migration stream for men of his caste, rural to urban migrants in search of menial labor in the big city. Weighing the trade-off between the particularly humiliating forms of caste discrimination in his village against a certain structured discrimination in the city that is coupled with steady waged work, the choice for Guru is clear. He regards the potentially complicated relationships among workers in Gitanjali with indifference. Relations with the other servants are, he says, "fine; they work; I work." He does not seem to meet any of them socially, although he does have a friend nearby, a "brother" from a neighboring village. In the city at large, Guru believes that they [his community] are treated well, remarking that when walking on the street, one can talk to anybody. In his father's time, however, "it was very different, a lot of untouchability. If I ate near the others, they would not like that. That was a whole different time."

Even as Guru is able to perceive some incremental change for the better in the condition of his community, and despite the however ineffectual support of the union, he is encumbered by a multiplicity of social, economic, and cultural constraints and feels trapped in a life that is certainly not of his choosing. And in this way Guru's story varies only slightly from those of other servants.

A World of "Unfreedom"

> If I ever asked her if I could go and get some news of my son, she'd say no, not right now, there's too much work. If I said I had to go out and buy provisions, she'd tell me to go and come back by a certain time. If I was late she would shout at me. I wasn't allowed to go anywhere, or to talk to any one.
>
> **Baby Haldar,** *A Life Less Ordinary*

In a recent celebrated autobiography, *A Life Less Ordinary*, a young woman who works as a domestic servant wrote about the sheer "unfreedom" of being a live-in servant. But, she concluded, "In some ways, things were not so bad. I lived in a large house. We ate reasonably well. I was getting paid regularly and I even managed to save a little bit. But I missed my son."[16]

The structural dependency of servants, of being caught in a work/home bind with nowhere to go, is a defining element of Kolkata's culture of servitude. This culture is premised to a significant degree on the employer conviction that servants are essential and "part of the family," bound to it by ties of affection, loyalty, and dependence. These characteristics arise from the past of the big house and memories of growing up with longtime, faithful servants, or family retainers, but also inflect the present. Servant indispensability means that their absence is regarded as a considerable inconvenience. Servant discourse mirrors this double-edged sense of dependency. Servants are well aware of employers' dependence on them—servants are essential—and acutely sensitive to the nature of domestic work, which they describe as *paradhin* (literally "unfree," or dependent) rather than *swadhin* (independent).

Employers commonly separate servants into two groups, full-time and part-time. Part-time is used to describe servants who work for multiple households every day as well as those who are on duty in one household, for example, from 8:00 A.M. to 1:00 P.M. and then from 4:00 P.M. to 8:00 P.M., a schedule that would make it nearly impossible for them to work elsewhere. The key here is whether or not the servants leave the employers' premises and go to their own homes in the afternoons and then again at night. Thus, part-time servants are actually live-out servants, and the conflation of "live-out" with "part-time," and "live-in" with "full-time" signals the extent to which employer understanding is bound up with the availability of labor. If a servant is in the employer's home, then the assumption is that he or she is there to work, regardless of the hours of duty.

For servants, *paradhinata* (unfreedom) is defined both by the nature of their work and by the fundamental difference between living in the home of the employer and living in their own home. Indeed, in Bangladesh, live-in servants refer to themselves as *bandha* (bound), and live-out servants are *chhuta* (free).[17] The primary distinction, then, for both employers and servants, depends on the servant's place of residence, although for employers the crucial matter pivots on access to labor, and for servants, access to autonomy. Such a distinction is also echoed in the lives of the nanny-housekeepers Hondagneu-Sotelo studied in Los Angeles.[18] In Kolkata, the continuum from bandha/bound/dependent to chhuta/free/independent parallels that from family retainer to freelancer, from greater dependency to greater autonomy, although all servants would describe their work condition as paradhin.

We have suggested that the category "family retainer" is employer defined and, as such, most fully carries the weight of employer expectation and desire. It is a category based on long duration of service in one home and/or to one family, often over the course of three or four generations, and is necessarily applied to a servant in retrospect. No one sets out to become a family retainer, after all, nor is anyone hired to be one. Lakshman, whose story we examine in the next section, was originally taken on as a child servant. Lakshman is considered to be the epitome of that most desired characteristic, loyalty, often understood by employers as a combination of constancy, which he has certainly demonstrated, and dedication to the interests of the employing family (often at the cost of the servant's own the family), which he has also exhibited over several decades.

Lakshman's Story

> *I do hereby give, devise, and bequeath my bangle [churi], which I have on my left hand, to [servant] for his dedicated service absolutely and forever.*
> **From a will (Kolkata, November 2000)**

Lakshman has been working for the same family for fifty years. He was sent by his parents to work in a big house in North Calcutta ("a man from the village brought me here"), since their land in Orissa was insufficient to sustain the entire family. He was ten years old when he came to the city, and he is over sixty years old now. "When I was young, I didn't have enough to eat in my village. So my mother said to that man, 'Take him and put him to work in a good home.'" Lakshman liked Calcutta as a boy, for his first impression was that people were nice and food plentiful.

As he told us his story, Lakshman spoke in a distant and flat tone, reporting his losses and decisions as if they had happened to someone else:

Who did you leave behind in the village?
My mother.

Only your mother? No brothers and sisters?
Oh yes, I had sisters; they were married off. I was the youngest. And then I came here [Calcutta] to Dadu's house, and then my mother died and I never saw her again. We were on holiday with the family in Hazaribagh when I got the news. I went back to the village to perform the last rites.

Didn't you have anyone of your own in Calcutta?
When this family became like my own, I forgot about everything else.

How did they make you their own?
When my mother died, I thought, "I have another mother and another father," and in this way I forgot the others. When my mother died, I thought to myself, "I will make these my own people."

So you decided this?
Yes, I did.

As a boy, Lakshman learned how to cook, even as he played with the daughter of the house. His employer showered him with affection and had him sleep on a little bed in the *puja* (prayer) room but did not allow him to "mix" with the other children in the neighborhood. He assisted his employer in preparing for the daily prayers and would even pray with her: "I used to make garlands for the goddesses."

He knew how to read a little in Oriya, but his employers never sent him to school. He lived and worked in Calcutta, returned briefly to his natal village to get married when he was twenty-six years old, but continued to live with his employers while his wife stayed in the village. While his wife was alive, he saw her once or twice a year. By this time, the first generation of employers had passed away and he began working for their daughter—his former playmate. "She loved me like a younger brother. They really loved me very much. Everybody loved me." Today, he works for the third generation of the same family.

Lakshman came alive only when we asked him if he felt that he had suffered. He asked, "Do you want to hear about my suffering? *My* suffering?" When he spoke, he made it clear that he suffered deeply and that his suffering had at least three root causes: "Once I left home, I never saw my mother again. . . . I have no son [who would be expected to take care of him in his old age], only a daughter, and that causes me sadness. . . . We've labored for the babus all our lives and yet we are left with nothing."

Lakshman cannot go home anymore. What, after all, is home to someone who left his natal village and family when he was a child of ten? Having sent all of his money to his family over the years, he has no savings in his old age. In any event, he now earns a meager Rs 400 per month from which nothing can be saved.

He does have opinions about the employers of the past compared to his employers today. They were better in the past, he says, more affectionate and caring, and now they work the servants harder and nag incessantly. He measures his life with the family of his employers both through their declining love for him and what he identifies as three betrayals. The first was when he was still a young man and, wanting a better life, decided that he would look for a factory job. At that point, his employer (Ma) asked him to stay on with them and promised him a job in her son-in-law's factory. So Lakshman waited, but the factory never opened. The second, many years later, occurred when he asked Ma's daughter, Didi ("elder sister," also a term of respect used by younger relatives, close friends, and servants), for more security; she pledged that she would give him land but had a stroke before fulfilling the promise. But that was not the worst, says Lakshman.

> She would lie there, we would hold hands, I would tell her about my sorrows, and she would cry. One day, I was sitting at her bedside and weeping, saying to her, "You promised me a factory job, and then land, and now you're sick, so what is to become of me?" She said, "You take this necklace." She tried to use her working hand to give me the necklace. I told her, "I don't want the necklace; I wanted a job. I don't have anything; I don't have a son." She was lying there, half-paralyzed, trying to give me this necklace, and then Sahib [Didi's son] said, "Why would you give such a valuable necklace to Lakshman?" Then she said, "I couldn't give him a job, so I wanted to give him this necklace." I felt hurt, but of course I didn't want the necklace. I also thought, how much is this necklace worth? I don't really need this necklace. So I said, "Didi, I don't want this necklace." Sahib pulled the necklace away, separating our hands, pushed me away and said leave this room. Even after Sahib did this, Didi tried to hold on to my hand. I told Didi, "Don't cry; you don't have to give me the necklace. Even if I get another job, I'll still stay with you." So the necklace was taken back, and I was shoved away. What can I say? It's just my fate.

If Lakshman responded vaguely to many of the questions we asked him during the course of our conversation, he described the previous scene with stunning visual clarity. It is a scene he has clearly replayed many times in his mind and is, for him, the moment of final betrayal. In Lakshman's reckoning, it is a life for a necklace, which the older woman offered him and which her son retracted. The employer's son, Sahib, now Lakshman's employer, indicated through his words and actions at the crucial moment that his mother had offered Lakshman more payment than Lakshman's labor—or his life—was worth.

Lakshman perceived that Sahib did not think a lifetime of service was worth even a necklace. This mismatch in the moral and political economy of servitude reflects a movement between the feudal and modern social imaginaries, to which servants and employers repeatedly return. Even the terms with which Lakshman addresses his employers denotes this shift. His first employer was addressed as mother, Ma; the second (Ma's daughter) as elder sister, Didi; the third, no longer familial—Sahib refers generically to the class of bosses. Later, Sahib, now his official employer, asked Lakshman to stay on and requested that he "see me [Sahib] off" before leaving the family's employ. Lakshman stayed on, although he wondered: "But what about me? I have no one to look after me. I can see you off [the great crossing], but what about me? So Ma has gone, Baba [father] has gone, Didi has gone, you'll be gone . . . and then what will become of me?"

Lakshman remained the loyal family retainer for his employers, although his narrative is punctuated by abortive attempts to leave, coupled with increasing resignation that he will never be able to do so. Moreover, his employer's plea that Lakshman continue serving until he, Sahib, dies reveals that rather than recognizing a lifetime of servitude by arranging to care for their loyal family retainer in his dotage as might be anticipated under the rules of feudal servitude, the tables are turned in an ultimate betrayal: Lakshman is bound and will sacrifice even his old age. The line between his life's work and some definitions of slavery is hard to draw.[19]

In the world of "unfreedom" in Gitanjali, a handful of other servants have worked for decades for their employers. Arun, nearing seventy years of age, is about to complete thirty years of service to the same family as a live-in servant. However, unlike Lakshman, he did not start out his working life as a servant but tried farming in his native village, factory work in Calcutta, and contract labor in different places in northeastern India, before beginning to work as a cook. His starting wage was Rs 80 and is now about Rs 550, most of which he, like Lakshman, sends back home to the village to support his wife, who does not work outside the home. His children, three sons and two daughters, are adults now; the daughters are married, and his sons show no signs of supporting their parents.

Could Arun also be considered a family retainer based on length of service and the fact that he, like Lakshman, has ostensibly devoted himself to a family that is not his own?

> This family is fond of me but not enough to give me more money. [They don't] even give money for medicine. They give us [referring to the other domestic in the flat, Shyamali] a few clothes. I suppose I'm okay here. I say sometimes that

I will leave. They [employers] say, "Where will you go? You have no other skills. Make the best of what you can here." And they are right. As I grow older, they will forgive me if I do less [work]. But who else would forgive me?

Sometimes, if I forget to put salt in the food, they still eat it. Others wouldn't let me get away with that. Also, if I'm ill for two days [and don't come to work], I can get away with it. I don't know if I would be able to with a new family. The old lady [his elderly employer] used to give me orders before, but now she is ill and she says, "Do everything by yourself." I know what they want, and I can manage without guidance.

Arun's words reveal a mutual dependency at the end of life, notwithstanding the chasm of class and the certainty that he will end his days as poverty stricken as when he was young. As both he and his employers age, they are willing to overlook small lapses and also to relinquish to him a degree of decision making about his tasks. It is quite conceivable that his employers would describe him as loyal, affectionate, and dependent—he considers himself entirely paradhin—yet while Arun is quite matter-of-fact about their affection for him, he does not express any in return. Perhaps unsurprisingly, few of the servants in this study mentioned affection for employers or the employers' children in their charge.

In contrast, employers' memories of the past of the big house highlight the love that family retainers had for the employing families and seeming indifference toward their own. Older employers, especially, emphasize the loving care they received as children from these servants, servants who somehow did not have families of their own. When questioned, some employers claimed that the servants' families were dead, and others that the servants did not have much contact with their families beyond sending money home to the village every month. This is a theme that will be explored more fully in the next chapter, but it is unambiguous in the story of a family retainer like Lakshman that it was precisely the pain of losing his own mother and being orphaned as a young boy that led him to adopt the employing family as his own. He describes his suffering: "Once I left home, I never saw my mother again. When my mother died, I thought to myself, 'I will make these my own people.'"

In Gitanjali today, the servants' world revolves around their families, which are the prime justification for engaging in paradhin work and staying with it in the hope that their children will never be forced to become servants. Not unlike their middle-class employers, servants speak of making sacrifices for their children and regret their inability to spend time with them. Indeed, as Aparna, thirty-five, says fiercely, when we ask her what she wants out of life:

> A nine-to-five job. I want holidays and health care. No one thinks that we, too, have a life. We do so much for their babies—what about ours? We come home, and we are so tired that we slap her [their daughter, if she is demanding] or yell at her. Poor thing. It is not her fault that we don't have any money.

Love for their children and the desperate hope that their sacrifices will not be in vain are the constant refrain in their conversation, even as they chafe at the lack of freedom.

Perhaps for servants, a family retainer is merely a servant who never left—and was not let go—and ends his days in the home of his employers, in many cases having nowhere else to turn. Other contemporary live-in servants are distinguished by the *possibility* of leaving their employers' homes and, indeed, quitting servitude itself. In Gitanjali, there are live-in servants who, even after fifteen years of working for the same family, hope to leave one day. Others have toyed with leaving but are now reconciled to the idea that carrying on is the only available option. Yet they are aware that loyalty, constancy, and service do not necessarily guarantee a home and minimal care for life—the imagined terms of being a family retainer in the past of the big house. Raghu's anxiety about being a live-in cook and man Friday for nearly twenty years involves both the state of unfreedom and the lack of any guarantee in return: "If they say I have to go, I have to go—there are no certificates or anything," while long-term live-in Kamal says, "They will either fire me or retire me."

Time and Labor Regimes

If one striking characteristic of domestic arrangements of the big house was that servants were always, as one employer put it, "at the beck and call" of the employer, the new temporality associated with flat living with servants' quarters has meant that servants are now on a schedule. There is more a sense of a work-day since servants come to work at a specific time in the early morning, typically take an afternoon rest period, and return to their quarters at night. In this new regime of regulated work hours, employers were seen to be obsessed with timing, and servants resented their constant nagging. One Gitanjali employer, sixty-five-year-old Sharmila, explicitly described to us how she scolded her servant for returning to work after her afternoon rest at 6:00 P.M. rather than at 5:00: "They think they have been here for a while and can take advantage of me. But if you are too fussy, they can't handle it." What she perceives as having to exercise restraint, servants perceive as harassment. Shyamali's employer, for example, always says, "Why can't you people come on time?" if Shyamali is late returning from her midafternoon bath. The employer's tendency to address a particular servant as "you people," as if referring to the entire servant class, was seen to be especially degrading. While employers continually complain about slowness, tardiness, and laziness, servants feel they have too little time to complete their assigned tasks.

The condition of unfreedom in everyday life means, among other things, that servants must submit to employers' inflexibility about working conditions and schedules and, often, to what they consider to be exploitation. There is a common understanding about the workday of a full-time servant in Gitanjali, but the time boundaries are elastic. Morning work may begin as early as 6:00 and may end as late as 3:00 P.M., and the evening shift usually begins after 4:00 P.M., but it may extend past 10:00 at night. Even if there is no task at hand, some servants cannot leave the employer's home during established work hours, and fifty-year-old Sunil finds it especially demeaning to have to ask permission to go out for even an hour.

> I work for a single man. I make morning tea, clean the house, do the marketing, make breakfast, and then I eat. I cook three or four dishes for lunch, and make Sahib a cup of coffee after lunch. Then I clear the table and wash the dishes before I leave. I return at 4:00 or 4.30 in the afternoon, make tea and snacks for him, and then I have no work until 7:00 P.M. But even though I have no work, I cannot return to my quarters; I have to stay there. At 7:00, I cook dinner, serve it, clear away the dishes, wash up, and then I can leave.

Durga has a particularly demanding work schedule since she is the cook and child minder for a household of six. She works from 6:30 A.M. until 2:30 or 3:00 P.M. and then again from 5:00 P.M. to 10:00 at night. In return she gets a salary, tea with two pieces of bread, and lunch, usually with one piece of fish or meat. "These people do not pay well, and they don't give food generously, but then who does?" she asks. This is especially grating since, as mentioned earlier, Durga's employers are quite demanding about meals, and she is required to cook five times a day.

Of all the workers in Gitanjali, thirty-seven-year-old Shibani is the most unhappy with her employers. She resents the way her employers own her time and insist that she work around their schedule, although as the person performing the work, she believes she knows the best way to do things. She attributes their often rude behavior to the fact that she is paradhin, and she states flatly, "I stay only because of my children." In particular, she resents her employers' distrust—though she is the cook, she is not allowed to open the fridge, which is kept locked—and their lack of generosity.

> They give me only stale food and not enough rice. If I tell them I need anything, they say, "You are greedy in everything [*beshi lobh*]." One time I told them I needed more rice, and she [the employer] said, "*Koto khao! Koto khabey!* [How much do you eat? How much more do you want to eat!]"

Employers' stinginess with food is coupled with their meanness with time and money. Servants point to the employers' desire to extract as much labor in as little time and for as little money as possible. Shibani is allotted a few days off a year, but her employers require that she complete the tasks she would have done in that time before she leaves. Shyamali's employers—who are particularly concerned with timing—have gradually eliminated the part-timers who did polishing and other such tasks, and these tasks have been added to her workload, but with no additional compensation. Tensions arising from unequal bargains over labor, time, and money pervade Gitanjali, as thirty-eight-year-old Kamal explains:

> Sometimes they say, "If you do these five things, I will give you this much money." And then they give you eight things to do. I have two choices. I can refuse and make her [his employer] angry, or I can do all eight and hope that she will be pleased and will give me extra money. If I can please you, you will be pleased with me.

Although Kamal presents this negotiation as an option, there is, of course, no real choice. His condition of dependency dictates that he choose the second option—to please his employer so that she will have an incentive to continue employing him or to treat him well—even though his acceptance creates a new, more stringent baseline for the next round of "bargaining." For live-in servants, then, despite customary regulation of work timing, tasks, and remuneration, their labor power is infinitely available to employers. In Gitanjali, there is less difference between full-time and part-time servants in this respect than in Kolkata as a whole, given that almost all are, in effect, live-in servants. Indeed, part-time servants such as Aparna, who live in Gitanjali's servants' quarters, complain of being treated as full-time servants—although they are paid only

Part-time workers in driveway of middle-class flat complex.

SOURCE: Photograph by Seemin Qayum.

for part-time work—precisely because employers always have access to their labor. Thus, Durga says with finality, "For those who have a place to live [of their own], part-time work is better, even if it is too much work."

The Transition to Part-Time Work

As the movement to part-time work becomes more predominant in the city, employers find themselves with less control over servants in both spatial and temporal terms. Not only do servants live out but since they work for multiple employers, no one employer can hope to command their full attention and loyalty. Because part-time workers typically work in four or five houses, performing a set number of tasks in each house, they are especially task and time driven. They are always rushed, since their livelihood depends on getting to the next job on time, and they know that they will be reprimanded if they are late. Because of the exigencies of their schedule, they are, in fact, often late. "Everyone hurries us all the time, and so I can't handle it. I just take my watch off and work at my own pace." The cultural dissonance between feudal peasant and industrial capitalist time and work practices discussed by E. P. Thompson are lived every day by Kolkata residents struggling to comprehend a not dissimilar transition.[20]

As they hurry from one place of work to another, part-timers realize that there is no place for them to rest, even in the street. "If we sit down on someone's stoop even for a minute, we are scolded, 'Who are you? What are you doing here?'" Yet the footsteps of the part-timers connect the different loci of the city—houses, flats, bastis, squatter settlements, markets, trains. In the expressive phrases of Michel de Certeau, "Their story begins on ground level, with footsteps. They are myriad, but do not compose a series. They cannot be counted because each unit has a qualitative character. . . . Their swarming mass is an innumerable collection of singularities. Their intertwined paths give their shape to spaces. They weave places together."[21]

Ganga and Sita live in the same basti, located a short distance from Gitanjali, and both began working as part-timers about twenty years ago because of their husbands' inability to provide a steady income. Forty-two-year-old Sita, who recently stopped working because of her health, says that she had no other option but domestic work because "I can't even sign my own name; how could I work in a factory?" Sita cobbled together a living based on a complicated rotation among six houses, an arrangement that endured for eighteen years. When she started working as a servant, she made a total of Rs 400 per month, and by the time she left, her principal employer alone paid her Rs 400. As a part-timer she never received vacation benefits but simply had to take time off when she could, incurring the employers' ire as a result. Nor was there a pension: "No one gave me anything when I left."

Sita counts herself as having been lucky in her employers because she was able to bring her small children with her to work, a practice that she notes is unacceptable today. Yet her working life, as she recalls it, was full of excessive demands on her time and labor, scoldings when she was late, and anger when she asked for a raise. She devised ways to swallow her own anger and resentment at bad treatment. She would go downstairs, wait until she recovered, and then go back to work. She says that she kept quiet because of her illiteracy, afraid that if she left a house, she would not be able to find a replacement. Hence she stayed with the same set of houses for nearly two decades.

Roy's interview with a part-timer who lives in a squatter settlement along the side of the railway tracks at Jadavpur station also shows the precarious livelihood of part-timers today:

> In those days, it was easier to find work. Now, I want to add one more household but I can't find work. There is so much competition from all of these women who come on the trains. They are so poor. They will take any rate. . . . That's how insecure we are. We miss work for some reason or other. Our bodies give out. Or the trains don't work. And we are fired. It is like living with a gun to our head. There are hundreds of others to take our place.[22]

The ease with which part-timers are replaced was confirmed by several part-timers in our study, many of whom began working at eight or ten years of age, who use a crèche in middle-class Salt Lake in the eastern part of the city: "If you are sick and you miss even one day, they [employers] will replace you, and when you come back to work the next day, they will say, 'Why are you entering the house? We don't need you. Go away.'"

Sita has an intimate understanding of what it means for "our bodies to give out" and underscores that part-time domestic work is strenuous. Only those who have been brought up to do it are able to withstand the bodily strain and pain. She has deliberately brought up and educated her daughters to attain better employment options, but, she adds with a laugh, they would in any case be physically unable to perform domestic work.

Fifty-seven-year-old Ganga, too, is tired and worn out after years of backbreaking floor cleaning, clothes washing, and spice grinding in five Gitanjali flats and hopes to retire soon. Ganga works six days a week from 8:30 A.M.

to 3:30 P.M. (for which she earns a total of Rs 1,000 per month) and then will sometimes eat with one of "the people who love me" in the servants' quarters. In her basti also, she says, people look after one another. Like every other part-timer in our study, Ganga recoils from employers yelling at her when she is late or misses a day because of illness. She wishes that employers would not take advantage by failing to compensate her for doing the work of another servant on leave. Yet she agrees with the other Gitanjali servants cited previously that it is preferable to work as a part-timer. There is less at stake if she decides she must leave one household, although as the sole support of her orphaned grandchildren, she has to work as much as she physically can. Ganga believes that despite the petty abuse of irate employers, she has more control over her life and work than those who are dependent on one employer. After all, she can leave Gitanjali behind every afternoon and return to her own home.

Conclusion

Servants and employers may inhabit the same culture of servitude but understand its terms differently. For employers, the family retainer is distinguished from the part-timer by his selfless loyalty, on the one hand, and his dependent presence, on the other. For the servants, however, the shift from live-in family retainer to freelancer is marked by differential autonomy and employer control over servant labor power. In other words, what is seen by employers as a fundamental difference of character between family retainers and part-timers is quite clearly seen as a difference in the labor regime by servants themselves.

What all the servants in our survey and in-depth study share is that they perform household labor in private space and that they can expect a lifetime of this labor. Neither marriage nor promotion will likely take them out of this job, though it is also likely that at least some of their children will not be servants. What differentiates them from one another is their degree of freedom and autonomy, and whether they sell their labor (their presence) or labor power (through their tasks). As the spectrum within one building shows, two different time and labor regimes may coexist, with servants who are strongly tied to one employer working alongside servants who have weaker relational ties to multiple employers. The coexistence of these dual regimes means that servants are aware of the gains and losses from each form of labor. While all agree that part-time work—freelancing—is preferable, they are keenly aware of the costs of autonomy, as we shall see in subsequent chapters.

4 Disquieting Transitions

Every upper-class household had a large fleet of faithful retainers whose
efficiency was unquestionable. It may sound incredible but in those days the
servants were proud of their work and their masters' social position. Some
of them were excellent advertisements for the affluence and stylishness of a
particular household. Our jamadar, Munshi, hailing from Aligarh, came
to work with my family in 1930, a year before I was born. He worked with
us with rare devotion for 60 years and died in harness in the mid Nineties.
There was no part of the house which was not touched by his vigorous broom
and there were no family secrets that Munshi wasn't aware of. . . . Today,
so many servants turn out to be marauders, grasping and bestial, ready to
become characters in horror stories.

Samir Mukerjee, "Vignettes of a Vintage Town"

EMPLOYER NARRATIVES of the past are deeply emotional. More than one employer
wept when remembering the servants of childhood. Others declared with certainty that servants loved their young charges as they would have their own
children. Many punctuated their reminiscences in Bengali with the explicit
phrase "like one of the family," in English.[1] Even if the famously difficult inter-
pretation of tears is put to one side, it would be analytically risky to take such
declarations at face value. If a culture of servitude normalizes domination and
inequality, employer insistence on affective and familial ties with servants could
be considered a maneuver to make the unacceptable acceptable.[2] Quite possibly
these are nostalgic representations of a world that is past, representations in
which servants are not simply the object of memory but the grounds for evoking through the magic of hindsight a different set of memories—of idealized
home and family, and an ordered and understood existence. An idealized past
is the inevitable backdrop and foil for employer claims about relationships with
servants and servant attributes in the present.[3]

We argue in this chapter that employers of servants deploy the "rhetoric of
love"—an ideological strategy that allows structural inequalities and domination to be perceived on an entirely different register such that relationships

of servitude are reinterpreted in terms of mutual trust, affection, obligation, and loyalty.[4] The rhetoric of love, a hallmark of Kolkata's culture of servitude, encompasses employer claims of affection and familial relationships that bind servants and employers to each other. It is not necessarily a deliberate strategy of dissimulation and denial, but rather, a complex discourse that both hides exploitation and makes it more bearable for some employers and, indeed, for some servants.[5] In what follows we explore the deployment of the rhetoric of love within a larger familial discourse used by employers to refer to the way things were, and compare it to employer perceptions of the way things are today. Above all, we ponder what the negotiations around love and money, devotion and betrayal, mean to middle-class employers and their servants.

Supriya's Story

"When he died, we were heartbroken," Supriya weeps as she recalls the part the family servant, Gostho, played in her life. Supriya, now an upper-middle-class social activist in her early sixties, was born to a prominent family. When they were young, each of the siblings was assigned a particular servant, and Gostho, who was hers, came into the family as a youth of eighteen when her parents married. He eventually married and had a daughter of his own, but his family lived in his native village in Medinipur. When Gostho was still a young man, the entire village was swept away in the monsoons, after which, Supriya says, "he adopted our family as his own." Because of his loss, she explains, he depended on her family for emotional sustenance and, unlike other servants who might have left after a time, Gostho stayed with Supriya's parents for almost his entire lifetime. The dependence was mutual because Supriya's mother also "depended on him heavily" and, as long as he was there, never had to enter the kitchen. In addition to being cook and child-care provider, Gostho was Supriya's father's right-hand man and "companion in all his hobbies." To indicate to us how close and familial her relationship was to Gostho, Supriya recounts that during her wedding, she performed *pranam* to him—a gesture of respect to parents and elders that involves touching their feet. Gostho gave her first baby a silver rattle and, during the course of her marriage, did not hesitate to "scold" her husband when he felt Supriya was being neglected in any way.

Late in life, Gostho adopted his sister's son. When Gostho was dying, because he now had someone of his own, Supriya's father took him back to the village; otherwise, Gostho would have stayed in her parents' home until he died. In Supriya's family history, Gostho fulfilled the ideal of the family retainer who was deemed "part of the family"—essential to the family's well-being, loved in life, and mourned in death—with a loyal and loving attachment to the family that was made possible by the disappearance of his own family. The actual or metaphorical disappearance of the servant's family, whether due to death, neglect, or silence, is a cornerstone of the family-retainer narrative—as Lakshman's story in Chapter 3 indicates—since it enables the seamless substitution of the employer family for the servant's own.

Gostho was succeeded by Indranath, who is of the same generation as Supriya and her siblings. Indranath, too, is seen as having been "devoted" to her parents and is expected to stay with the family as long as her widowed mother is alive. Supriya emphasizes the familial elements of their relationship by reminding us that Gostho and Indranath ate the same food as the family, except for rice, in contrast to the servants of other families, including those of relatives, who were given stale food and meager portions and were mistreated.[6] Indranath has been more like a friend than a servant, a close companion to one of her brothers when they were growing up, and someone who embraced Supriya and wept with her upon her widowhood.

But now times have changed, continues Supriya ruefully, and the affection and loyalty demonstrated by Gostho and Indranath are no longer available. Her own husband was uncomfortable with her attempts to have a close relationship with their servants; his doubts stemmed from a lack of trust. Today she finds that "every time the maid goes home, I don't know if she'll come back. I don't expect loyalty—you love them and you look after them, but still they don't stay."

The quality of the interaction with servants has also changed, say employers; along with the family retainer, the historic attributes of love and loyalty are also disappearing. In the case of her maid, Supriya finds herself encountering impertinence—something that clearly did not come up in her memories of the old days—and in her brother's house: "The maid is given any amount of latitude—not because they love her but because they are dependent on her." Thus, in this view, mutual caring has been replaced by an instrumental appearance of caring, and the moral economy of obligation and love is disappearing.

There is a sense of inexorable change in Supriya's narrative, change upon which she has reflected. She points to the breakdown of the joint family and smaller apartments, on the one hand, and the absence of better livelihood options for men, on the other, to account for the disappearance of the male family retainer and the rise of the female part-time domestic worker and, ultimately, the sorts of part-time arrangements prevalent in Mumbai—the quintessential modern city in the Indian imagination—where part-timers, according to Supriya, work in three or four houses and earn up to Rs 4,000 per month. The prospect that Kolkata will inevitably become like Mumbai was echoed in several employer narratives, even as they mourned the passing of the old order.

Yet Supriya is a person who thinks about issues of fairness and justice. Thus, that old family retainers are being replaced by part-time servants who set their own conditions is a positive development, in her view: "They have been oppressed for so long that it is good that they can." Yet she is quick to point out that Indranath "may or may not think of himself as a kajer lok, but he certainly does not think of himself as oppressed or exploited."

Even as she muses about her affection for Indranath, doubt creeps into Supriya's voice as she wonders how Indranath's wife can manage on his salary, and she suggests that it is "better for things to become more contractual." What will become of Indranath, whose sons are "useless"? "We should have looked after Indranath's children," Supriya rues. Indranath married off his daughter at age thirteen, and she now has two children, but "the only good thing is that her husband doesn't hit her." Indranath was very determined that none of his children should become servants: "So somehow he must not like what he is doing—we failed in our duty." Even as Supriya recognizes the existence of oppression or exploitation in general, she cannot let go of the countervailing affective assumptions of the feudal order in the particular. It is, she believes, a sign of her family's failure that Indranath, who has been more a beloved friend than a servant, should so desperately want his children not to become servants.

Supriya's eloquent words reveal the stakes of "the emotional economy of the everyday" that surround the culture of servitude of the old and the emergent order.[7] In Chapter 1, we outlined the two social imaginaries that Kolkata's culture of servitude bridges. Building on Supriya's comments, we can probe further into the still prevailing assumptions of the feudal order in which servants are considered part of the family, and servants and employers are bound to each other by the rhetoric of love. In this transition to what are considered more modern working relations governed by the market—part-time domestic workers, for example, as explored in the previous chapter—we find deep employer ambivalence about a relationship with servants based on the assumption of a wage contract rather than the rules of the rhetoric of love. We should recall that actual contracts are rare; what is paramount is the contract as symbolic.

The contract between employer and servant is imagined as representing the impersonal rationality of the market and is embraced by some young employers who are weary of the emotional exigencies and reciprocal ties of the old order. Yet employers who may well embrace the market outside the home, and whose class position depends on the capitalist economy and global financial flows, also express unease with the calculus of cost/benefit entering the home.

Like One of the Family

The phrase "like one of the family" is a constant refrain in employer narratives, certainly in Kolkata but also used in many other parts of the world to evoke the quality of the relationship with domestic workers.[8] In the United States, such a qualifier tends to be used exclusively for child-care workers—nannies, babysitters, and even au pairs—but in Kolkata it covers both child-care workers and servants who have simply been with their employers for a long time.[9] It is a convenient and often comforting fiction of which everyone is aware, yet the phrase indexes certain stock characteristics that family members are meant to possess or display: love, loyalty, generosity, and the recognition of mutual obligation. Families are not meant to be sites of disloyalty, treachery, indifference, and selfishness, and these are the very traits that employers fear in servants.[10] Thus, one meaning of "like one of the family" is affective, referring to the idealized emotions that family members are expected to manifest toward one another. Inasmuch as servants demonstrate loyalty, love, and a sense of obligation toward their employers, they may be said to be "one of the family."

The phrase, however, does evoke another element of familial structures. Families are hierarchically organized, headed by parents who are expected to educate and discipline children, keep them safe, and provide for them. Relationships with servants, who are often treated as dependents—like children— no matter their age, have been considered paternalistic or maternalistic.[11] Thus, the second, more hidden meaning of "like one of the family" refers to the fact that the servant falls within a familial hierarchy, albeit on the lowest rungs.[12] Employers often reminiscence about the servants who "brought them up," but even those servants forever remain in the limbo of childlike dependency.

Nevertheless, the discourse of being like one of the family is not rejected out of hand by servants themselves. Servants certainly have a complex relationship to it, but perhaps, as Saubhagya Shah so eloquently remarks in his essay on domestic workers in Nepal, it gives servants a claim, however tenuous and partial, on the home in which they work and on the employers on whom they depend.[13] This very claim, however, is contested by some young employers as they seek to lessen the sense of responsibility and obligation that the discourse of family entails.

More commonly, as discussed earlier, the servant was considered the child or dependent of the employer, a relation codified in the domestic manuals that came into vogue in the late nineteenth century when servants had become the norm in middle-class households in Bengal and women were given advice on servant management.

> Servants too are part of the family. Unable to feed themselves they submit to us and receive minimum wages in return. A sympathetic housewife affectionately serves them food and never says harsh words to them because of their low birth. You [housewife] must love the servants as if they are your adopted children.... If you win their hearts with love, the servants will willingly do everything you want them to do. Love works more than wages.[14]

The sentiments expressed here reflect an understanding of the servant as a dependent, vulnerable, and perhaps incapable child, who has been incorporated into the family on that basis. It is also instrumental in nature, deploying the rhetoric of love in reminding the housewife that "love works more than wages." At the turn of the twenty-first century, Lily, the sixty-year-old wife of a prominent Calcutta judge and daughter of a magistrate, similarly emphasizes the mutuality and obligation owed to servants because they had given their entire lives to employers—not just their labor.

> In those days we didn't just look after the person working in the house; we looked after the entire family—we looked after the children, the mothers. While this has changed in many families, both my husband and I were brought up to run our households this way. We feel that if they give their lives to us, we should give something in return.

Not only do employers assume that servants give up their own families for them; they admit that they often forget that the servant might have "a house of her own, her own family, and children." Ritwik, the fifty-five-year-old head of a charity, compared the expectation that a maidservant forget her own home to the expectation in patrilocal Bengal that upon marriage, a girl leave behind—indeed, forget—her natal home. If the place of work is to be likened to the marital home, then the maid (the bride) must be given love in order to secure her commitment to the home of the employer. Ultimately, the aim is to get the most out of her (servant or bride), he explained, "but she can't give it all to you in the absence of an emotional bond."

Love, loyalty, and mutual obligation, then, are seen to tie servants and employers to each other in a way that is characteristic of a feudal mode of servitude. The employers of the older generation express anxiety about more contractual relations, for if love and loyalty work better than wages, then the contract should be viewed with suspicion because of the change it inevitably brings to the bond between servants and employers. Employer discomfort with the fact of wages in return for care and service, the setting of wage scales, and the market overshadowing relations with servants appears in many accounts of paid domestic work, thus setting it apart from other forms of wage labor. It would, after all, be inconceivable for factory bosses to feel that the fact of the market somehow damages the relationship between worker and employer, or indeed the quality of the work.

It is the figure of the family retainer that represents the much-sought love, loyalty, and mutual obligation and that has attained, in Bengali myth and memory, an iconic status.

The Old Faithful

Schoolchildren in Bengal inevitably memorize (and often recite at interschool elocution competitions) a poem by Nobel laureate Rabindranath Tagore called "Puratan Bhritya" (The Old Faithful Servant). It tells the story of a buffoonish, often incompetent servant whom the mistress of the house always accuses of thievery, but who ultimately sacrifices his life for his master by nursing him through smallpox when everybody else abandons him. The master recovers, but Keshto, the servant, dies of the disease. This poem has come to represent the ideal family retainer, and indeed, several employers would say, when referring to a family retainer in their past, "Oh you know, he was a real Puratan Bhritya type."

The faithful family retainer is the archetypal servant of the feudal social imaginary.[15] Loyalty was this servant's main characteristic—loyalty to the point of self-sacrifice, for he would be willing to put the employer's family before his own, and indeed, his employer's life before his own. Self-sacrifice as a motif occurs in many stories of days past told by the older generation, as Mala, sixty-eight years old, recounts:

> Let me tell you a story about my uncle's family. They had a Nepalese maidservant to look after the child. One day, the maid and child were watching a

procession while leaning over a wooden railing, which gave way. But the servant held on to the little child so tightly that he survived the fall but the maidservant did not. That is how devoted and loyal servants used to be in those days.

The family retainer was usually, but not always, a man, and many of the older generation of employers recalled the ways in which their old servants were tied to their families. Seventy-five-year-old Subhas describes his family's relationship with their old faithful servant in the first half of the twentieth century, acknowledging the not fully reciprocated self-sacrifice on the part of the family retainer:

> We knew he had a wife and children somewhere, but he only went to see them once a year and never extended his visit. He never begged for any help for his family and never brought them to Kolkata. He was a typical family retainer. My younger brothers took the place of his children. We paid him until he died. We didn't know about his family so couldn't give anything to them. Looking back, we could have done more. We were good but not kind enough.

Jyotsna, seventy years old, contrasts the faithful servants of the old order with the threatened disorder of today:

> In my father's time there were more servants, and they all lived in this house. There was so much love and affection then. The servant who raised us also had the right to punish us. If we were upstairs studying and the cook called us to eat, and if we were late or spilled rice, then we would be hit. Servants had the same rights as parents, and they loved us. They were more dominant and very independent; they had rights over us. But things have changed; the whole country has changed. There is politics now, and so you have to exercise discipline. Otherwise they [servants] will go out of control, and we will have to leave the house.

In the previous descriptions, family retainers may sacrifice their own families for the employers'—indeed, the few family retainers we spoke with had had little contact with their own families—but, in turn, receive a modicum of respect and are granted a certain authority in their roles as guardians of children. Some employers, such as Supriya, weep as they remember their old servant. Others, like Subhas, regret that they never really gave back to the servant the kind of consideration they had received. Yet others are proud of fulfilling the terms of their particular arrangement of feudal reciprocity. But all mourn the disappearance of the Puratan Bhritya, and with him a time when everybody lived together and yet knew their place. With the passing of the era, Kolkata's employers describe themselves as left with servants who "go out of control" or "turn out to be marauders, grasping and bestial, ready to become characters in horror stories," as quoted in the epigraph of this chapter. If the male family retainer is the idealized servant of the past, then the female part-time servant is the anxiety-producing servant of the present and future. The alterations in the rhetoric of love are disquieting for both employers and servants but are experienced differently by servants and by the younger and older generations of employers.

"They Don't Love Us Anymore"

Sitting around a dining table one balmy Kolkata afternoon, sipping hot tea just served by the maidservant, three elderly middle-class employers reflected nostalgically on the affection between servants and masters in days past and grappled with the perceived changes in this relationship.

> Kakoli: In my husband's family, the servants treated the child of the master as their own. The old servants had so much gratitude.
>
> Mila: Nowadays, [the servants] don't care, they just don't care, whether you hire them or not. . . . It's becoming more and more westernized. They just don't want to serve anymore. They have got their own identity—"we are also human beings." That feeling, whether it is due to communism or westernization, I don't know.
>
> Kakoli: Nowadays the masters love the servants, but the servants do not love and respect the masters.
>
> Damayanti: Actually, I don't agree with that; it happens from both sides. We don't have the same affection as we did. We are also to blame.

Clearly for these employers something has been lost, but they are puzzled by the reason for this loss. These three women, who came of age in the era of the Puratan Bhritya, agree that things have changed, but they differ about the source of change. While Mila and Kakoli single out perceived alterations in servant behavior and identity, Damayanti insists that the turning away from the affective bond is mutual. However, Mila's ruminations also point to institutional sources outside the employing family for the apparent changes in servant attitude and affection. Living in the state of West Bengal, which has been governed by an elected Communist Party for twenty-five years, the CPI(M), Mila uses "communism" as a code for worker rights, and "westernization" for the loss of older values and an increasing social awareness of human rights. She recognizes that the rhetoric of rights disrupts the rhetoric of love and has the potential to destabilize the culture of servitude with which she is most familiar.

Indira, an upper-class social worker in her seventies who lives in the family mansion, expresses concern about servant well-being in line with Damayanti's views: "Today's employers don't treat servants well. We should treat them as members of the family because they have given up everything." For Indira, being an employer of the old order requires a sense of noblesse oblige. Indicating the trembling old man who served tea and snacks from a silver tray, she said that he had been with the family since he was a small boy, and she expected that he would live out his days in her house. Like Damayanti, she blames present-day employers for the deterioration of the servant-employer relationship:

> [Today's employers] say to servants, "We have an expensive television; don't touch it." Lifestyles have changed so much. If someone is very poor, starving, how can you say "no" when he asks you for five rupees when [you are] spending five thousand rupees. Young people do not feel compassion. I don't want to be unpopular and sound aged, but there is such a difference [in generations].

But in a milieu that is so often represented as one in which "servants are part of the family," what was the reality for servants? In an essay written for the popular Bengali magazine *Desh*, economist Pranab Bardhan recounts a remarkable anecdote about a servant his family had many years ago.[16] They knew him only by one name, Monglu. One day when he was asked for his full name for registration on the electoral rolls, he gave his name as Monglu Half-Bardhan. On being asked about it later, Monglu explained that in every home in which he worked, it was his policy to take on half the family name. Thus, Bardhan concludes, with this move Monglu marked both his closeness to the family that had employed him as well as his distance.

The rhetoric of love and family with its patriarchal overtones—more characteristic of the big house—is offset, both by employers and servants, by the rhetoric of an increasingly contractual relationship associated with contemporary apartment living. Employers of full-time servants today are expected to offer, in addition to a wage, meals, including tea; oil and soap; an afternoon rest period; annual gifts of clothing; and a certain number of vacation days. Employers of part-time servants are expected to give no more than a wage and tea. Yet many servants expressed a yearning for something more than a wage.

North Kolkata big house today.

SOURCE: Photograph by Seemin Qayum.

Aparna, who works part-time for several employers in Gitanjali Building, said, "Suppose I work for you and you give me two hundred rupees[a typical monthly wage for a daily two-hour shift]. That's good. But is that all? Are we not human beings? I say this to you even though I have been lucky in my employers."[17] Her husband, Kamal, a full-time worker in the same building, confirms this: "It used to be that in the early days, they didn't pay very much money, but they really cared for you. Now, especially in this 'high society,' they will give you one hundred rupees instead of ten rupees, but nothing else. In middle-class houses they still give us a little tea and bread to ease their conscience [*atmar shanti*]." Kamal casts an ironic eye on the paltry offering of tea and bread by present-day employers as compensation for the absence of genuine care. Even this trifle, he seems to indicate, is actually a balm for themselves. What servants miss in the new order are precisely the intangible benefits that accompany the rhetoric of love, which in some ways serve to recognize that they are persons who feel and suffer, not merely wage workers.[18] Against the backdrop of an uncertain and sometimes inhumane present, workers summon up images of an ideal feudal past as one where employers more readily accepted responsibility for the well-being of the servant.

A New Feudal Contract

In an old crumbing North Kolkata house, we find a somewhat unusual system that seems to work for employers and servants alike. This rambling house is occupied by different generations who belong to the extended joint family that once lived there with a large staff of servants. The house has now been filled with perhaps a dozen full-time and part-time servants. Some are men who live in the house rent-free and have jobs outside the home during the day but have specific household chores assigned to them, such as the daily marketing or other errands. Others, mostly women, live in the house and take turns looking after the ailing brother of the mistress of the house. A few of the women do not live in the house but come during the day to help with the cooking and cleaning. The mistress of the household, Jyotsna, a retired librarian, has made the best of her circumstances. She has, in effect, traded the one asset she has, real estate, for labor. She runs the home, she believes, with exacting democratic discipline and maternal affection:

I am very strict about discipline and timing. Everything has to be in its place. When I need it, I want to be able to find it, so we have to be disciplined. The advantage of having so many people is that when one is absent, others fill in. I tell them [the servants who do not live in] if you want to leave early, fine, but you can't be even a minute late [in arriving]. If they are late, then I have to prepare and send the food upstairs myself.

But I don't keep a difference, a distance between us and them. We eat exactly the same food, even the same rice, even chicken, even sweets. All sit down to eat, and I serve them all at night. I do not make any difference or distinction regarding clothing. The material my nephew's shirts are made of, I give them the same. If the nephew gets two shirts, they get three because they don't have any, and they work outside and thus their clothes get dirtier. Every week everyone's clothes go to the dhobi so they never feel they are different.

In compensation the servants provide security and care. Her siblings are old and frail, says Jyotsna, who is herself spry and energetic at seventy, and the house is an old one that needs maintenance. Thus, she has deliberately established what we think of as a new feudal contract, re-creating a rhetoric of love and loyalty that binds the household together, precisely out of the awareness of her vulnerability. Yet for Keshto, in his thirties, who has an outside job as a handyman and does jobs around the house in return for food and shelter, this is a good arrangement: "I really feel this house is my own. If there is something missing, I tell them. We are happy here because they [the employers] maintain the house well and give everybody love."

The other servants elaborated on what love means in a fundamentally unequal situation. Anu, who takes care of the invalid brother, articulates the nature of this relationship:

The relationship is so good that you can't possibly say no to her [Jyotsna], and that is why I am here. I do all the work that women of the house would do for the older brother. She is very good as long as we do as she says, but if we don't, she gets angry as parents do, and we don't dare talk back. I want to say one thing very clearly: if you are obedient, she will be very good to you, like parents, but you have to do things her way.

Though Anu uses the same discourse of family and maternalist love that her employer might also employ, the conditional nature of her employer's affection is not lost on her, nor on Kapil, a male servant in his thirties, who says, simply, "She who loves you also punishes you." In these servant representations of the rhetoric of love, there is skepticism certainly, but not necessarily rejection. Servants take on the rhetoric of love, however partially, because, as in Bourdieu's analysis of the master/*khammes* (bonded laborer or sharecropper) relationship in Algeria, "nothing suits the *khammes* better than to play a part in an interested fiction which offers him an honorable representation of his condition."[19] In this sense, servants accept to a degree what Bourdieu would call the "collective misrepresentation" that they are part of the family.

The End of Loyalty

> My father tried to educate the servants and their children a bit, get them jobs outside the house. He tried not to keep them as domestic servants, but some of them had this total loyalty thing. "No. This is where we want to be, and this is what we want to do," they would say; "someone has to stay in this house from our family."
>
> **Lily, age sixty**

> Today she's with us; tomorrow she may not be.
>
> **Keya, age thirty-four**

Lily's words imply that for those who worked in her father's house for her family, domestic servitude was their life, not just their work. Those servants chose loyalty over upward mobility, unlike servants today, of whom employers from a younger generation, such as Keya, believe there can be few expectations of loyalty. It is precisely the change from live-in to live-out, and more so to part-time domestic work, that seems to account for the decline of loyalty. Employers note that there is a market in part-time work such that part-timers will simply follow the money, "so the question of living in a house and having loyalty to a family is totally gone." In addition, given the wealth of intimate information that servants have about the families for whom they work, the employer desire for loyalty should come as no surprise.[20] The only way to ensure loyalty and continuity, then, is to "develop that kind of bond," as Lily puts it—referring to the rhetoric of love and family ideology of the past. Otherwise, the market wins.

The professed loyalty of employers was premised on the loyalty of servants, for "if servants are loyal and dutiful, then they are looked after," says Vijay, a thirty-year-old engineer who was raised in a big house and now lives with his wife and two small children in a flat. In the case of his family, this means a certain level of responsibility for the welfare of servants and their children's employment and marriage costs: "These are small things for these people who have been with us for the past fifteen or twenty years who have literally proved their loyalty to the family." Raised in a culture of servitude that idealizes family retainers, loyalty, and obligation, Vijay and others of his class and generation inhabit a neoliberal corporate world as adults. They thus effortlessly translate the ideology of noblesse oblige—taking care of servants' marriages and children—into managerial discourses of benefits and merit increases, medical care and holiday leave. Indeed, they reinterpret the past in terms of corporate management. Thus, family servants of a generation ago are referred to as "supporting staff with no critical responsibilities. . . . My mother and grandmother called the shots, they decided what to do, and these people merely carried out the orders."[21]

The meaning of loyalty is somewhat idiosyncratic in narrations of the past. In the history of the big house, a very good servant could steal and still be kept on—and his children as well.[22] Loyalty is not diminished by petty thievery, but, rather, is characterized by constancy, fidelity, and the willingness to stand by the employer. Indeed, it is typified by the poem "Puratan Bhritya." In turn, older employer stories are punctuated with feudal paternalism, such as employing successive generations of the same servant family, overlooking petty theft by otherwise respectful servants, or allowing old servants to die "at home." Bankim and his wife, Madhumita, owners of a North Kolkata mansion, emphasize that servants who were considered part of the household lived, worked, and died there: "We never thought they were outsiders; that is why they came back here to die." After forty years or more of living with the employer's family, and often having been obliged by circumstance to cut ties with their own family and natal village, servants in fact had no other place to go.

If petty thievery did not disqualify servants of the past from being considered faithful and loyal, it has an entirely different status today and is the topic of constant concern and conversation among employers. Some employers keep the kitchen pantry locked and hand out to the servant only the amount of flour, oil, sugar, and spices she would need to prepare the day's meals. Part-time servants are seen as particularly likely to steal. Further, since they work for multiple employers, they cannot be expected to be loyal to just one employer. Sona, an advertising executive in her thirties, uttered a common theme: "There is the risk that when they [servants] leave, you don't know what they're carrying with them—we'll find almonds, spices, other expensive items missing. They come with a purse and leave with a bag—but we're not checking bags." At times employers seem to agree that the way to manage petty pilfering is by turning a blind eye in order to keep the servant. Yet employers feel trapped and constrained by this concession. There is a sense that servants are implicitly blackmailing employers so that relatively minor misdemeanors must be overlooked in order to retain them. This resonates with multiple conversations employers constantly have with each other about the "servant problem"—the scarcity of good servants, of servants as they used to be.[23]

Even though part-timers are seen as a problem for many, some older employers now prefer part-time workers for security reasons. Suniti, an upper-middle-class widow who lives alone in a flat, cautioned: "With live-ins you can't control who comes in or is let in by servants. There have been two cases of murder, one by a servant who had been working with the family for twenty years." Indeed, the employers we spoke with seemed obsessed with the end of loyalty and the disappearance of trust. While servants have always been accused of stealing, here petty thievery serves as a metonymic representation for the dislocations of modernity. Whereas for big-house employers like Bankim, a loyal servant's petty theft mattered little, for the apartment dweller thievery is the first step on a teleological path to betrayal and even murder. This is particularly true at a moment when there is rising social concern for elderly parents who are living alone. The social institutions of Bengal have yet to come to terms with a newly mobile generation whose parents must now either live alone at home, increasingly dependent on their servants, or perhaps move to one of the few homes for the elderly that have begun to appear. Thus, newspaper accounts of servant crime are almost always about crimes against the most vulnerable—widows or elderly couples whose children are abroad or in another town.[24]

When servants were recruited from the villages in areas where the employers owned land, they were a known commodity; the families of the servants and the employers had typically known each other and had working relationships for generations. Today, servants are recruited through servant and neighborhood networks and, say employers, cannot be trusted as they were in the more feudal arrangement.[25] Rather than a "part of the family," servants have become strangers who enter the home. As outsiders in a space meant to be intimate and safe, they are now viewed as a clear expression of threat to its most vulnerable members. The official Kolkata police website encourages registration of domestics with the local police station, and the U.S. State Department similarly warns travelers to the city to be aware of servant criminality.[26] Thus, servants in Kolkata today are being recast by both employers and the state as potential threats to domesticity.

Kolkata police warning about servant criminality.
SOURCE: Kolkata Police website: http://www.kolkatapolice.org/download.html.

The End of Life

> [T]he following amount shall be distributed to the following persons in the
> following manner:
>   (a) Rs 10,000/—(Rupees ten thousand only) to [name] my maid who
>   served me well.

From the will of an upper-class employer (Kolkata, 2001)

One source of anxiety for servants is, of course, what will become of them at
the end of their lives. The feudal order promised that they would be looked
after until they died. Employers also relate stories in which servants stayed with
them until they were gone or were made comfortable in their natal villages so
they could die there. For some employers, certainly, the phrase "like one of the
family" is not taken lightly. To Indira, a widow in her seventies from an old
zamindari family, it means the obligation to take care of servants, who are after
all one's dependents, until the end of their lives.

I remember my grandfather's old bearer, Alokda. Alokda had a great personality. We respected him, confided in him. He was very loyal. He came to my
grandfather when he was twelve and retired at seventy with a pension. He was a

great loss for me. My last connection with him was when I sent him money for dentures because he had lost all his teeth.

My grandfather lived in Assam surrounded by tea gardens. He employed three boys from tea laborers' families, and when one of them died much later, my father did *mukhagni* [lit the body] for him and a *shraddha* [Hindu ritual for the dead]. At the time I didn't think of it as anything unusual. Now when I see how servants are treated, I think how good that generation was. I didn't know until later how badly people actually treated their workers.

Mila, another widow in her seventies, recalls:

There was a widow who came to my husband's family when she was thirteen and stayed for sixty years. She brought up my husband and maybe others. She was pensioned off by the siblings, and when she died, my husband performed the mukhagni and shraddha for her.

The performance of mukhagni, the privilege and right of an eldest son within Hindu tradition, was, in these and other cases, the final act that acknowledged the servant as part of the family. In the performance of the funeral rites, the male employer enacted the role of a son.

Neither servants nor employers are sure that this sort of guarantee for old age will continue to hold. Srilata, a young woman who was raised in a lower-middle-class family, explained the problem involving the old woman servant *Mashi* (aunt), who had been with them for many years and can no longer work:

So, for the last four or five years, we have been trying to get Mashi's daughter to take her away, but the daughter refused, saying, "She's been living with you, and now you're sending her back to me?" But we finally persuaded the daughter to take her. My mother wanted to do things for Mashi but couldn't take responsibility for her life. After all, it's her family's responsibility. At the end, it was a gradual, difficult parting. Mashi was torn. She would say, "I can't live there [her daughter's house]; this is my house," and yet also, "I can't work anymore; why would you keep me?" . . . But what we did was not right. Mashi had no savings and now feels like she is a burden on her daughter.

Mashi had been considered like one of the family because she would report for work even when her own children were sick, just so, according to the story, Srilata's mother could go to work. Mashi was a widow who gave all of her meager salary to her married daughter, even as Srilata's mother advised her to keep some money for herself. Mashi worked for the family for many years, and the house eventually became like her own. As Srilata tells it, she "realized" that Mashi was not really a member of the family when, only a few days after Srilata's father died, Mashi urged Srilata's mother to give her red saris to Mashi's daughter since widows in India traditionally do not wear red.

The salience of this story lies in its recognition that the rhetoric of love is a convenient fiction for both employers and servants. The relationship of dominance is unmasked when the servant makes the slip that "proves" that she does not deserve to be thought of as a member of the family, in this case by grasping after the red saris at a time of family mourning and grief. The fiction is readily dispensed with once it becomes too costly, for example, when it involves bearing not only the living expenses but also the presence of an old servant "in retirement." Given that Srilata's family felt they were no longer in a position to look after Mashi in her old age, the sari incident allowed them to believe that Mashi had proven that she was not a genuine member of the family—"after all, it's her family's responsibility"—and helped assuage their guilt about shirking their own obligations as longtime employers.

Although liberalism is classically associated with a language of rights, it is evident that the very nonliberal relations of servitude in the past also contained within them a concept of rights. Within the moral economy of the zamindari household, servants believed that they had a right to expect to be taken care of in their old age.[27] Another younger employer, Rohan, told us of his struggles with Ganesh, the old family retainer with whom he had grown up and who had served his parents for decades. Feeling obliged to look after the aged servant once the family home had been sold, but not wanting Ganesh to become a fixture in his own flat, Rohan decided that a retirement home would be the best solution. Rohan deliberately chose one of the better homes in the city for the man who had served him and his family for so many years rather than an institution for indigent people, as he might easily have done. What he could not understand, therefore, was why his old servant was so angry and expressed such a sharp sense of betrayal. In this case, Ganesh believed that by sending him away, Rohan had acknowledged that Ganesh had never been one of the family and had violated the promise of the rhetoric of love.

The End of Maternalism

Even as the rhetoric of love is acknowledged to be gradually disappearing, young women servants in particular are attracted to a "maternalist" discourse in which employers scold them and show affection as if they were daughters.[28] Mitali, who was orphaned at eight, knew that she had to seek protection in order to survive and thus had worked in other people's homes since that time. Eventually, she came to work for an older woman who became very fond of her and whom Mitali called "Ma" (or mother). Mitali confesses that she frequently lied to Ma in order to be able to go out to the movies, much as a daughter would: "I earned two hundred rupees, and I thought, 'Good! One hundred for the movies and one hundred to be saved for my marriage.'" And when she finally fell in love with a local night watchman, she turned to Ma for help. "I told Ma that I liked this boy, but how could I know whether he would take advantage of me and then abandon me?" Ma sent for the young man and ensured that he would agree to marry Mitali. She then accompanied the couple to the court to legalize the marriage. Mitali had effectively called upon precapitalist modes of loyalty and employer responsibility to enforce an agreement that would guarantee her protection beyond the affective safety of Ma's household. Today, Mitali is still married and has a son, and she still works for Ma. She wishes her husband were not so poor, so she could stop working, but she considers that she has achieved what she could given her circumstances: "No one, after all, wants to make a living working in people's houses. But that is fate. I was so worried that no one would marry me because my parents were dead, but that worked out."

Situations and responsibilities such as these are precisely what younger women employers seek to avoid. Like the employers that Hondagneu-Sotelo studied in Los Angeles, many younger women employers in Kolkata express discomfort with expectations for a relationship that extends beyond the contract. Keya, who runs a social development NGO, explained: "There's far more tension with women [servants] around because they open up and talk to us a lot more as women, whereas men [servants] wouldn't communicate innermost problems to us. . . . You get so involved with their personality, their personal problems, they expect you to understand them more as women."

Keya went on to compare her relationship with servants to those of her mother-in-law, with whom she shares a home:

> My mother-in-law does far more for the servants than I do in terms of looking after their needs. She will inquire about their home life, if they have enough to eat. I don't need to know that. I simply say: "You need food; take it." [One is] not looking at it as a family relationship. . . . [My attitude toward servants is] "If it's not suiting you, then you leave. . . . As a human being, if you have problems,

I can help you to a certain extent, but I cannot solve your problems for you, if you don't begin to help yourself."

Older employers, such as Keya's mother-in-law, and their servants may cultivate affection toward each other, as Dickey has also described for Madurai.[29] While her mother-in-law operates within a code of encouraging emotional reciprocity and care, Keya resists such attachments and opts for a neoliberal discourse of women's self-empowerment increasingly prevalent in nongovernmental organizations (NGOs): Keya will support her maid Mumtaz to an extent, but Mumtaz should make efforts toward independence rather than be dependent on Keya for maternalist protection and affection. This attitude is consistent with the exhortations of the entrepreneurship, microfinance, and other self-help programs for women that are such a prominent part of the international development agenda in the global South.[30]

In turn, these young women employers, especially those with professional careers, often resent their dependence on servants. Ayesha, who works for a cosmetics company, elaborates on this point:

> I am constantly trying to attain that level where I am least vulnerable to them. So it's not person-oriented; it's just job-oriented. I want it to be much less of a relationship, and much more of, "Just come, do the job, take your money, and that's it." I can't afford to devote time to building relationships. . . . I'm a worker; she's a worker. I don't tell my boss my problems; I don't want to hear hers.

Ayesha uses the language of corporate management to compare, without a trace of irony, her work and the work of her maid. In contrast, we might expect the employers who worked with NGOs to have a different sensibility. Yet here, too, the positionality of being an employer overshadows the possibilities of putative solidarity among women. Keya, in common with other younger women employers, believes that servants make use of employers' reliance on their labor: "Mumtaz knows that one is dependent on her to a great degree, and she is playing on that to see how much I will give her." The crux of the matter for Keya is that she believes that her responsibility for Mumtaz, who works full-time but lives out, should end with paying her a decent wage and providing her with a meal. On the other hand, she believes that Mumtaz would like Keya to be responsible for her entire family. Thus, what Keya says is her repudiation of Mumtaz's manipulative demands, is in many ways Keya's reluctance to acknowledge Mumtaz's dependence on her and Mumtaz's more feudal expectation of the employer-servant relationship. Unlike employers of the older generation, who may be more anxious about the commercialization of the relationship, Keya appears relieved by it. Says another younger employer, who works for a women's NGO, "If you are very friendly with them [servants], they will take what they can. They will exploit you, and they have exploited me." These young professional women rearrange the discourse of dependence and exploitation to index their own vulnerability rather than, as might be expected, the servant's. Uncomfortable with the legacy of the rhetoric of love and obligation, they are attempting to construct a new conception of the servant-employer relationship—one in which, as Hondagneu-Sotelo eloquently puts it, "a new sterility prevails."[31]

In discussions of affective ties with servants, there is a recognition among some employers that the affection and authority given to longtime servants worked in the past only because there was a perceived consensus about status: "We are masters. They are servants." In today's presumably more democratic world, such closeness and the ceding of authority to servants are considered dangerous. Several employers had cautionary tales to share about servants who "got out of hand," engaged in power games with their employers, and then left them in the lurch. In these last cases, the employers express a sense of betrayal: as Supriya, whose story opened the chapter, notes, "You love them and look after them, and still they don't stay." The servants are seen to have violated the terms of the rhetoric of love, loyalty, and (mutual) dependency.

Grappling with Changes

> It is a matter of our upbringing. We think we have to have a whole horde of servants trying to help you. You grow up thinking that you need them, that they are a must in the household. But that's not true. It requires a change in your own mental makeup. So if we do just this extra bit, maybe our dependence on them will decrease just that much.
>
> **Sona, age thirty-five**

Sona looks ahead and, although she cannot quite imagine a future without servants, understands that what has occurred in the past is a certain construction of household need—what we have called "the essential servant." She can envision reconstructing the way the household functions to the extent to which the perceived reliance on servants lessens. For younger-generation employers like Sona, this reimagination of the household would respond to both the exigencies of modern-day living and, more important, the perceived changes in servants' identities and desires.

Our survey shows that a significant majority of Kolkata's servants are now part-time, live-out workers; they work in several homes every day and live either in nearby bastis or commute to the city from adjacent rural areas. This has meant a decline in employers' expectations of loyalty and love and, correspondingly, employers' sense of obligation. Yet this move to part-time servants is still a source of unease for many employers, old and young. If, as we have seen, Kolkata's culture of servitude reflects a rootedness in a feudal past even as the material traces of that past disappear, then employers are faced with learning how to lessen the cognitive dissonance between the new conditions of existence and the culture of servitude with which they are comfortable. Thus, though the theme of loyalty does not automatically arise in a situation where part-time servants work for wages for a few hours a day in each of multiple homes, employers return to it repeatedly, and their very utterance, "We don't expect loyalty anymore," signals the extent to which loyalty continues to be a crucial attribute of their understanding of the employer-servant relationship.

There are, in effect, two primary changes of note that shape employer strategies for coping with the disappearance of the rhetoric of love and loyalty. The first is the recognition that servants have changed, and the second, for the younger employers, that their needs as employers have changed. Employers recognize that servants are different in multiple ways from those of the remembered past. Servants today are described as "answering back," dangerous, interested only in money rather than an affectionate loyalty to the employer family. Employers sense a seller's market and believe that servants no longer need to bend over backward to placate employers: "They now have understood that wherever they go, however they go, whenever they go, they will find work." This is seen as giving servants more bargaining power and putting the onus on employers to be more careful with them. Indeed, some employers now feel their dependence on servants so keenly that they are prepared to tolerate a poor worker rather than no worker. Says Ratna, who is the sole income earner in her household:

> I have a part-timer who works very badly, even in our small house, but I will not say anything to her. I have no relationship to her and do not make even minimal demands of her. I never ask her to do a single task beyond the tasks she was hired to do, and if she does, she is always compensated for it. My husband doesn't want me to even occasionally say something to her. He'll just do the dusting

himself. The whole thing is too unpleasant. If I had the time and money, I would prefer to do it all myself with a vacuum cleaner and a washing machine.

Here Ratna is trying to come to terms with both perceived servant scarcity and what she thinks of as the rules of a contract with a servant who is now more like the wage worker of capitalism. Ratna believes she upholds her end of the new bargain by never asking the part-timer to exceed the terms of the contract and compensating her when it happens. But in this story, it is the worker who does not fulfill the terms of the contract. Rather than address the issue of worker inefficiency, however, Ratna retreats, trapped in her present circumstances, and finds "the whole thing" too distasteful. She would rather have no worker than a worker of the new order, yet since she must work outside the home and is unable to recast the domestic division of labor with her husband, she feels that she has no choice but to put up with the current situation.

This attribution of bargaining power and personhood to women part-timers means that there is now an awareness that they will put their own family first. Many women prefer not do full-time work precisely because they can hurry home at different points in the day to tend to the needs of their own families. Indeed, some husbands of part-time workers told us that they had only given permission to their wives to work on condition that family duties not be neglected. Mira, for example, juggles her exhausting work schedule in five houses during the day plus a night shift as an ayah in a sixth by being highly organized, and she manages to cook lunch and dinner for her family as well.

Part-time work itself operates on a different temporal cycle, so those who do not adjust to the new logic of work are doomed to have servants who do not last. Says Srimati of her mother-in-law:

> She didn't understand that you couldn't just give part-timers more and more to do like you could live-in servants. She thought that through small gifts of clothes and money part-timers could be induced to do extra work. The result was that they became greedy. They would agree to do extra things in return for gifts but did not have the extra time to do the extra tasks and would be late for the next house. Part-time servants are so time bound that if there were any delays, everything would fall apart, and then there would be bitter words with my mother-in-law. So servants simply do not last in our house.

In other words, Srimati's mother-in law continued to try to impose the logic of a full-time servant who is paid for his or her presence on a part-time servant who is paid by the task. This fundamental change, which has necessitated a reorientation of the employer-servant relationship, is one with which Srimati's mother-in-law, raised as she was in a more feudal culture of servitude, could not cope. Srimati herself, however, has gradually learned to do so, adjusting her expectations to an emerging culture of servitude.

> I used to once scold them when they disappeared. I expected them to always be present! But now I say: "You do whatever you think, go wherever you want, but I have these things you have to do." They also understand me, and they always honor what I ask of them.

However, as we have noted, the new part-time workers, ostensibly armed with rights, are not the only ones who have changed the rules of the game. Employers are ambivalent about the decline of the rhetoric of love. On the one hand, younger employers now actively seek a more impersonal relationship with a domestic *worker*, rather than a servant as understood in the conventions of Kolkata's culture of servitude. Yet dual-income couples' reliance on servants to look after their young children conflicts with their desire for an impersonal, professionalized relationship with servants that is restricted to the temporal, spatial, and cultural limits of the working day. Though these younger couples are attuned to the exigencies of the modern contract, they wish for affectionate, attentive child care from servants—the sort that they themselves grew up with in joint families with old-fashioned family retainers—which in itself implies something rather different from a "clinical" or "impersonal" relationship.[32] According to Ayesha, the cosmetics manager, "I would prefer my child to be at home, with one person who is like a grandmother—so I'd like to build my relationship with that person, as an exceptional case, for my child. I would still prefer him to be at home rather than at a day-care center. But all other jobs should be done along the Western model." In this case, "Western model" implies contractual, managed relationships of work. For Ayesha, westernization is clearly positive (except for child care), but to seventy-two-year-old Mila, cited earlier, westernization is clearly negative, implying the loss of valued rules of comportment and a worrying assertion of the worker's personhood.

However, when servants act as if they do not wish for love but prefer money, employers are made uneasy. They believe that servant demands for more money prevent the sort of idealized bonding they had with servants earlier when employers gave of their own free will and servants never asked. Employers complain that now one has to "make contractual arrangements with the servants. They are only worried about money." And others like Srimati, who feel they have been burned by trying to be caring and affectionate to servants in the past, now say directly to the part-timer, "How much money do you need? Because I need you to come on time so I can get things done." Other, perhaps more perceptive employers understand that what servants want today is not just more money but security, which is now only available in monetary, market terms: "I think they want more money, not salary money, but money to buy land or for their daughter's marriage." In the past, servants may have relied on their employer to provide this security. Today, they must figure out how to save enough money to provide this for themselves—a task that falls outside the realm of possibility for most.

Young women part-timers, gathered at a crèche where they leave their children each morning before embarking on their rounds of part-time jobs, spoke to us most clearly about operating outside the rhetoric of love. Without hesitation they expressed their distrust of employer claims of affection and obligation: "Frankly, the rich don't like the poor. They only like us as far as we work for them. They say they love us to make us work."[33] They explained that employers are able to treat them thus because "no one thinks we are human after all." These women not only assert their "humanness" but also negate the idea of a distinctive servant nature (a premise of the culture of servitude that we shall explore further in Chapter 6). They are profoundly skeptical about the possibilities for change in the employer class. "If the employers read an article about us in the newspaper, do you think they would treat us better or with sympathy? No. They will beat us down more." It is employers' awareness that servants are articulating their consciousness and condition in new ways that heighten employer nostalgia for the past and anxieties about the present.

Conclusion

> *Should I take the Lord's name first thing in the morning or the name of my servant?*
>
> **Comment by employer on her servant in survey**

In the past summoned up by employer narratives, infused with the rhetoric of love and mutual obligation and loyalty, the fact of the relationship between employer and servant was given, and certainly viewed by employers as less contentious. Today's older employers struggle with the implications of the different temporal rhythm of part-time workers. Younger professional women, struggling to manage multiple demands, would like to dispense with both the inequalities of the old order—servants sleeping in the corridor with no fan, eating different food from different plates, suffering abuse—as well as its reciprocal ties. Yet their need for servants to provide child care, and consequently to love their children, further complicates this uneasy relationship. They recognize that they cannot escape the web of dependency and need without jettisoning the essential servant—and this they are not willing to do.[34] What employers appear to want is a contract that has loyalty and affection contained within it, the very qualities that cannot be captured by a contract. Older servants long for a modicum of security while younger and part-time servants seek a still-elusive, fair contract that would be honored. Thus, in contemporary Kolkata, employers and servants living in a culture of servitude in the interstices of two social imaginaries, the feudal and the capitalist modern, find themselves in daily confrontation. Both are losers in what Hochschild has called the "economy of gratitude," in which neither party feels that reciprocity or fairness has been achieved, and both resent the unequal ties of dependency.[35]

Will you not hire me to work, oh mother
Will you not hire me?
There was a flood in Kishore Ganj
And we lost our home
My husband has turned me off
What else can I do but come to you for work?
Runa Laila, song of lament[1]

◆

We meet Zeenat in a room in her employer's house. As a live-in servant, new to the city and entirely dependent on her employers, she has no separate space, no place of her own, to which she can take us to talk. A few minutes into the interview, she leans forward and whispers, "Can you please get me out of here!"

Zeenat is a young Muslim woman who grew up in a small town in northern Bengal, now working in her first job as a domestic servant. She is not accustomed to this life yet and, indeed, never imagined she would be doing this sort of work. Zeenat's life, like the lives of many women servants described in this book, has followed a certain trajectory. Her parents died when she was a child. Her brothers, unwilling to bear the burden of an unmarried sister in the house, married her off very young, although she just wanted to go to school—"I wanted to study." Of her married life, she simply says that she moved to Delhi with her husband. He ultimately used her illiteracy to his advantage, tricking her into a divorce by obliging her to sign a piece of paper renouncing the marriage. Young Zeenat was thus left in a new city with a small daughter, no education, and, of course, no job.

As a divorced woman, she was a disgrace and an embarrassment to her brothers in the town of Asansol, and they refused to have anything to do with her. The only person who did not turn her away was her sister, who lives in a town some 350 kilometers (about 220 miles) from Kolkata. While with her sister, she was

119

"recruited" to work in her present employer's family. Thus, she found herself far away from her daughter and working as a domestic in a large crumbling house, learning with some resentment to work, live, and be like a servant.

Zeenat cannot get used to this work, and she is not yet used to this life. She misses her daughter, whom she has not been able to see in the month that she has been working in Kolkata. As the only full-time servant in the house, she lacks sufficient food and rest. During Ramzan, she wakes up at 4:00 A.M. to break her fast, works until 10:30 P.M. without the customary afternoon rest period, and is therefore constantly weary. She is bewildered by her employers' behavior toward her. She can't understand why they insist that she bathe in the afternoon and not in the morning like a "normal" person, and why they accuse her of using too much laundry soap. "After all," she muses, "I live in the house. It's not that I work here and then go away. If they want me to care about them and what they eat, then they should treat me well." It is a reasoned caring that she seeks and fails to find in her employers.

She says fiercely, "I don't want to do this work. I have to do this work. I am not an old woman. I am young and *shaukhin* [I have fancies]." She is unwilling to give up her dreams and desires the way servants inevitably must do. In her dreams, she would marry again, but a man of her own choosing. And she would work hard, but only in her own home.

Her sister is a vendor who sells clothes on the street for a living. Zeenat is uncomfortable with the idea of working on the street and thus finds herself with no choice but to work as a domestic servant. She sounds so bereft as she tells us her story that we try to encourage her. What about her sister? Yes, she tells us, her sister loves her very much, but "who will keep me all my life?"

Indeed, who will keep her, cherish her, provide for her? In her life Zeenat has had three potential candidates to do this for her—her father, who died early; her brothers, who treated her as a burden and washed their hands of her; and a husband, who abandoned her with a baby. The patriarchs in her life have collectively failed her, but still she dreams of a home where she would be cared and provided for, and longs for a husband for whom she would work within the home.

While this ideal is unavailable in her present circumstances, she urges us once more, at the end of our conversation, to help her get out, to find a "good" employer for her. She is a good worker, she promises; she is just too unhappy working for her current employers.

We leave Zeenat, considerably shaken. We have done so many interviews, and heard so many tragic tales, that we have begun to develop a certain distance for self-preservation. Zeenat affects us because we see in her the humiliation of having to learn to become a servant, of having to learn, in effect, to have one's humanity systematically ignored or even denied. We are reminded of Fanon's words: "As soon as I desire, I am asking to be considered. I am not merely here-and-now, sealed into thingness. I am for somewhere else and for something else."[2]

That evening, we are quiet at a social gathering. When pressed for an explanation, we tell Zeenat's story in brief. Several people present nod and shake their heads: "Well, she'll just have to get used to it." "There isn't really anything to be done for these people." "Oh, is it her first job? She'll have to learn to adapt; the other servants on the street will tell her what's what."

◆

Zeenat's narrative brings to the fore the tensions involving dependence and independence, work at home and work outside, abandonment and protection, desire and servility, that mark the life of a female servant. It points to the power of an idealized patriarchy, with its bonds of dependency and security, and to the poignancy of women's yearning for elusive patriarchal protection. This chapter analyzes patriarchy as it impinges on the lives of servants in Kolkata, a social structure and meaning system that has created not only dependent women, children, and servants but also those "male losers" referenced by Steve Stern—male servants who have failed both in the world of home and in the world of work.[3] It thus offers a deeper look at the structures of feeling through which Kolkata's particular culture of servitude must be understood.[4]

It has been some time since feminist scholars jettisoned the analytical concept of patriarchy, only to reintroduce it as a loose descriptor rather than as a useful analytical frame.[5] While we agree that the conceptualization of patriarchy as a unitary universal phenomenon obscures more than it reveals, specifying the multiple forms and loci of masculinist domination that prevail remains a necessary task. In this chapter, we show that in Kolkata, a particular, contextualized form of patriarchy, as a set of social relations imbued with meaning, has structured identities and social relations, while it is itself a site of contention, resistance, and even mockery. As such, we take due note of Olivia Harris's commentary, which today is as or even more relevant than it was when written nearly thirty years ago:

> The assumptions made today about the natural—and proper—organisation of
> family life can be shown to have arisen in particular historical circumstances.

The definitions of motherhood, childhood, fatherhood, the representation of the home as a "haven in a heartless world," have been forged out of veritable ideological and legal campaigns, and are subject to constant renegotiation as needs and circumstances change.[6]

In this way we attempt to specify the nature of bhadralok patriarchy as it was forged as the hegemonic domestic ideology of the dominant class discussed in Chapter 2. We analyze its operations across the social formation as it impinges on and is deployed—and indeed renegotiated and refashioned—by the subaltern classes.

Bhadralok Patriarchy

Kolkata's evolving culture of servitude is inserted in patriarchal hierarchies that operate on multiple levels within both employing and serving households. Contemporary household ideologies hark back to the emergence of Kolkata's bhadralok culture and patriarchy in the nineteenth century. We have elaborated this emergence and the "astonishing consensus" that was created around domestic labor and domesticity by the end of the nineteenth century. The losers in this consensus were those women without protection and those who could not afford to stay at home—and were consequently excluded from the domestic sphere and proper domesticity—as well as the men who were unable to provide women with that protection. Working women were thereby also easily excluded from the purview of labor laws.[7] The continuing power of the consensus is reflected in current workforce statistics, in which urban women's labor-force participation in West Bengal remains at just over 11 percent.[8]

The domestic consensus meant that even as middle-class women began to enter the labor force in the twentieth century, "their responsibility for domestic labour, and its construction as a wholly female domain, remained inviolate."[9] For both men and women, the construction of Bengali patriarchy into the twentieth century has emphasized duty—the duty of women to be exemplary wives and mothers and manage their households efficiently and smoothly, providing proper child care and home-cooked food:

> What is the prime duty of women?—*grihadharm*. Today, disorder and revolution will be unleashed if women abandon their households. What is *grihadharm*? To run a peaceful home, not to waste time, not to gossip maliciously.[10]

Sanjay, a lower-middle-class employer and intellectual—he is a schoolteacher—noted the comparability between the accepted definitions of respectable womanhood and of servant:

> In our society, it is the assumption that a girl gets married in order to do housework for her in-laws—this is shown in films and so on. So, in fact, the woman is coming [to the in-laws' home] as a domestic servant, but can she be called that? Through one gaze, obviously she is a servant, but most of society sees with another gaze—so how can we think that she is a servant? The husband's family, in having her work for them, is not, after all, violating society's norms. She is simply fulfilling society's role [as woman].

In contrast to the duty of women to serve the home, the duty of men to earn an income to support the household is encapsulated in the following comment: "I think I do the major part of the household work. I am earning money. If I did not do that, no household tasks could be done smoothly. I spend the major part of my time earning."[11] Young male employers today continue to significantly take on the role of patriarch, assuming, even if their wives earn as much as they do, that the responsibility for the economic well-being of the household is theirs alone. In this way, hegemonic ideals of masculinity and femininity are likewise sustained. Even in those cases when women are the only, equal, or primary wage earners, their duty to family and home continues to be supreme.

The cover of an issue of the women's magazine *Sukhi Grihakon*, for example, shows a split photograph of one woman. On the upper half of the page she is at work, speaking on the phone. On the bottom half, she is dressed in the customary red-and-white cotton sari, cooking at home. The cover story, "Chakure Meyer Sonar Patharbati," is written by Bani Basu, a writer of some distinction. The title refers to the impossibility of a *sonar patharbati* (stoneware bowl made of gold), and metaphorically to the situation of *chakure meye* (women who work outside the home, literally working women). Basu argues, in effect, that the problems of working women arise from the fact that their status is still not quite legitimate:

> A sense of diffidence, a touch of becoming modesty, and a demonstrative dependence on men—these traits ultimately define a woman. . . . Earning women need a "motive" as justification [for gainful employment]. To phrase it more charitably, they need an apologia. A deep-rooted anxiety to find vindication for all their actions dominates the lives of working women. But make no mistake. Women do not need these "apologias" just for the outside world: They need

them for themselves. There is a symbolic spring balance suspended between their domestic lives and their life away from home. How much to give to the home? How much outside? . . .

She tiptoes into the house after work, has a quick change of clothes, and then immediately plunges into some domestic chore. The kitchen shelves need cleaning, and by tonight. Nobody has really asked her to do this job, but in reality, in cleaning the kitchen shelf she is actually salving her own pricking conscience. When she tidies up the table, she is in effect assuaging her guilt-laden heart.[12]

It may be supposed that the labor of servants helps working women to avoid the often bitter disputes over the domestic division of labor that are so commonplace in the United States, in situations where middle-class women can use their class advantage to overcome their gender disadvantage. However, Hilary Standing's analysis of Kolkata households with employed women in the 1980s produced the perhaps surprising result that women with servants do not spend less time on the domestic sphere than women without servants. In the first place, having servants does not affect women's designated responsibility for household management and supervision; and second, "the employment of servants only 'frees' [middle-class] women for other aspects of social and cultural reproduction, while poor women must, of necessity, cut their domestic chores to a minimum."[13]

Some female employers in our study effectively excused themselves from household responsibilities, such as Nilima, an upper-middle-class woman in her sixties who recalled: "I never had to do much after I was married because we had four servants [cook, ayah, bearer, and sweeper]." However, this vision of careless idleness is contradicted by others who note that in their families, however elite, women have always been actively involved in household management and supervision. Notwithstanding, some patriarchs of the old school do consider the purchase of a servant's labor as a direct substitute for their wife's labor. They have servants so that their wives can dispense with taking care of the home, even when the women might wish to manage their own households. One of the employers, a woman in her late thirties, reports: "My father always said to my mother: 'If I've got someone there who I'm paying to cook for you, why should you be in the kitchen? I want you to sit with me.' He used to get really annoyed if my mother went in to help [the servant]." Slight variations on this kind of reasoning among contemporary male employers point to the continuing potential of patriarchal authority in the household whereby both servant and wife bend to the will of the husband.

In contrast, in ordinary middle-class or lower-middle-class homes that can no longer afford a full-time servant, the housewife retains responsibility for child care and cooking. Harking back to nineteenth-century ideology about the position of middle-class mothers and wives, popular sentiment decrees that "you can only eat food prepared by your mother's caring hands." In these homes one or two part-timers are typically hired to take over the least desirable tasks, such as washing the dishes or sweeping and mopping the floors. Finally, for the women servants in this study who live in their own homes and work in others', the "double shift" is surely a double ordeal.

Indeed, the situation of women servants in Kolkata clearly corresponds to the imperatives of the dominant ideology that women should work for a wage only if obliged to do so out of economic necessity; normally, they should be maintained by fathers and husbands as part of the latter's patriarchal familial duties. This ideology is bolstered by the material conditions of a labor market in which the expansion of female employment has been in the worst-paid service occupations. As Standing concludes, "[M]arriage and motherhood remain the most reliable route to security" for both working and middle-class women.[14] For the women servants in this study, the security of marriage is a hollow promise. Yet, as we shall see, the combination of poor working conditions and hegemonic domestic ideology serves to heighten the need to avoid having to work outside the home rather than to underscore the importance of a political struggle for better working conditions.

We have seen that Kolkata's culture of servitude had its origins in a colonial feudal patriarchy in which the employing family had ties of obligation and duty toward the families that served it. In its ideal form, the patriarch was responsible for the well-being of servants and their families who, in turn, owed him loyalty and obedience. The decline of this relationship is a source of concern and regret for some older employers and relief for many younger employers. Even as they decline responsibility for servants' welfare, employers blame servants' dysfunctional families, and especially the failed patriarchs, for the plight of women servants and their children. Patriarchal relations within the employer home remain relatively unchallenged even as the shaky or failed patriarchy of the servant home comes under scrutiny.

Stern notes in writing about gender hierarchies in colonial Mexico that elite claims of paternal concern are often belied by indifferent and sometimes abusive behavior. Yet, he asks, why does a certain popular openness to paternalist visions of loyalty, deference, and rightful authority persist? "Why, if subalterns knew that most elites failed to live up to paternal pretense, did they nonetheless develop a partial receptivity to the premises of a paternalist political culture?" We would agree with Stern that this "receptivity" gives subalterns—in our case, servants—a shared language and means to contest forms of perceived injustice and to make demands upon elites or employers that had to be met to maintain a measure of elite/employer legitimacy. In addition, we argue, ascription to patriarchal discourse and practice within servant households grants a certain cultural legitimacy to the subaltern, working-class family, even as women are relatively powerless to enforce patriarchal support and protection.[15]

Women servants are considered, and, indeed, consider themselves, to be particularly ill-fated not only because the men in their lives are incapable of sustaining them or their children but because they must work outside the home. In this sense, both male servants and the husbands of women servants are failed men and patriarchs, and their very masculinity is questioned. The first because the demeaning domestic—read as feminine—tasks a male servant must perform compounded by the very characteristics that make him a good servant—loyalty, subservience, obedience, placing the employer's family before his own—make him a failed patriarch. And the second because these men cannot support their wives and are, therefore, in the judgment of many employers and wives, "useless"—and their masculinity undermined.[16] Hence employers and women servants are unhappily joined in their condemnation of what we have called "the failure of patriarchy," with censure in the first case and reproach in the second.

When women servants narrate their lives, they inevitably note the failure of patriarchs—fathers, husbands, and brothers—to perform their prescribed familial and social functions and duties as the cause of their unfortunate circumstances. Thus, these women end up taking on "patriarchal" responsibilities of supporting their households. When they envision what they would wish for their children, especially daughters, they almost always summon up a functioning, idealized patriarchal family—what Radha Kumar has called "utopian patriarchalism"[17]—where good husbands cherish and provide for their wives and children. Simultaneously, and no less strikingly, men servants express with resignation their own as well as their fathers', and often their sons', inability to properly make a living—be it from the land in the natal village or in Kolkata's offices and factories. Indeed, male servants think of themselves as failed patriarchs and feel doubly diminished. Above all, they bitterly regret that their wives must work and fear that their children will follow in their footsteps. The inept and hapless working-class man has become the abject subject of Kolkata's modernity.

Responsible Women and Incapable Men

Caught in a web of structural and personal causality, subaltern husbands and fathers repeatedly fail to take on their prescribed responsibilities to support and take care of their families—wives, children, elderly parents, and younger siblings. As outlined previously, this inability primarily lies in the lack of access to the means of production, originating in landlessness or near landlessness and consequent rural out-migration. Men working as servants have found employment in what is generally considered the lowest of urban livelihoods, above begging and menial, casual labor such as transporting loads on their backs or pulling a rickshaw, but well below other working-class jobs such as factory or office work. Of course, as servants, their economic, social, and personal situations are precarious indeed. Yet, as will be seen, men in this situation of relative powerlessness and dependency are concerned to ensure that their children—both male and female—do not follow in their footsteps, that their sons become gainfully employed and their daughters safely married and protected in the husband's home.

Women who are obliged to go out to work as servants in the absence of a wage-earning father or husband feel the failure of patriarchy acutely. Across the board, women servants aspire to marrying and staying at home as wife and mother, not to working outside the home. Adhering to a hegemonic family- rather than work-devotion schema, which Mary Blair-Loy has analyzed in an- other context, women servants are continually unhappy with their work lives.[18] The failure of patriarchy represents not only the involuntary or voluntary der- eliction of fatherly or husbandly duty in terms of financial support and fam- ily security but also lack of consideration and neglect. And women, like men, desire to do their utmost to ensure that their daughters are not faced with the same plight.

The women servants in this study unanimously explained their condition as servants as an instance of the failure of patriarchy, manifested in the absence of protection by parents, brothers, or husbands. Women typically end up as servants in the context of being orphaned, abandoned by husbands or in-laws, or married to a husband unable to provide for them. In this sense, women's servanthood is rarely seen as a question of their own shortcomings but rather one of men's uselessness, pithily described by an older woman servant: "Men don't want to work. They just want to hang out, go to the cinema, drink, and mistreat their wives." This sentiment is echoed by employers such as Sunita, who declaimed, "Women are workers; men are drunks."

Many women servants were married off at a young age when their parents could no longer afford to keep them or, indeed, because they had no parents and were considered a burden on the extended family. Some, like Shyamali, found themselves, at age eleven, the third wife of a much older man; others, like Krishna and Mira, were married off early because their relatives decided that a male guardian was necessary after their father died. However, marriage did not guarantee security for either Krishna or Mira, both of whom had to start working because their husbands were unable to provide for them. In Mira's own words, "It never occurred to me that I would have to work after marriage, but my husband is incapable [aksham]." She comments that there is not a penny left for her after attending to the needs of a five-person household, six when her mother-in-law was alive. Referring to those servants who commute into the city by train, she empathizes: "Their husbands are not worthy. If the husband is unable, then it is fine to work outside the home. But if the husband does work, then he will be suspicious of the wife who works outside, thinking, 'What is she up to?'" Mira makes clear that while she has nothing against work, she would have liked her work to have been in her own home as a wife and mother, looking after her husband, children, and in-laws.

Mira's sentiments are echoed by the train commuters, such as the woman who recounted that she had been doing domestic work for several years, but only after her marriage. It would have been unthinkable that she do this work before she married, as her family was relatively well off and she was loved and, by implication, protected. Even now, she said, her family cannot believe that her husband is unable to support her and she must work as a servant. At Canning, the last train stop on the South Kolkata line (see Map 1 on page 28)—about an hour and a half from the center of the city—the rigors of the daily schedule of the train-commuting part-timers are well known. A tea shack owner, a woman, pitied their hard lives:

> These poor girls, they wake up at 3 A.M., they walk for an hour to catch the train, and work so hard all day. Then they come back and have to ford the river [because it is too expensive to take the ferry], and when they get home, they have to go to the bazaar, and bathe, and cook, and look after their children and husbands, and don't get to sleep until midnight. And the husbands stay home and drink all day.

When asked whether the men farmed while the woman went out to work in the city, she just laughed. There is little land, and farming clearly does not provide a subsistence income.

Some women servants do find themselves accountable to their husbands, who may not be able to provide for them yet retain the authority of the patriarch. A case in point is Bulbul, who presents herself as the daughter and wife of Brahmins. Bulbul's husband, a temple attendant, permits her to work outside the home as long as it does not affect her ability to look after their own children. Krishna's husband reluctantly agreed to allow her to work outside the home but insisted that she quit temporarily to look after his ailing parents. Nevertheless, most women servants either do not have husbands or fathers or cannot rely on their incomes. A pervasive sense of the failure of an idealized patriarchy and of their men's inability to protect them permeated women servants' conversations with us: "I don't have parents to protect me—how much can I bear? If my husband were better, then life would be tolerable." Even as women servants bemoan the lack of patriarchal protection in their own lives, they strive to provide the necessary protection and security for their children.

The implications of the failure of patriarchy in the lives of women servants and their families are multifarious, and women attempt to compensate for the painful gap between their lived experience and the expectations of a dominant ideology that demands that women tend to their homes, husbands, and children. Many seek to create a home life of their own under circumstances that militate against it. Paromita finds herself in a cycle of failed protection. Not only was she widowed young and left with a small child but her now grown-up daughter has been deserted by her husband. Paromita is the sole support and protector for her daughter and grandson: "Here I am—I have no parents, no husband; my daughter's life is a disaster. I can only depend on myself. My daughter has nobody. If I die, she has nobody." Yet Paromita made a conscious decision not to do live-in work, in order to practice a domestic ideology of her own, and has done full-time live-out work for thirty-five years: "I've never done *raat/din* [night/day or live-in] work. I like to go home."

Mira, who as noted earlier is the sole earner for a five-person household, rejects full-time work altogether in favor of the flexibility of part-time work that allows her to perform household tasks for her own family during the course of a workday. She works from 8:30 A.M. to 4:00 P.M. every day, in five houses in her neighborhood. She usually has no time to eat, and none of her jobs provides a meal, which is the rule with part-time work. As she rushes between the five houses, she picks up the rations and vegetables for her family's meal. She goes home from 4:00 to 7:00 P.M. and does the cooking for her family. But her day is not over. During the night, from 8:00 P.M. to 8:00 A.M., she works as an ayah (in this case, an attendant to elderly or ill people). She is only able to sleep intermittently. As an ayah Mira earns Rs 1,800 a month (60 per day), and from part-time work she earns Rs 1,240, for a total of some Rs 3,000.[19] Therefore, only by making intricate arrangements between home and work—and working a triple shift—is she able to fulfill her expected responsibilities for the family and household. Mira is fully aware of the costs: "You have no idea how much I have suffered. . . . People who used to know me don't recognize me because after doing this work for so many years, my posture and face have changed and I have aged."

A common assumption is that women servants must have a female relative living with them who can take on child-care responsibilities in the absence of the mother, but this is often not the case, especially for new migrants to the city.[20] Mira is fortunate enough to live close to her employers' homes. Most part-time workers, however, who live in bastis and squatter colonies in the city, usually do not have the possibility of attending to their families during the course of the workday. Since it is their responsibility to protect and care for their children, they try to avail themselves of the few crèches in the city that will accept their children. One such crèche in Salt Lake, run by a prominent social work organization, serves primarily to provide a safe space for servants' children, and secondarily to prepare children for school.[21] The women who use this crèche for the most part have been abandoned by their husbands—even though they would not want to admit it—and the husbands who have stayed earn a pittance as rickshaw pullers or casual laborers. When asked about what their husbands think of putting a child in the crèche, they shrug to indicate that husbands have little to say about such matters. On Sunday, when the crèche is closed and part-timers have to work, they manage in makeshift ways, which may include leaving the child with a neighbor or, as one said, "If you are unlucky like me and have no one you can leave the child with, you take the child with you to work." The part-timers prefer not to take their children to work: "It looks bad and hurts our dignity. The employers become upset if the child touches anything, creating tension for everyone. Some employers send the child outside, saying they don't want the child to pee inside. Although it is dangerous outside, what can we do? Sometimes the children are unhappy in the crèche, but we want them to be there so they can be educated."

Even though the safety and education of little children are of constant concern, some women servants have had to pull their young daughters out of school and send them to work, an action they bitterly regret. As daughters grow up, their parents are filled with anxiety about their futures. Lakshmi worries that her three unmarried daughters are unprotected in her absence. Krishna, like so many other women in her position, desires the security of both marriage and an income for her daughter.

> I want my daughter to be good and to study. For myself I accept my woman's fate. I tell my daughter that if she doesn't study, I'll send her out to work. For if she drops out of school and stays at home alone, she might go astray since there are bad people around. But what I want is for her to finish class twelve and then get married so that she can stay at home and be a tutor. I don't want my daughter to work outside the home but inside the home. She is my only child; I want her to stay at home.

Thus, women servants, who have learned to survive in the absence of male patriarchal protection, wish for their daughters that which they were denied. Despite their experience of the home as a problematic site, the street, not the home, is seen as the primary danger. Listening to her mother describe her desire to educate and marry off her daughters, Sita's daughter interrupted to ask why her mother could wish for this, given that marriage for so many women in their basti has meant abuse and abandonment.

The dependence on men for protection sometimes fails in particularly ugly and horrific ways, as in the case of Ganga and her daughter. Ganga, nearing retirement age, works as a part-timer in the Gitanjali Building to support the five grandchildren who were left in her care upon their mother's death. Although the daughter was clearly burnt to death by her husband, Ganga speaks of it as suicide because she cannot afford to point a finger at her son-in-law. Who, she asks, would look after the children if he were sent to prison?

Women servants may be aware of the lack of protection in their own homes, but for many young women, employers' homes are actually fraught with danger—another reason women want a home of their own. For Mitali, who was orphaned young and had no family home, her only option was working as a servant and seeking protection in employers' households. Yet she had to leave a home in which the employer's son "kept trying to get under [her] mosquito net." Other servants also recounted tales of sexually predatory employers but were reluctant in most cases to refer to their own experiences, a pattern that Ann Stoler also found among Javanese servants, who spoke of sexual relationships and violence that had happened to other servants, but not to themselves.[22] Employers, however, confirmed that sexual exploitation, albeit clandestine and a forbidden topic of discussion, has not been uncommon: "All men joke and talk about maidservants. If a young man managed to do it with a maidservant, the others were jealous. It wasn't looked down upon. Men servants had liaisons with maidservants, too."

In the absence of male protectors, then, women servants make their own way, while determined that their daughters not follow in their footsteps. Yet few dream about their daughters becoming economically independent. Rather, they wish for them the life they sought but were denied.

What Do Women Want?

The dominant development paradigm promises that should women be educated and work outside the home, they can overcome their oppression in patriarchal households and family structures, and at the same time become the agents of social and economic progress.[23] Not only does the philosophy of the overarching importance of women's empowerment through education and work underlie much of Western feminism and development theory and practice, but it has been taken on—partially—by the postcolonial Indian national project, and certainly by the women-in-development and gender-and-development frameworks in which women rather than men are considered the ideal workers.[24] As we shall see, however, the "astonishing consensus" around domesticity created in the nineteenth century retains its hold over even the sections of society it was designed to exclude—namely, women of the laboring classes. Primarily interpellated as daughters and mothers, women servants are obliged to work outside the home by familial duty and economic necessity, while longing for the possibility of working at home for their own families rather than those of strangers.

Even as their words make evident that daily hurts, neglect, and violence are often inflicted within the family, the only imaginable alternative for most women servants is a more tolerable version of the culturally sanctioned patriarchal relations of authority. As such, they illuminate a central contradiction of the gender politics of the Indian nation-state: The nationalist movement situated women firmly within the family, and it is to the family that women continually turn for both security and affective ties, more than to the workplace and the relationships of work. In what are manifestly trying circumstances, women servants cling to hope, desire, the possibility of love and, perhaps, of upward mobility—a safe home of their own.

It is unsurprising that young women like Zeenat, whose story opens this chapter, would seek not just familial protection but love. Yet middle-aged women with grown children also regret the dearth of husbandly affection. Lakshmi speaks with great sorrow about her husband's failure to love and appreciate her, his jealousy and possessiveness, and his will to dominate. When asked what she hopes for in the future, she says:

> Just some love. One can't live without love. Just like a plant or a tree, one withers and dies. There is a man who loves me now and does a lot for me, but he is not my husband. . . . But tell me this: Am I wrong to accept love from someone else when my husband has refused it to me for so long? If a thief steals, will you punish him or find out what the circumstances were that led him to commit this act?

While Lakshmi may have the courage to seek love outside her marriage, justifying her actions in the absence of husbandly affection and care, others simply long to be loved. Shyamali, married to a man more than three times her age, believes that the emptiness in her stomach can be filled only by happiness and love. Durga moves fretfully from a discussion of work, to home, to love:

> I just don't like this work. What will it take for me to be free? I have never received anything in my life. I don't get love from anybody—not parents, not husband. And now my children resent me because I am not there for them. All homes have their own sorrows. Mine is that the man who took my hand never gave me love.

Zeenat, despite being cheated and abandoned by her husband, as recounted in the beginning of this chapter, is simply not willing to give up her dreams and desires—above all, to marry a man of her choice. Repeatedly, then, women servants replace the failed patriarchy of their experience with the utopian one of their fantasies.

In seeking love within an idealized familial context, as we have shown in Chapter 4, some young women servants willingly participate in maternalist discourses, thus mirroring the rhetoric of love that employers articulate. Denied patriarchal protection in their own families, some, like Mitali, find a substitute in the relationship with an employer. To avoid the risk of sexual assault in the houses where she worked, she persuaded a trusted woman employer to let her sleep on the kitchen floor while she continued to work as a part-timer for other families. Mitali gratefully recalls her employer's anxiety when she returned late from a film one night. The relief that somebody was looking out for her more than compensated for the employer's reprimand.

The desire to re-create a family in the workplace takes other, troubling forms. We found in our survey several young servants who did not receive a wage. The employers explained that they were putting aside the money to spend on the servant's eventual marriage. Roy notes a similar circumstance, which she calls "a fantasy of domesticity," among young workers who justified the absence of a wage by arguing that generous employers were saving the salaries to give them as dowry.[25] This fantasy of domesticity assumes that employers will, in fact, secure a husband for their maid, a patriarch to replace the presumably failed patriarch of her own family. Yet this manifestation of the collective anxiety about protecting women denies the young woman's agency—taking her from one patriarchal family to another—and reinforces her dependence on the benevolence of the employer, since with no money, she cannot leave. She is in fact the object of exchange, and never the recipient.[26]

Domestic fantasies indeed constitute the imaginary of most women servants, but going out to work has become an unexpected source of pleasure for some and an escape route for others. Krishna, whose story is a classic one of being married off by her brothers after their father's death to a man she does not respect, now lives and works outside the home. She enjoys the money she earns and the opportunity to get away from the unpleasantness at home. Similarly, Shefali, who initially resented having to work outside the home when her husband fell ill and could no longer sustain the household, is now grateful that she works in a big house with other servants: "We laugh and joke for two or two and a half hours. I would have no friends if I didn't work, and I sometimes think if I were at home, how would my time pass?"

Nevertheless, most are resigned to their "woman's fate," having given up their own aspirations in hopes of creating a better future for their children. Mitali declares that she may be ignorant and uneducated but she will make sure her son completes his schooling, and she will work in other people's houses as long as needed to realize that ambition. However, their constrained circumstances mean that servants often cannot afford to keep their children in school and are obliged in the interests of family survival to send out nine- and ten-year-olds to begin work as servants. The children who are able to study further often begin to fail when they reach the eighth and ninth grades for lack of extra tuition and family cultural resources.[27] Recognizing this situation, Shibani wishes she had had the opportunity to study so that she could help her children get through their school years. Shibani's is not a romantic ideal but a clearly practical one. Only a place of her own would make possible an alternative life for herself and her children: "If only I had land or a home, I would do part-time work, study a little, and then I could help the children with whatever knowledge I have."

Children's prospects constitute the alternative pathway to the future, and some employers do indeed exercise a patriarchal duty or sense of noblesse oblige and support the education and marriage of servants' children. Only rarely do servants—with or without the help of employers—manage to jettison servitude in favor of a more secure and independent life. In one such unusual case, Rita's female employer became so fond of her that she encouraged Rita to train to attain a marketable skill, personally made all the arrangements for a wedding when Rita fell in love, and helped Rita set up her new home. The employer considers Rita lucky to have found a good man who did not reject her for her servant status. Today, Rita earns an income as a beautician, and she and her husband, a pharmacist's assistant, have a home of their own—albeit a rented room. Because both her former employer and her husband's employer are willing to back them, they may actually qualify for a loan to buy a house on the outskirts of the city. Rita now visits her former employer as a friend, chatting, exchanging gossip, and eating at the same table. Rita's husband wants her to engage a servant to help her with daily chores, perhaps because he wants to claim middle-class status, but Rita resists, protesting that she can easily take care of one room. Rita, then, has actually been able to enact the desired domesticity, taking it out of the realm of fantasy, with the constant backing of an exceptional employer.

Another story of upward mobility has yet to reach a felicitous outcome. Nita has worked in the same house for eighteen years, since she was a child. As a young woman, she asked her employers to send her to school. With their support she was able to attend night school after the workday was over, and eventually she graduated. To pass the demanding class 10 and 12 exams, however, she had to subcontract a domestic worker to cover some of her chores to give her time for the necessary preparation—the only case of subcontracting that we have encountered. She then wanted to go on to university, but her employers were unwilling to pay. As an alternative, she herself paid for a tailoring course, and seamstress work has provided an additional income. Yet now that she wants to get married, the stigma of being a servant makes her unmarriageable—unless to another servant. Nita's education has not allowed her to move out of the servant class, and marriage, that "most reliable route to security," is fraught with complications.

The Lament of Failed Patriarchs

A servant is not really a man, a human; a servant is a servant.

Mila, age seventy-two

If the essence of domestic service is subservience, and less about the completion of tasks than being at the beck and call of the employer, then it is also a job that runs counter to hegemonic ideas of masculinity, both bhadralok and other.[28] Male domestics (33 percent of West Bengal's servant population in 1991) recognize that theirs is clearly a bad job, an awareness that coincides with popular opinion that less demeaning jobs for men can readily be found. Some of the older generation of male servants regret that the job is being progressively deskilled as domestic service becomes an increasingly feminized, task-driven, and part-time occupation, and consequently consider it even less desirable for men than it was previously.[29] Hence, male servants, enmeshed in a discursive web not of their making, struggle to make sense of their positionality in spaces that are demarcated as both feminine and inferior.

Held up against the bhadralok model, male servants who work as cooks, factotums, or sweepers fail as men on several counts. Bhadralok were and are considered men of culture and education, professionals if successful, and clerks if not—but bhadralok never work with their hands. In a caste-inflected social structure, manual labor is customarily associated with menial work or servitude. Bhadralok occupational privilege is matched by patriarchal privilege at home. The bhadralok naturally assume responsibilities as protectors and providers of their households and, in turn, are served by their dependents. Aspiring bhadralok are vigilant about not compromising their status. A young, university-educated peon (lowest-level office staff) at one of Kolkata's premier companies, while fulfilling duties such as photocopying, sending faxes, and running errands, refused to perform another typical task, serving tea, since he was himself served tea at home. He declined puja (festival) bonuses for similar reasons of patriarchal status, indicating that he was the one to give such bonuses to others in his household. As this young man's liminal case exemplifies, bhadralok standing means engaging in swadhin rather than paradhin work, refusing menial labor, and being able to support and protect a household.

These are standards that few working-class men can attain and are essentially beyond the reach of male servants. Factory or office employment, recognized as relatively independent and decent work, is the prized working-class job but is not easy to find in liberalized and globalized Kolkata. This and other, sometimes informal-sector, work may allow men to be more swadhin, without necessarily providing enough income to support wives and families. Yet there is no job that fails to meet acceptable standards as thoroughly as domestic service, and thus the men engaged in this work are often profoundly bitter and frustrated.

Men often end up as servants after failing to find or keep less paradhin jobs, typically having started their working lives as young migrants sent to Kolkata by families faced with land scarcity and rural crisis. As middle-aged and elderly men reflecting upon their lives, they narrate sequences of misfortune, failed promises, and personal shortcomings that only the next generation may overcome. Although some men servants were initially reluctant to discuss their problems with us, it was the concept of *koshto* (to suffer) that transformed their silence into speech. When we asked if he had suffered, Lakshman, the family retainer presented in Chapter 3, switched seamlessly between his suffering as a servant, a son, a father, and a poor man:

> Servants suffer because we work and work for the babus all our lives. I never got to see my mother before she died. I have no son, only a daughter; if I had had a son, would I still be doing this? Would I not have had a place to stay? Of course cooking hurts my body. It hurts a lot, especially in the summer without a fan [there was a fan, but they took it away], but I suffer the most because I have no land. I suffer because it is hard work; it's my fate, my fate to suffer like this.

The lament of the failed patriarchs operates simultaneously on multiple levels. Lakshman laments fate, the pain of hard work, the subservience to the babus, his personal losses still felt keenly after decades, and ultimately, "most" of all, the absence of the land that might have sustained his family and his masculinity and provided an alternative to servitude.

Arun was the youngest son of eight children, born in the district of Medinipur east of Kolkata to poor farmers who, having little land themselves, had to work as farm laborers for others to make ends meet. As the youngest, he was able to study through the fourth grade and, still a child, became a soldier in the underground struggle for Indian independence. After several years of guerrilla warfare, his father, increasingly afraid for his son's safety, helped him escape to Calcutta where he joined his older brother. Arun's summary of the next fifty years of his life is an account of his failure to keep a succession of jobs through lack of skill, illness, or sheer bad luck. Finally, he began work as a cook, and today, twenty-six years later, he still works for the same family. Nearing the end of his working days, he admits: "I have lived my life with my head bowed, but I will not bow my head at the end of my life. I have lived paradhin."

Sunil, born in Bankura (southwestern West Bengal) into a farming family that was unable to manage with the small plot it was allocated when the joint family's landholdings were divided, also sees himself as having failed. By age fifteen he had begun working in an eyeglass factory in nearby Burdwan (central West Bengal) and eventually moved to Kolkata where, because he was Brahmin, he found a job cooking in religious festivals. He then found a regular job as a cook for a family with whom he worked for twenty-five years. Quiet and bespectacled, Sunil acknowledges his failure as a father and as a husband:

> We have no choice, and we have to keep going. Somehow we have to keep going because we have absolutely no savings. The girls have to be married, and I am afraid we can't afford to keep them in school much longer. There is no future in this work. What if I fall ill? In any case we have to pay all the doctor bills ourselves. I am growing old, and yet I cannot manage to do anything for my girls—we have no house, but we have daughters with no one but me to look after them.
>
> If I could just find a way out. If I only had a little education, I would have been able to get some kind of job. My future almost opened up in Ranchi [Bihar, where he went for six months], but someone ruined it for me. If that had happened, my wife would not have had to work. In my family, she is the first wife to work. I am the only weak [*durbal*] one of the lot. All my brothers and cousins have a pukka house and their wives don't work.[30] Mine is the only one that has to work.

Sunil's failure as a patriarch, in his eyes, stems not only from the fact that his wife is obliged to work outside the home coupled with his inability to build a future for his daughters, but from the shame of being a servant. Balai's in-laws, for example, do not know that their daughter works outside the home, and they think he is a driver—a job that is perceived as having more dignity and more independence. Drivers occupy an intermediary space between paradhin and swadhin work since they are skilled and work outside the home. Balai knows that his daughter also tells her friends that he is a chauffeur. He is embarrassed but understands his daughter's reluctance to acknowledge the less-than-bhadra work he does.

These themes appear repeatedly in the lament of male servants, especially of those who do not have sons, for within the rules of patriarchy, sons may share their fathers' burdens. As Lakshman explains: "If I had had a son, would I still be doing this? I don't have a son, so I have no one to call my own; after all, my son-in-law cannot be my own." He would have never let his daughter work as a servant, sacrificing himself instead; now that she is married, he cannot assume that she and her husband will look after him in his old age. Yet as Arun's case shows, fathers cannot necessarily rely on sons. Arun is bitterly disappointed in his sons, whom he classifies as "useless," and does not believe they will look after him once he stops working. In a slightly different situation, Raja does not know whether to be proud or anxious about his sons. He worked doubly hard so that his sons would never have to become servants, giving them the opportunity to study and train for a trade, but now he worries that they are too soft to do any hard work at all:

> My oldest son started working in [a five-star hotel]. He joined as apprentice steward, but the work was too strenuous and too much like a bearer [waiter/butler] and he couldn't handle it. You see, though we didn't have much money, I saw to it that [my sons] didn't have to work, so [now] they can't handle it. I have been working since I was twelve, not as swadhin, but in others' houses. Naturally I have had to take the employers' wrath. I told my sons that as long as I am alive, you can study, and then you can maybe enter "service" [as an office clerk].[31] They want it, and I want it for them. I do not want my son to work in another's house. If I don't have clothes, I ask [for my employer's] help, but why should my son be in that situation? I never had the opportunity to study after all, so I have to do what I do—but not my son.

For working-class fathers, as Sennett and Cobb argue in their fine analysis in *The Hidden Injuries of Class*, the overriding motivation for sacrificing themselves for their children is to ensure that the children will not be like them.[32] Whether or not they have managed to protect and support their own families, Arun, Lakshman, and Raja are joined in their fear that—despite their sacrifices—the next generation may not after all achieve the elusive benefits of swadhin work and an idealized patriarchy.

Reconfiguring the Patriarchy of Servants

Even as male servants lamented being trapped in cycles of dependency and failure, a reconceptualization of the nature of paradhin work, and the conditions for supporting and protecting a household, emerged in their stories. Within an unfavorable context, some male servants were able to consolidate their position as heads of households through revaluation of the terms of work, status, and dependency. Lowly or undesirable tasks become ordinary work, individual aspiration gives way to familial responsibility, and the condition of servitude is offset by employer reliance on servants.

Raja, while resigned to being a servant, expressed a calm acceptance of all labor as labor—including the commonly reviled task of washing dishes—and even a certain satisfaction in a job well done:

> There is no task that is the worst. Madam doesn't make me do things after all—I do them myself. If I see something dirty, I call the sweeper to clean it or I do it. I don't mind washing the dishes either, though I don't do it all the time, just in the evening, after the sweeper leaves. I have pride in my work and don't want to leave the kitchen dirty for Sahib to see when he makes the tea for himself in the morning. What is there, on the other hand, to like? I work because I have to. I neither like nor dislike anything.

Yet Raja is perhaps an exceptional case, with achievements few of his fellow servants can hope to attain. Despite his concerns about his sons' capacity to make a decent living, he has managed to educate them, as well as send his younger brothers to university and find them employment in local government offices, acquire land and a house in South 24 Parganas from whence he commutes every day, and support his wife (who works at home as a seamstress)—all with the help of generous and appreciative employers. As discussed previously, ties of dependency and mutual need can bind employers and servants, especially in the case of long-standing male servants such as Raja, who has worked in his present position for twenty-five years and is prized by his upper-class employer: "Raja does a lot for us because we really look after him. He likes to live beyond his means. It doesn't bother us because we want him to live that way. Poor chap, he does so much for us. We are extra dependent on him. We cannot do without him." Raja's employer also validates his masculinity, expressing a clear preference for him over any female servant, who, she says, would tend to "embroil" employers in personal problems: "Women are too much trouble. They gossip and listen to telephone conversations. . . . A woman would never be as good as Raja." Because he takes pride in his work, is efficient, attentive, and reserved, Raja is indeed the "perfect servant."[33] Yet this does not preclude simultaneously having to come to terms with the nature of his work and, within its limits, fulfilling to a significant degree his patriarchal responsibilities.

Kamal lives in the servants' quarters in the upper-middle-class Gitanjali Building with his wife, who does part-time work there, and daughter. He is another male servant who has made his compromises with paradhin work and dependence on an employer for food and shelter. By holding his widowed employer's ignorance and neglect of the household in contempt, he reverses the relation of dependency: "She knows nothing and understands nothing, not even where things are kept. She asks me everything." In Kamal's eyes, his employer's reliance serves to dilute her power over him; in effect, he feels in control of the household and could even be seen to occupy, in a peculiar way, the place of the man of the house. Kamal's dominance of the domestic realm is reflected in his appraisal of even the most menial and feminized tasks as "simply work":

> I don't feel I have any [problems] really. This is simply work. And no work is bad. One has to survive. Many think, "There is no dignity in this work." I don't have that attitude at all. If I can do it well and earn enough money, then I am willing to do anything. . . . I don't agree that there is a difference between this and other work. Some feel *ghenna* [disgust] that a man should do *barir kaaj* [housework], but not me. People think sweeping, mopping, and washing dishes are women's work. But why shouldn't all people do everything? If my wife is not at home and I don't have the money to pay someone to [do a domestic chore] for me, then must I not be able to do it for myself? I find that ninety-nine percent of people feel ghenna, but I am not like this.

Kamal recounted that his wife at one point wanted him to leave domestic service to become a driver "outside." He learned to drive and got his license, but then he decided that he preferred live-in work for Rs 2,000 to the uncertainty of finding a driver's job for a maximum pay of Rs 3,000 as well as finding a place to live and incurring the attendant expenses. He once did find a job in an office but did not take it up for the same reason—he would have far greater expenditures given the cost of rent, food, electricity, water, and transport—and would give up the security and benefits of working "inside." Similarly, Raghu, another live-in servant, also realized after getting his license that a driver's salary would not be sufficient for him to afford a place to live in the city.[34] Moreover, in order to prevent him from quitting, his employers gave him a raise, hired his wife, and contributed to his children's schooling. As Kamal corroborates: "What would make me choose the outside? Here my daughter is safe. She is learning so much, getting so much help from everyone [the residents of the building]. Who will do this for her on the outside? I could not. All I want is for my daughter to get a decent job. If she can also make a good marriage, then even better." Both Kamal and Raghu, in the end, determined that they could best fulfill their familial duties by remaining within the confines of dependency and servitude—what to others is ghenna and to them is simply work—rather than opting for the precarious independence of "outside." It is precisely in fulfilling their duties toward their children and making decisions that others may consider shameful that a few men servants have been able to reconfigure their own patriarchy to avoid failure.

Servants' Critique of Employer Patriarchy and Privilege

Just as some male servants essay subverting a masculinist and classist discourse that denigrates their work, a comparable critique is extended to the framework of bhadralok patriarchy itself and its avatars. In Kamal's judgment of his employer in the preceding section, she has failed in her duty as a housewife and is thereby diminished in the eyes of her servant. Mrinalini, a bohemian employer in her sixties who was widowed young, frankly envisions the potential for servants to actually run the household, influence its moral tone, and even intervene in the employer's finances:

> Speaking of myself [as a single woman], if I were to have a lover, I don't have
> that privacy; it's not possible, because what would the servants say? So you see,
> I really have an extremely limited existence. . . . My daughter was appalled that
> my servant knows so much about my financial affairs. She told me that I was
> completely in his hands now. The relationship is not an easy one; they have a lot
> of power over me. . . . The other day he told me that since I have so much money
> in my savings account, I should have put it in a long-term or recurring account
> and got more out of it.

Indeed, the tables are turned when servants patrol the boundaries of acceptable sexual conduct and money management (and would justify, if it became commonplace, employers' fears about the stability of this culture of servitude).

Paromita, who has worked as a servant for most of her sixty-plus years, dismissively compares the younger generation of employers to the housewives of yore who shouldered the burden of domestic chores: "Now women do not suffer; they have all those machines to do the work. This generation doesn't know how to work. These girls go to the office but can't do anything at home. They scream if they have to work." Sardonically deploying her untutored status— "but then I'm illiterate, so how can I know what is good and what is bad?"— Paromita effectively equates illegitimate patriarchal authority in the servant and the employer homes but, in the employer's potential for violence, sees the power of class hierarchy even as she deplores it:

> You don't stay when your husband slaps you; why should you stay when your employer slaps you? They slap you because they have more money. We're poor—that's why we're abused. But if it wasn't for us, they wouldn't get their work done. . . . It [sexual abuse by employers] happens often; then the girl gets pregnant. You know what happens then—you have the money and we don't—but wife abuse happens even in your houses. . . . We're all human, so why make distinctions?

In this way, Paromita rejects a discourse, often used by employers, of domestic violence as endemic to the servant class and deftly identifies it with the exercise of power. Servants recognize the irreconcilability of bhadralok patriarchal pretensions toward servant well-being and lived practice: "Sometimes I am treated so badly that I wipe away my tears with one hand and work with the other," said one part-timer as she waited to pick up her child at a crèche. The other servants gathered at the crèche chimed in with a veritable barrage of stories about employer hypocrisy and ingratitude.

The part-timers commuting daily between their villages and Kolkata offer the most trenchant social critiques and most noticeably stand outside the domestic consensus engendered by bhadralok patriarchy. In the space of the second-class "ladies' compartment" for the duration of the journey back home, liberated both from the duties and obligations of their own households as well as the exigencies of employment, they are lively and talkative, full of energetic denunciations of the failure of patriarchy. One young woman tossed her head back and declared defiantly, "If only my husband would die, then I could get rid of this *sindoor* [vermillion on the hair parting that is the sign of Bengali Hindu marriage]"—implying that life without a failed patriarch is preferable to life with him. A more middle-class appearing woman in the train compartment was offended: "These women are *asabhya* [uncivilized]. They speak a foul tongue and use words that I couldn't imagine using." The attitudes of the train commuters afford the sharpest contrast with the bhadramahila, and, coupled with the fact that the commuters travel alone so far from home, they arouse suspicion among some urban elites who question their morality. As one well-known physician exclaimed:

> You rode on the train with them? You probably caught something from them. They are dirty, foul-mouthed, *bidi* [hand-rolled cigarette]-smoking, and smelly.

There is plenty of work to be done in the villages, but they want to come to Kolkata for *certain* reasons. Here they work for only a few hours and then run off home. The women who come into Kolkata in the evening *say* they are ayahs on night duty.

By casting aspersions on their morality and identifying them with prostitution, the employing classes ensure that the train commuters do indeed fall outside the domestic consensus.[35] Yet the street—as they go from house to house in the course of the workday—and the train are spaces of only intermittent freedom. The women undergo a transformation in the course of their journey from the city to the country. During the passage, they are working women, relaxed and united at the end of their workday, drinking fizzy drinks, eating snacks, and swapping stories about markets, men, and miracles. They alight from the train, now changed into wives and mothers, looking toward doing the marketing, cooking the evening meal, and snatching a few hours of sleep before they return to work the following day.

Conclusion

The absence of economic alternatives combined with unusually successful hegemonic ideologies of domesticity and class have conspired to make it difficult for servants to change their circumstances. Male servants are uniformly considered losers within the bhadralok patriarchal consensus, while the majority of women servants consider the fact that they have to work outside the home more problematic than the nature and conditions of their labor. Although certain spaces and times enable moments of insight and mutiny, the primary ideology that prevails is one of "utopian patriarchalism." Women servants long for an idealized, patriarchal fantasy in which they would be both respectable and protected. These hegemonic ideologies of domesticity and class serve to dissuade women from working outside the home, reinforce Kolkata's culture of servitude, and partially explain the extent to which, unlike in some of India's other metropolises, Kolkata's domestic workers are less actively engaged in seeking their rights as workers.[36]

6 The Cultivation and Cleavage of Distinction

And we do not yet know whether cultural life can survive the disappearance of domestic servants.[1]

Alain Besançon, quoted in Bourdieu, *Distinction*

WE HAVE SEEN how the institution of domestic servitude has undergone transformations associated with processes of urbanization and the move from the big house to the flat since the 1960s, but especially since the beginning of the 1990s, and concomitantly how the rhetoric of love, family, and loyalty has coexisted uneasily with an emerging, market discourse that seeks to identify the servant as a "contractual" worker rather than—or in addition to—as "part of the family."[2] In Kolkata, the practices and ideologies of "modernization" and "modernity" have not by any means led to the obsolescence of the servant, as the narrations of postwar optimism in the United States presaged.[3] Indeed, middle- and upper-class life at the beginning of the twenty-first century continues to seem inconceivable without servants. As we have seen, keeping servants not only confirms the attainment of middle-class status but also confers attributes of prestige, cultural capital, and civilization on employers of all classes.[4] Bourdieu's insertion of the above epigraph at the beginning of *Distinction* is telling: Class domination is sustained by distinction.

Domestic servitude has been equally if differently sustained in the past and the present by the operations of distinction. For what expressions of familial ideologies and loyalties cannot conceal, nor the wage contract disguise, is exploitation; above all, domestic servitude is a class relation rooted in extreme inequality and expressed through class distinctions that have been carefully nurtured and maintained over time. As we have noted, a culture of servitude is one in which domination/subordination, dependency, and inequality are normalized and permeate both the domestic and public spheres.

We borrow from Bourdieu to elaborate the third premise of Kolkata's culture of servitude—that the cultivation of social and cultural class distinction normalizes, and sometimes naturalizes, the relationship of domination and exploitation that undergirds the institution of domestic servitude in India and elsewhere.[5]

Distinction as Distance

In Kolkata's culture of servitude, class distinction can take myriad forms, but the notion of *distance* between employers and servants—be it literal/physical or metaphorical/emotional—is critical. In the spatiality of the old order—the big house with servants' quarters—servants are meant to be everywhere and nowhere; even in the absence of quarters, their presence should be unobtrusive since ample space allows servants to sleep and live anywhere in the house and grounds. In the relatively curtailed space of the flat, servants are considered to be intrusive and infringing on privacy, especially if there are no separate quarters for live-in servants, and the distinction of physical distance becomes acutely problematic. In both old and new spatial contexts, then, distance is a paramount concern.[6]

In the past, the space of the big house provided the distinction of physical distance coupled with comparatively unquestioned employer control and power to dictate the servants' way of life. Servants belonged in a separate category with distinctive dress, manners, and habits in the big house, with a well-regulated, recognizable place in the order of things. Indeed, when twenty-first-century employers lament the fact that "people do not want to work as live-ins, do not want to work as domestic servants," they are feeling the loss of that unquestioned categorical separation, power, and control. At the same time, employers are nostalgic for a time when servants "were a part of you," but this yearning, we would argue, is precisely for a time when servants had a well-defined place in the space of the big house.

Today, as employer and servant coexist in the more limited space of the flat, and servants increasingly live in their own homes, the very edifice upon which the institution of domestic servitude was built, distinction, can appear to be crumbling. Bhagat Singh, the retired bachelor who grew up in a plantation house and laughingly admits that he has very fond memories of that "feudal agro-based existence which I miss very much," now lives in an upper-middle-class apartment building. He is concerned about the constant intermingling of live-in servants and employers in the relatively confined spaces of the complex—the flats themselves, as well as the communal stairs, elevators, and entryways:

> The servants had their own place [in the zamindari system in the plantation where he grew up]; they didn't have to live on the fringes of our society. Here they are unavoidable nuisances. It is better for servants to live in slums apart or in village communities. It is worse for them growing up as a fringe class amidst middle-class apartment complexes. The tendency in India is to have high rises [apartment buildings] with the feudal order imported in. . . . If the servants coalesce into a real class, it is a real threat. There is definitely a feeling amongst employers of us versus them. Servants see it the same way.

[handwritten margin note: why?]

Bhagat Singh prefers servants to live apart (as many servants themselves prefer a home of their own). He offers a social-psychological explanation for his preference—if servants live on the "fringes" of employers' lives without the possibility of growing independently into their own selves, it may create the sorts of resentments and envies that could "coalesce into a real class threat." Recall Judith Rollins's brilliant evocation of *ressentiment* to analyze in another context servants' challenge to the operations of distinction that underlie class domination: "But domestics do exhibit the extreme consciousness of the Other that is characteristic of those in a subordinate position; and they do express the *ressentiment* of oppressed who do not accept the justness of their oppression."[7] Although other employers may not share Bhagat Singh's logic, they have in common with him the fear that the absence or erosion of distinction as distance leads unavoidably to heightened tensions and conflicts between employers and servants. As such, it becomes imperative that both servants and employers learn distinction and reproduce distinction.

Mrinalini, the artist in her sixties whom we first encountered in Chapter 2 living in a big house, has identified and to some extent transgressed the distinction of distance in a way that neither her mother's nor her daughter's generation could do. Speaking of her longtime manservant, she makes clear that he defies many of the barriers servants confront—cleaning bathrooms, work that only jamadars do, or dealing with the employer's money, which servants never do:

> There is an invisible line that separates servant from employer, but nobody knows where it is, because I am confused myself. I've got them [servants] all confused. They don't know how far they can go, and then they begin to offend me. Sometimes I get very annoyed because they don't do their job; then I have

to do it myself, and I get angry and I feel like saying, this is not my job. This is what you're here for, this is what you're paid to do, but I can't say that. But it's not that I'm so decent that I don't think this. It comes to mind, but I control myself. [We ask why she controls herself.] How can I say, "You're paid to do this?" What I say to them is, "How can I do my job *and* your job?". . . Arjun cleans my bathroom and handles my money—he handles all my money. My daughter is different. She keeps her distance from servants like my mother did. She believes that there is a master-servant relationship. She thinks I spoil my servants. She takes good care of her servants, but they would never dare tell her what to do, like my servants tell me what to do.

Mrinalini's unusual situation helps to throw into relief the circumstances of physical distinction and emotional propriety that can be observed in most other households, even across generations. Mrinalini knows that there is "an invisible line" that structures the master-servant relationship and defines employer and servant duties, obligations, and behaviors, a line that both her mother and daughter knew not to cross. It is quite possibly because she has become "confused" that she and the servants in her household are able to break new ground—the same servant cleaning bathrooms and acting as financial adviser—as we shall see further in the next section.

The Politics of Sitting

There are rules, at once explicit and unspoken, that are meant to govern servant comportment in the space of the home. One clear rule concerns where servants are allowed to sit. The simple act of sitting, the question of where one's body may be placed, like many of the other practices embedded in unequal relationships of power, turns into what we have called the *politics of sitting*. Mala, an elderly, middle-class employer, remarked that in her childhood the maidservant would sit on the floor, "but with great satisfaction." Now, however, "they say, why, why should I sit there?"[8] But Mala exaggerates, for servants are well aware of these rules. Paromita, a full-time, live-out servant in her sixties, explained:

People don't like it if you sit on chairs. . . . Do you understand what I'm saying without having to say it? Here [in the apartment of her employer] they don't let us sit except on the floor. In other houses they don't even let us eat the same food or from the same plates. As a rule, we don't sit on chairs in case somebody says something—it hurts our pride. In many houses they insult you, which is why we don't do it.

Indeed, in most houses, servants sit on their haunches on the floor of the kitchen or on low stools provided for them. This habit or custom is, again, unquestioned and unspoken, the *doxa* of the employing household, if you will. Hence Paromita declines to explicitly state the condition of being placed in a separate, inferior category despite—or perhaps because of—her shame and anger.

The practice of the employer sitting or reclining while the servant must stand or sit on the floor is an unmistakable embodiment of hierarchy, inequality, and subordination/domination. That it has been virtually unchallenged is a sign of the literal/physical distinction at the core of the culture of servitude. Even when there is emotional proximity, the physical distance is rarely bridged. Rohan, a young doctor, explains the politics of sitting as it relates to Ganesh, the family retainer who brought him up:

> Yes, the relationship is very, very close with him, but there's always a distance. Even now that he's seen me growing up, and he's brought me up, but even today, if I'm at home, and I'm sitting and talking, he will never go and sit; he'll still stand and talk to me. Because he's been brought up with that type [of behavior].
>
> [We asked if he would care if Ganesh sat down and started talking to him.] Not anymore, now that he's old; I mean, it doesn't make a difference to me. In fact, now when he does [stand], I'll tell him to please sit down, because I see he's old.

Habits of a lifetime, both for servant and young master, very nearly take precedence over competing claims of respect and deference for the elderly and of intimacy with the child one has brought up to be a man.

Artist Mrinalini confronted honestly the politics of sitting:

> In my heart, I'm sure I'm feudal. I would not want Arjun [live-in servant] to sit on my bed. I don't mind him sitting at my table, but as yet I would not like him to sit on my bed.[9] We watch TV together, and I make him watch Discovery channel. Now he is addicted to it. Before that he would watch cricket. This is a promotion because we are both watching together, and he is sitting on a *mora* [stool] rather than on the floor. When we watch TV, I sit on the bed, Arjun sits on a mora, and Saraswati [live-in maid] always sits on the floor. Two days ago, Saraswati went and got a mora for herself. I was happy. It is good. I would love to say that it is all equal and democratic; it's not really, it's all on the way to . . .

In common with several other employers in this study, Mrinalini self-consciously contrasts feudal with modern, democratic ways of being. Her description of television watching reflects two key developments within the home: a contemporary iteration of colonial and nationalist civilizing reform—by introducing the servant to science—and a gradual, but incomplete, erasure of spatial distinction between the servant body and the employer body as the servant moves up from the floor.[10] It should be noted, however, that only in one or two of the dozens of households observed in this study was there any alteration in the politics of sitting.

Mrinalini's advocacy of shared viewing of television, science programs or otherwise, with servants may be the exception that proves the rule. In fact, most middle-class employers are annoyed by servant expectations that they be allowed to watch television in the employer's home, even though it is an increasingly unavoidable practice. A middle-class employer recalls that before she acquired a television, she found it difficult to get a maid: "They would come to my house, look around, say, 'You don't have a television?' and then never return!" One affluent couple analyzed servant television watching as an inescapable tangent of the rampant consumerism that has swept through the middle and upper classes in Kolkata over the past several years, joining employer and servant desires. At the same time, this couple is clear that even though servant television watching has become a social phenomenon that is discussed in their circle of friends as a necessary evil, it is something new to Kolkata's culture of servitude and has yet to be fully absorbed.

> Consumerism, as it's hit us, has also hit them [servants]. So today their wants and needs are far more than when I was a kid. For example, a young girl servant that we recruit, she's seen good things around, she's aware that there's something called the television, the Star TV, and there are Hindi movies playing, and I watch it at home (even though I never saw my parents watching), so [she thinks] why shouldn't I watch it, too. So their wants and needs are also increasing—that's a big shift, I would say. Therefore, they also expect that they get the good things in life. Now salary can meet a certain amount, but there are a lot of perquisites that I don't remember my parents having to worry [about].
>
> But I know of friends who say, "I've got this very loyal servant, but there's one addiction, she must watch this soap [opera] between seven and nine, so I can't entertain [company] then. I have to keep her happy, because she's with me. Or Saturday evening, they [the servants] have to watch the movie on television."

You want to keep them happy, because we are all nuclear families and both go off to work—you don't want to upset the apple cart.

In our survey, over 50 percent of the servants reported that the chance to watch television was the only good thing about their job. Yet this "entitlement to leisure" is disputed by employers for different reasons. While some employers simply express disapproval of servants desiring to be "entertained on the job," perhaps a deeper objection stems from the servants sharing the same viewing experience as the employers, at the same time and in the same place. Practices of cultural consumption serve as markers of class distinction, and the shared consumption of television serials and movies—entertainment and leisure—makes employers uneasy.[11]

The imbrication of the politics of sitting with the problematic of servants watching television in the employer's home reveals yet another complication of distinction. How can social distinction in the smaller spaces of the flat be maintained, especially when shared television watching could mean shared experience and greater emotional proximity? For many employers, this involves policing their own behavior as well as that of the servants. Vijay, the young engineer, disapproves of any tendency for employers and servants to behave as friends and harks back to the strict distance observed by his parents in the big house of his childhood, once again focusing on the charged point of shared television watching. In the following quotation, Vijay filters his parents' behavior in the past through his sense of appropriate distance in the present:

My parents were strict in the sense that there were timings. Everything was an open system, yet no indulgence, but not that much differentiation either—what we ate was what they [the servants] ate. Today I see, for example, that servants and the lady of the house are friends; they share a TV soap together. My mother wouldn't sit and discuss with [her servant] some family problem. She wouldn't indulge in allowing them to get too close beyond a certain point. You do your job and then you go, you're paid, we're taking care of you, you take care of us—it's very clinical. . . . I don't remember Gautam [the family retainer in his parents' home] insisting that he must have a TV or, in those days, a radio. He didn't expect to be entertained on the job, just as we don't expect to be entertained at the office.

Yet while young employers, who are often imbued with a corporate ethic, may not want to be "friends" with their servants, they do want to be friendly. Viji, an office manager in her thirties, is dismayed that her mother-in-law talks to servants as if they were lower beings and hers to command: "My mother-in-law, when she talks to the servants, she talks to them as servants, and then expects them to take it, whether she's right or wrong. They can't reply [talk back], and if they do, there is a fight and then you have to cope with it." In contrast, Viji's own mother "does not give [their longtime cook and family retainer] the opportunity to talk back, because she does not talk like that [like Viji's mother-in-law]—she talks to him one to one." The contrast Viji sketches is between treating the servants as an inferior class or group, or as individual persons with rights and feelings. As we have noted in Chapter 3, servants resent acutely being addressed as "you people," as if they could be dismissed as an undifferentiated and homogeneous lower order. Viji's account also reflects the incorporation into employer discourse of new management practices that emphasize treating workers and support staff as valued individuals rather than as interchangeable—and dispensable—components on the plant floor. We have considered the contradictions of this discursive change in Chapter 4.

Caste Withers but Lingers

While Saraswati and Arjun, servants in Mrinalini's singular household, have worked themselves up from the floor to the stool, most other servants are categorically prevented from breaking barriers of class and caste hierarchies.[12] In particular, low-caste servants associated with cleaning bathrooms and taking away refuse are strictly regulated. When asked whether she ever talked to the jamadar of her childhood, Mala, a middle-class woman in her seventies, remembers:

> Oh, yes, because he couldn't touch anything. I would have to pour water over his hands and into the container he was holding so that he could wash things. But he didn't mind that he couldn't touch anything—he himself would tell me that he shouldn't touch things. These days, however, things are different. I said to my jamadar the other day: "Don't touch my curtain," and he said: "Why not? Am I not a human being?"

The issue of caste clearly shapes this issue of contamination, and there are those who would desire to maintain distinction on the basis of caste. Recall that the main caste distinction insofar as domestic work tended to revolve around those who cleaned bathrooms and performed other ritually impure tasks, especially washing dishes, and belonged to low castes. In upper-caste households, members of low castes were traditionally not allowed to touch certain things and enter certain sacred or ordinary spaces. In order to overcome the ritually imposed caste barriers in daily life, the women and girls of observant Hindu households practiced routine and ritual procedures, such as pouring (clean) water over the (unclean) jamadar's hands. In general, in the big house of the past, the jamadar came from outside the home to clean specifically that space, and no other servant would touch the bathroom.

Today, the bathroom cleaner or sweeper continues to be someone who will go from home to home, flat to flat, almost exclusively dedicated to the task of cleaning bathrooms. In only one case did we encounter a middle-class employer who cleaned her own bathroom. Similarly, as we have seen, washing dishes is considered the most menial and lowly of household tasks, and all who can possibly afford it will at the very least hire a part-timer to clean the dishes. It can thus be affirmed that the caste strictures involving the ritual contamination presented by dirty dishes in observant Hindu homes pervades the wider culture. In virtually all houses, servants eat separately, in the kitchen, often off plates and glasses specially kept aside for them. Therefore, the distinction between employer and servant may be clearly marked by notions of caste contamination.[13]

The servant body is considered to be weak, susceptible to illness, and unclean, but servants are expected to do work that requires them to be strong, healthy, and clean. Most employers recognize that servants have grown up in poverty, lacking nutrition and health care, and hence are liable to fatigue and ill health. Yet this recognition is often overwhelmed by the pervasiveness of the notion of the intrinsically unfit and unclean servant body. This contradiction is thrown into relief by employers' lingering revulsion toward the unclean servant body even as that servant performs tasks that demand cleanliness—meal preparation and cooking, making beds—and simultaneous employer awareness that their live-in servants certainly bathe daily.

Zeenat relates that her employer did not allow her to bathe in the morning but insisted that she bathe in the afternoon, like the other servants did. Zeenat, for whom this was her first place of employment, bitterly resented not being allowed to approach a new day freshly bathed and dressed. Her attention to personal care—in the manner of a middle-class person—irked her employer, who accused her of using more laundry soap than the entire family did. Zeenat asked, "Is it a crime to want to keep yourself clean?" Paradoxically, it may be: Zeenat's concern with personal hygiene and cleanliness too obviously belies employer assumptions about the unclean, and thus distinct, servant body.[14]

Many of the employers in our study were originally from East Bengal. Gopa, an elderly feminist and Communist, recounts that in the rural East Bengal of her childhood, most servants were "untouchables" and some were Muslim. The "untouchable" servants washed dishes and put them aside, and then the women of the house would pour fresh water over the dishes before touching them. She remembers once when her mother's aunt came out of the prayer room and saw the shadow of a Muslim servant, the servant was verbally abused. Says Gopa: "The fellow was shivering with fear. You see, the employers didn't want to touch Muslims so they would serve them food from above. There were no Hindu servants because women of the house did the cooking [thus obviating the need for a Brahmin cook]. The women would even purify the boiled milk delivered by noncaste persons." In those contexts Muslims apparently were as beyond the pale as (or even more than) low-caste persons.

A retired banker in his eighties, Subhas described the rigid caste barriers in the rural feudal estate were he spent his early childhood: "The cooks were Brahmin and Kshatriya, the Rauts were carriers of water, and all other domestics were tribals.[15] Champa, the ayah who looked after the little children, was a tribal." As he recalled, "The servants themselves imposed the caste system." The hegemony of the caste system, Subhas's words imply, did not require employers' impositions or interventions to enforce it and its practices. In Calcutta, where he has spent most of his life, similar caste conditions prevailed.

A female employer in her thirties, Srimati, who works for a women's NGO, analyzed the caste rules observed in her paternal grandparents' household and how this observance made life difficult for her mother in the joint family and was a source of shame for her generation:

> My paternal grandparents were strict Brahmins and didn't like servants to touch things. So, the daughters-in-law and women of the house had to do a lot of work. This is why my mother didn't finish her [college] degree. . . . My paternal grandmother and widowed aunt lived with us. No one could touch them because of the rigidity of purity/pollution.
>
> [We asked whether the widows had a special servant.] Yes, the daughter-in-law! My mother was cultured and modern but had to look after the widows as well as cooking and making the beds for all. My mother never had much respect

for them [the older, less educated women]. Servants did the dishes, the dhobi washed the clothes, and all were purified by water from the Ganges. The milkman was not allowed into the house. Whatever came from the outside had to be washed again by my mother.

My father's family had money but no culture, and so they were fixated on purity/pollution. *So* horrible! My brother once said to my grandmother, "It is my sorrow and shame that I have Brahmin blood in me because for generations we have tortured people."

Many of the employers we spoke with told us stories of the kinds of caste regulations and prohibitions practiced by their family in the past. Yet, in our observation, these strictures were more readily rejected in theory than in practice. While employers easily speak of discarding old caste habits because of their liberal and modern outlook, the perceived rejection by servants of "things as they should be" is undeniably disturbing.

While Ayesha, the cosmetics manager, seems to actively seek an impersonal and contractual modern relationship with her servants, this desire is overridden by the importance of maintaining distinction.

I am very keen that my child shouldn't be neglected, but at the same time I am very strict about a servant being a servant. I don't want them sitting on my sofa or my bed. But I've had to make compromises in the sense that I've had to give them one of the bathrooms to use.

I've had to because you constantly have to balance between practicality and your ideology and principles. . . . The other day, [my child minder] said, "Can you wash my shawl in your washing machine?" I didn't like that, and I haven't washed it even today, but I can't say to her, "I'm not going to be washing my clothes with yours, however nice I am with you," you know?

This section illustrates some of the tensions between the old, feudal, big-house order and emerging, modern, apartment living in a caste-ridden society. Whereas the first is fundamentally based on hierarchical and unequal relations, the second assumes a certain equality among individuals despite class or caste differences. Nevertheless, traditional caste taboos continue to shape everyday life even among social sectors that consider themselves to be part of the democratic global modern. Concerns about contamination of bathrooms, clothes washed together, or dirty dishes—consciously or unconsciously disguised as the ideology of hygiene—must be directly confronted in a small apartment, and compromises must be made in order to ensure kindly child care.[16] Yet egalitarian treatment of the caregiver—which might help to achieve the desired good care within a more contractual relationship—continues to challenge the employer imaginary in Kolkata's culture of servitude, especially given the contradictory "modernity" employers inhabit.

Class Bodies and Servant Spaces: "They Dress, Use Cosmetics, Want to Be Like Us"

> [A] variant of the master-slave dialectic [is one in] which the possessors affirm their possession of their possessions. In so doing, they distance themselves still further from the dispossessed, who, not content with being slaves to necessity in all its forms, are suspected of being possessed by the desire for possession, and so potentially possessed by the possessions they do not, or do not yet, possess.
>
> **Bourdieu, *Distinction***

> This chap makes extra money in a covert way through the bazaar book.[17] His wife [who works in another household] also makes extra [money], I'm sure. How do they keep their daughters in such style? Where do they get their money? They are either starving, or . . . they live beyond their means but live well.
>
> **Bhagat Singh on his manservant**

In Bengal, the distinction between the bhadralok and the others, that is, those who are poor and uncivilized, is "naturally" reflected in a caste-inflected class divide within the bhadra home.[18] Precisely because they are not bhadralok, servants' bodies, dress, behavior, and aspirations by definition ought not to be similar or identical to those of employers. And when those distinctions begin to blur—or are perceived as such—it makes employers, both old and young, nationalist and globalized, anxious.

Kakoli, an older employer, recalls the obvious difference in clothing that once marked the women of the household from the servants.

> When we were young, the maidservants came to us bare bodied [without a blouse], with no slippers, and with just a sari to wrap [themselves in]. Now you can't tell the difference between the servant and someone who is part of the family—they dress, use cosmetics, want to be like us—before, they didn't have the money or the idea [that they could be like us].

What is particularly noticeable for the older generation of employers is the perceived change in servant dress over the past several decades. They remember servants in the past of the feudal big house as immediately recognizable as servants because of dress, manner, bearing, and so on—visible markers all.

The younger generation of employers perceives as well a temporal change in servant desire. Unlike servants with the self-effacing gratitude of the past, employers see servants today as having expectations of a different order as far as clothes, appearance, and, ultimately, status:

> There was never a question of choice in what [clothes] my parents gave servants when I was young. What my parents gave, they [the servants] took or they threw away. They never had the audacity to come and say I don't like this, please give me that. Today servants will come and say I want this sari of this make, or I need this shawl of that [type]. They will make their choices, and they expect you to adhere to that.

Tensions over the perceived erosion of these markers of class distinction and efforts to maintain them permeate daily life. Three elderly ladies chatting over tea one day remarked that young servant women "learn how to do makeup but not how to read; . . . they send their children to school but not themselves." The feeling is that servants' scarce resources should be spent on something uplifting, like education, not on makeup and clothes that can only cause confusion and consternation by enabling servant girls and women to acquire a middle-class appearance. Yet even when servants spend on education rather than middle-class frivolities, they are questioned.

One of Aparna's employers—she works in several flats in the Gitanjali Building as a part-time servant—commented that she was "a bit arrogant and not servantlike," which meant that Aparna's discourse, posture, and demeanor were not conventionally servile and self-effacing. She lacked what Thorstein Veblen has described as "an acquired facility in the tactics of subservience."[19] In contrast, another employer, who appreciates Aparna's honesty and efforts to make the best of limited circumstances, especially in terms of educating her daughter, thought she walked "like a queen." Perhaps in light of these contradictory employer responses, Aparna's position was understandable: "What is the point of being a smart servant? You might as well be stupid." Servants repeatedly emphasized that their circumstances kept them *murkha* (stupid, uneducated), and indeed, the servant body is constructed as a stupid body. However, when servants focus on the education of their children—as does Aparna and as do Bhagat Singh's servants referenced in this section's epigraph—employers wonder how servants could possibly come up with the funds to send their children to school with the proper uniforms, books, and other paraphernalia.

Unease with the blurring of well-established class lines makes Bhagat Singh wonder about the children of servants who live in buildings like his. "Today, children of servants grow up in the midst of affluence. How do they cope? Instead of growing up in a 'natural way,' they dress up smartly, change themselves. Sunil's [his servant's] girl couldn't get through her exams but has become fashionable." He then went on to tell the story of an encounter with a little girl in a school uniform in the apartment elevator. He asked her where she lived, expecting her to respond with the apartment number. He was surprised to hear that she lived in the servants' quarters, and his discomfort came through in the telling. As we will see in the next section, both the employer and servant classes learn distinction and reproduce distinction, yet Bhagat Singh and other employers face situations in which those learned assumptions no longer seem to hold.

Is it possible for someone to shed the servant body and acquire another class embodiment? It must be admitted that in the several years covered by this research project, we have met only one young woman, Rita, whose story we told in Chapter 5, who was able to do precisely this with the help of a remarkable employer. When we first met Rita, she was a young maidservant, and now she is a young woman with her own business as an independent beautician who, with her husband, is about to make a down payment on a flat. To fully take on the guise of their emerging middle-class status, Rita's husband suggested that she might want to hire a servant—although this has not yet happened.

The confusion and consternation felt by employers are not just a matter of social embarrassment but signal a threat to bhadralok identity. For if servant children can be mistaken for the pampered children of the upper-middle classes, and if female servants "pass" as middle-class women, then employers could mistakenly socialize with them, talk to them as peers, and, most worrying of all, conceivably fall in love with them. The construction of social life relies to a great extent on the traditional hierarchies and markers of class, caste, and gender. The erasure of such distinctions would inevitably impinge on the identity and hegemony of the employer classes—and their endogamy—hence the countervailing efforts. And here we can once again follow Bourdieu: "[I]t is an immediate adherence, at the deepest level of the habitus, to the tastes and distastes, sympathies and aversions, fantasies and phobias which, more than declared opinions, forge the unconscious unity of a class."[20]

Learning Distinction

Some employers remember a time as children when they did not understand the distinction between themselves and servants. In two cases, they recall touching the feet of servants—a gesture of respect made in Bengal to those older than one—and realizing, by the sudden silence of the adults present, that this was an inappropriate gesture, indeed an unacceptable one. Thus, it is in small gestures and unspoken moments that children learn about the hierarchical and unequal order of daily life.

For example, Srimati, the NGO worker in her thirties, told us that she was taught to respect servants, especially the older ones. Her mother instructed Srimati and her siblings to address the family cook, a widow, using the formal "you." Yet Srimati also remembers the time as a small child when her leg touched a servant's, so she automatically wanted to do pranam, but her mother indicated that she should not. Srimati said that even though she obeyed her mother, she could never truly accept that injunction. Now that she is an adult with her own servants, however, she recognizes the need for "a line." Srimati stressed to us nonetheless that because of her upbringing and mother's influence, she uses a soft tone in speaking with servants and makes requests—as opposed to the harsh, barked commands used by the older generation in her paternal family.[21]

We asked Mala how she realized or understood that the jamadar of her childhood more than sixty years ago was an "untouchable": "We just knew, from when we were very young, our mothers told us, 'Don't touch them; don't let them touch you or anything else.'" An elderly employer in his eighties directly linked learning about class distinction with gender distinction, in relation to servants and female siblings, respectively, within the patriarchal context of the large joint family household of his childhood:

> How did we learn how to treat servants? We realized we were superior to them. We thought them beneath us. They were obedient. We saw how parents, etc., treated them. We were taught never to abuse them—scolding, calling names, and hitting—by our father. Since very young, I remember ordering them about. There was nothing wrong with it. Boys ordered servants more than girls. If the servant wasn't there, we would tell the sister to do it. Girls were less aggressive.

Children learned by observing their parents the habits, discourses, and practices of Kolkata's culture of servitude. And in this culture of servitude rooted in feudal patriarchy, the hierarchies and distinctions of caste, class, and gender constituted the very fabric of daily life and relationships. Just as children learned that servants constituted a distinctive class, so, too, they learned that girls were closer to servants than boys, both as beings and as labor.

Many employers of the younger generation are caught between the learned assumptions of Kolkata's culture of servitude and emerging discourses of equality and democracy in the public and domestic spheres—this last particularly an ambition of feminism and the women's movement. Being caught betwixt and between is reflected in gender and generational conflicts within middle-class homes. Viji is as perturbed about her son's as she is about her mother-in-law's behavior. She believes that she has tried to set an example of more democratic and courteous treatment of servants, but she is dismayed by signs that her son seems to be learning from his grandmother to distinguish servants as a separate class.

> Aditya now tells me things like "Maya has to do this because she's a servant." And I really get annoyed because I take pains to explain to him that just because she's working for us, you shouldn't think like that. Aditya is imbibing values about servants in his grandparents' house and says a lot of things which horrify and stun us. It's really upsetting; . . . here you're trying to bring up a kid with different values, trying to make him understand that these people are coming to work for you just as much as we are going out to work. This has no effect because of the way he sees servants treated by his grandparents. When he says, "She's a servant," there's a clear class distinction—there's a clarity: he can do things [with Maya] which he can't do with me or anybody else who is older under normal circumstances, but he can do with them because they're servants. [Aditya says] "Maya doesn't listen to Dadi" [paternal grandmother], because Dadi is constantly saying that Maya doesn't listen. He's not hearing the other side of the story—Maya's also got reasons not to listen. . . . [Aditya says] "Maya should do this because we pay her, because she's our servant," . . . passing comments that to me are so racist in content.

Note that Viji's use of the word *racist* to stand in for categorical prejudice, in this case toward the class of people who are servants, reveals an absence in contemporary vocabulary of the means to speak about class discrimination. Since she is speaking in English, she reaches for the word in global circulation that effectively describes such categorical prejudice.

Viji is certainly not alone in her worry about bringing up a child who is learning distinction despite her best efforts to inculcate more egalitarian values and perspectives. Yet for the most part, children in our study do learn distinction, to distinguish between servant and employer categories, and to convert these perceptions and practices into internalized dispositions about what it means to treat a "servant as a servant."

Servants' children and children who live and work as servants, of course, all too painfully learn about distinction from a young age. Srimati told us about her childhood friend Hari, a young boy servant who was treated affectionately by her mother. He ate with the children of the family and, according to Srimati, was so used to being loved and indulged that he would not clean up after himself. On one cold night, he got into bed with Srimati to keep warm. Srimati had already been taught that boys did not sleep with girls, so she yelled, "Look Ma, Hari has come into bed with me." Young Hari, unsurprisingly, thought that if he could eat with Srimati, he could sleep in the same bed with her. Srimati's mother could have explained to Hari what he had done wrong, but she decided that he would not be able to deal with the hurt of being told that he was different from Srimati, that he was a "servant boy," so she dismissed him and sent him home to his parents.

Indeed, it was because he was a servant boy—not just a boy—that Srimati's mother had to dismiss Hari. There is a common folktale in India about a man who adopts a tiger cub. This cub, when brought home, plays and gambols around with the family, much as a dog would. Then one day, the man cuts himself, and the tiger licks the wound. The man immediately returns the tiger to the jungle. For the tiger has tasted blood and will now revert to the behavior nature had intended for him. Despite her fondness for Hari, Srimati's mother believed that she could no longer trust him to be around her daughter. Despite displaying a child's innocence, once Hari had crossed the line from play to bed, the belief that he had a different and potentially threatening class nature could not be ignored.

Some employers also believe that the fact that servants no longer want their own children to become servants is one more reason for the perceived scarcity of servants. Elderly employers note that in the past, when a servant's child came to be a certain age, the child would often be placed in another house as a servant. Today, however, servants send their children to school. It is not surprising that servants try to protect their children from learning distinction in this way. The three elderly tea-sipping ladies explained that even though servants routinely brought their very young children to work in the past, now they prefer to leave the children at home or in crèches because "they [servants] fear that if their children come, they will pick up a servant's mentality." Indeed, as a group of women part-timers who had dropped off their children in a local crèche told us, the crèche served two main purposes, to provide child care and to prepare small children for school. Education is quite possibly the only means servants have available to try to ensure that their children will avoid learning "a servant's mentality" and distinction. While schooling may not ultimately "unlearn" distinction, it is one of the few egalitarian and democratic resources accessible to servant families regardless of caste, class, and gender—and a way out of servitude.

Beyond Distinction

> *When you go to interview her, please don't tell her you are interviewing her as a servant—she would be hurt.*
> **Employer on servant who has been with her for twenty-eight years**

Servants perceived as rejecting "things as they should be"—the bathroom cleaner who asserted his personhood, the young maids who could pass for middle-class women, or the interchangeable servant or employer children—is rather disturbing to employers. Yet what does give servants the possibility of lessening their dependence, untangling themselves from the rhetoric of love, and imagining a different future for their children? We argue that changed urban spatial arrangements and housing forms are crucial for reconfiguring distinction. Unlike servants who live in servants' quarters of a big house or a flat, those who live in a basti or a village have a home of their own. This reality has profound implications for the relationship with employers and the barriers of distinction. The ability to leave the employer's house every day for one's own home means that the employer's control is finite. The three ladies quoted previously, for example, contrast a previous situation of an abundance of live-in servants to the present where servants say, "Why should I leave my home and live in yours?"

This perception of servant autonomy based on having a home of one's own heightens employer perceptions of their own relative powerlessness. "If the servant doesn't come to work, you can't say 'why didn't you come?' You have to be meek and submit to them." Elderly employer Kakoli recognizes that servants are not "meek" anymore because they have a place of their own, which to her signifies an inversion of the customary relations of power between employers and servants. If servants do not submit to employers, her words imply, employers must submit to them. In this hierarchical dynamic, as posed here, there is no possibility of a more equal coexistence. Employers realize to their dismay that part-timers with a place to call their own can "escape," as one employer put it. The choice of this word reflects at the very least the employer's awareness that there is indeed something worth escaping—be it from the work or from being at the beck and call, or being enclosed inside a house. By the same token, while recognizing that part-timing signifies more work overall because of having to attend to multiple houses, servants uniformly agree that for those who have a place to live, part-time work is better.

Keya, who would like to be thought a benevolent employer, cannot come to terms with increasing servant demands. Like several other employers, she believes it is her obligation to help the servants with their financial difficulties but is made uncomfortable by the perception that servants now feel they have the right to make demands on her. Relating an account of her failure to inculcate a degree of financial resourcefulness in her maid, Mumtaz, Keya queries why her full-time, live-out servant cannot help herself more given that she has the possibility, for example, of opening a bank account and saving money: "I cannot solve her problems for her, if she doesn't begin to help herself. At some point, shouldn't she be responsible for her life?" In this way, some employers conveyed that if servants now had increasing access to the discourse and practice of rights, and a new capacity to make demands on employers, some of the deeply rooted employer obligations should wither away.

Other employers, such as Mrinalini, had a more equanimous view of changing servant expectations: "I think they want more money, not salary money, but money to buy land, to get married. Our requirements and their requirements are different, so I always ask them, 'how much do you need?' and if I am able, I give it, and if I can't, no." Similarly, another employer said that her servant "wanted to build a house for himself so I gave him the fifteen thousand rupees he asked for because everybody has to think of their future security." In some cases, therefore, employers are coming to terms with the reality of servants' increased autonomy and having a home of their own, as we also saw earlier in Rita's story. Many employers, young and old, do recognize that in a modern, democratic world, servants should be considered persons with rights. Yet when servants claim modern collective or workers' rights, employers are threatened precisely because the possibility of a rights-bearing individual in one's home imperils distinction.

While West Bengal's ruling CPI(M) does not appear to have much interest or success in organizing domestic workers, employers who speculate that "communism" might introduce servants to ideas about workers' rights—recall the three elderly ladies' conversation in Chapter 4—are perhaps not far from the mark. As we saw in the same chapter, one such employer is Jyotsna, the middle-class retired librarian living in an old North Kolkata family home, who is perhaps overly dramatic in her fears. She worries that political changes and levels of grassroots engagement both locally and nationally mean that if employers do not exercise discipline—implying as individual households and as a class—they will lose control and servants will take over to the point of banishing employers from their own homes. Jyotsna, like Bhagat Singh, sees politically aware servants as a potential class threat.

From an alternative point of view, Gopa reflects on her fellow Communists, "Party people have many drawbacks, but they do have certain principles"—indicating that some Communists with means kept few or no servants and treated them better. Gopa approves of the new political consciousness, even though she, like other employers, overestimates the consequence: "There has been an attitude shift amongst domestics starting about ten years ago. Previously they were meek, docile, and terrified that they would lose their jobs. That fear has been replaced by the certainty that they will get another job, so they have more bargaining power, and employers must be more careful because there is a very high demand for domestic servants." Again, servants' recourse to rights is equated with a decline in employer control in an illusory context of servant scarcity.

Yet the politics of parliamentary democracy that flourish in Kolkata do in fact spill over into neighborhoods and households. Some low-caste servants are mobilized by caste-based political parties that have recently gained in power and popularity, while others may well be attracted to the CPI(M). For example, Lakshmi remarked that her husband would go to "those Kanshi Ram meetings sometimes."[22] Bastis have neighborhood clubs supported by various political parties.[23] The thriving political culture of Kolkata is the source for an alternative discourse about personhood and human rights that is unevenly taken up. Although, as one would expect, few live-in workers deploy this alternative discourse, servants who live in bastis and squatter settlements frequently do have recourse to it.

Servants also seek the support of the CPI(M) party or union apparatus when making claims on employers. Lila, an upper-middle-class employer, described part-timers as "more powerful and more threatening" than full-time and/or live-in servants. She had a part-timer who started "pinching things." When Lila tried to dismiss her, the servant said, "You can't sack me. You'll have to pay me." The part-time servant turned to the local party offices of the ruling CPI(M) to back her up, and Lila ended up paying her the Rs 400 that she had demanded as a sort of severance pay. Bhagat Singh, the affluent retired bachelor, told us the story of the euphemistic "gentleman" who hit a maidservant. She promptly

complained to the police and to the party. According to Bhagat Singh's narrative, "[This] servant who had worked for him for fifteen years, whom he trained
thoroughly, now demanded compensation when asked to leave, making his life
miserable." In both these employer accounts, servants who have recourse to
rights discourses or to related institutional support, be it from the party or a
union, definitely have the capacity to alter the status quo.

As we saw in Chapter 3, Guru, who has worked for the Gitanjali Building
cooperative as a jamadar since 1978, is one of the few servants who belongs
to a union. Although the union has been able to achieve a measure of results
from collective bargaining, such as contract and salary agreements, holidays,
and uniforms (which help to ameliorate the status of this degraded occupation), it has not been able to negotiate pensions for its members. In a city where
workers' rights have been at the fore of public debate and consciousness for
most of the twentieth century, it is remarkable that in the course of this study
we encountered only one unionized domestic worker.

Some employers who are involved with the CPI(M) or NGOs have attempted
to organize workers, quite often with contradictory results. We were intrigued
by the absence of a domestic workers' organization, so we asked, among others,
Srimati, the NGO worker, about this. She spoke in some detail about her effort
to form a union of servants from squatter settlements as well as bastis. It was
almost entirely a story of her expectations being dashed. Servants found it very
difficult to attend the meetings she set up because of the strict timings to which
part-timers must adhere and the difficulty full-timers face in getting away from
the houses where they are employed. Srimati emphasized that she tried to con-
vince servants to negotiate time off with their employers, but was unsuccessful.
Against a backdrop of stories about slavery and black workers in the United
States, she tried to show Kolkata servants what their rights as workers were, for
example, in terms of workloads, hours, and maternity and sick leave. (It was
interesting that she did not choose lessons from Kolkata's own labor history.)

At the same time Srimati stressed servants' responsibilities to employers so
that "servants would not simply take off without notifying them." She explained
about union dues and how members are compensated through union services.
She told them that they would have to do their duty well; otherwise, the union
would not support them. Srimati said she did this for months and then began
to realize that they really did not want a union. She believes that her mistake
was that the servants did not necessarily agree that what she thought was good
was, in fact, good: "Maybe they prefer the status quo, meaning, 'I cheat them,

and they cheat me.' Perhaps cheating is not the word, rather, a level of acceptance. Maybe I should have taken them to a union meeting. They don't trust
us. They don't believe a word we say, but perhaps if girls from the union had
explained it to them . . . after all I come from a class of employers."

Such distrust is neither rare nor perhaps surprising. Another servant, Shibani, who is a part-time cook for an employer she regards as rather unkind, is
skeptical about the putative ambitions of this book and equally negative about
employer nature:

> Who will read this book? You won't really educate them [employers]. They are
> not good people. Your book won't teach them anything. I read things with a lot
> of "criticize." I know what social problems are, but these people don't care. They
> will probably roll their eyes and say to you, "Why are you writing about *those*
> people?"

Shibani and many of the other servants in this study have in common a clarity
about their circumstances and the class relations and distinctions in which they
are embedded. For some employers, this new consciousness is a positive sign,
but they struggle with its implication for their relationship with their own servants. Older, upper-middle-class employer Suniti expressed this ambiguity by
positing that as servants gained access to education, they desired love, affection,
and help less, and independence more: "Women do not want to work in the
house. They say, 'I want to better myself. I don't want to be anyone's underling.'
Before there was selfless devotion. Now they think of themselves. Quite right.
They are human beings; why shouldn't they? It is quite fair." Suniti's choice of
the word *selfless* is revealing of the larger, historical tensions in the employer-
servant relation. She does not see servants' previous devotion as enforced or
servile but, rather, as voluntary effacement; similarly, the efforts to educate oneself and get out of servitude on the part of some of today's servants is seen as
rejection of the rhetoric of love in favor of financial gain and greater access to
rights and autonomy. Employers' uneasy reckoning with servants' assertions
of personhood—in contrast to the expectation of relinquishment of self that
marked an older culture of servitude—throws into relief the contest in Kolkata's wider political culture over modern rights and democracy.

7 Traveling Cultures of Servitude

ROHAN, AYESHA, KEYA, and other young globalized Indians we have met in the preceding chapters embody a changing culture of servitude. It is recognizably Kolkata's culture of servitude in that relationships between employers and servants continue to manifest a normalized domination, dependency, and inequality, but these employers enact servant keeping differently—often deliberately so—from the way their parents did. Yet as globalized Indians, adherents of the project of modernity, they nonetheless live in the spatial and social formation in which they were born; hence, the continuity in the culture of servitude may not be particularly surprising. But what of those young Indians who grew up within one particular culture of servitude but have been transplanted into another? How do first-generation Indian immigrants with the economic capacity to hire paid domestic workers enact the employer-servant relationship in New York or London or Singapore? In other words, does Kolkata's culture of servitude travel, or is it peculiar to Kolkata? These queries help to reveal the elements of a culture of servitude that are specific to the labor relation itself and those that are specific to the historical spaces in which the labor is performed. We thus turn in this penultimate chapter to an examination of the lived experience of the relations of domestic servitude by Indians who grew up in Kolkata and now live in New York City. At the same time we compare them to local practices of New Yorkers against the backdrop of the emerging or reemerging culture of servitude in twenty-first-century New York.

Situating Domestic Servitude in the United States

> *When I was growing up in New York City in the 1960s, I remembered the*
> *Upper East Side as purely white-bread, upper crust, bourgeois. . . . I do*
> *remember the white people and the snooty looks. It was clear, even to a seven-*
> *year old, that brown people didn't belong here. Today, one can hardly walk*
> *up Park or Madison Avenues without seeing black and brown women behind*
> *strollers or with bigger white kids in tow. They are hypervisible reminders of*
> *a largely invisible working-class of 200,000 women throughout the city who*
> *do the essential work of childcare, cleaning, cooking, washing, shopping, and*
> *whatever else their employers might demand of them.*
>
> **Robin D. G. Kelley, *Home Is Where the Work Is***

Much of the recent attention devoted to the institution of paid domestic work
in the contemporary United States highlights the racial and ethnic divide between employer and employee—the former almost always white, privileged,
and upper-middle class; and the latter, Latina, Caribbean, Asian, and to a much
lesser extent African American (a historical decline that merits fuller scrutiny).
Employers who are people of color rarely figure in the academic and popular
literature on U.S. domestic servitude.[1] While acknowledging the structuring
force of class and gender, many scholars have invoked race, ethnicity, national
origin, and immigration to explain the prevalence of paid female domestic
labor, the gross distinctions of power, status, and autonomy in the employer–
domestic worker nexus, as well as instances of deplorable working conditions
and abuse.[2] As Romero asserts in considering the history of the United States,
"[W]e find the proliferation of master-servant relationships in which race, ethnicity, and gender replace class as immutable social structures dictating a person's place in the hierarchy."[3] Undeniably, existing race, citizenship, and gender
inequalities explain which groups typically perform paid domestic work in any
given historical moment, as well as their different trajectories. Romero notes
that for white domestics the occupation served as a bridge to upward mobility, whereas for women of color, domestic work rapidly became an "occupational ghetto."[4] Although most working women were domestic servants in the
nineteenth century, surpassing the numbers who did factory and seamstress
work, by the latter part of the century native-born white Americans increasingly declined to work as domestic servants, and Irish and other mostly European immigrants competed for these jobs. Yet there was a continuous perceived
shortage of domestics, because up to one-third of urban households included
live-in servants, and immigrant women for the most part worked as domestics
only until they married. After the abolition of slavery, between 1870 and 1920,

African Americans began to enter domestic service, which eventually became "black women's work" as the numbers of immigrants declined; this coincided with the move from live-in to live-out workers.[5] In the decades after the Immigration Act of 1965, most U.S. domestic workers have gradually become immigrant women of color.

Yet to argue that the inequalities that produce and are reproduced by the institution of domestic servitude are attributable primarily to racial hierarchies and citizenship status involves, we suggest, a certain misrecognition. Other scholars, such as Ruth Milkman and her colleagues, have given primacy to class and class inequalities in accounting for the "macrosociology" of paid domestic labor, while affirming the significance of race/ethnicity, gender, and citizenship in its "microsociology."[6] In fact, we suggest, the employer–domestic servant nexus is profoundly racialized to *substantiate* the inherent relation of domination/subordination.[7]

Kolkata and New York

> The women's stories seemed to come from a backward country, or from a shameful time in the United States that many would sooner forget. . . . Listening to domestic workers talk about their jobs can give a rude jolt to assumptions about social progress and the civility of the rich and upper middle class.[8]
>
> **New York Times coverage of first National Domestic Workers' Congress, Manhattan, June 2008**

If in Kolkata it is a truism that everyone has a servant who is not himself or herself a servant[9]—recall that in our fieldwork spanning several years in the city we came across only one couple who deliberately chose not to keep a servant, and all the five hundred middle-class households in our survey had at least one servant—that was not the case in New York in the postwar period, when keeping a servant was the province of the wealthy.[10] However, the situation seems to have changed significantly in the 1990s and into this century. The *New York Times* notes that "entire industries and neighborhoods would collapse without paid domestic help" in New York City.[11] Milkman and her colleagues have argued convincingly against modernization theorists who hypothesized that paid domestic work would inevitably decline and disappear with capitalist industrialization and modernization by demonstrating that income inequality and class polarization in the United States account for the geographic variation in the proportion of the female labor force employed as domestic workers, with increasing numbers in certain metropolitan areas such as the greater Los

Angeles area. In so doing they also provide an important corrective to the recent feminist scholarship noted previously that has tended to rely primarily on the dynamics of discrimination and exclusion based on race/ethnicity and national origin/immigration to explain the prevalence of female paid domestic labor.

Milkman and her colleagues' analysis has clear salience for New York City, and similar trends can be observed in other cities and countries of the North. Helma Lutz argues persuasively for Europe: "For a long time during the 20th century it was expected that technological progress would eliminate the need for assistance from humans in households. However, today, at the threshold of the 21st century, the numbers of domestic helpers working in European households in the Era of Technology are very similar to what they were a century ago."[12] Writing about Britain, Gregson and Lowe show that the demand for waged domestic labor expanded considerably in the mid-1980s and early 1990s.[13]

Table 7.1 is based on table 1 in Milkman, Reese, and Roth, which shows the decline in the number and percentage of women employed in "private household service," in U.S. Census Bureau terminology, from 1940 to 1990. They note that the number of private household workers in the 1990 census is almost certainly significantly understated when compared to the figures from the Cur-

Table 7.1 Women employed in private household service in the United States, 1940–1990

Year	Number of women	% of all employed women	Number of men	% of all employed men	Total	% of all employed
2000	843,000	1.3	40,000	0.1	884,000*	0.7
1990	494,920 (753,066)	0.94	(28,934)		(782,000)	
1980	562,886	1.4				
1970	1,109,855	3.8				
1960	1,664,763	7.9				
1950	1,337,795	8.5				
1940	1,976,078	17.7				

SOURCE: U.S. Census Bureau, Census of Population, 1940–1990, as cited in Milkman, Reese, and Roth, "Macrosociology"; Current Population Survey 1990 and March 2000.

NOTE: The first row includes figures for the year 2000. Figures in parentheses in second row are from the 1990 Current Population Survey. Year 2000 numbers were given in thousands, which may account for the discrepancy in the total.

* The New York State AFL-CIO estimates that there are more than 800,000 domestic workers in the state of New York alone (Legislative Alert, January 26, 2004).

rent Population Survey (as we have indicated in parentheses).[14] We have added the top row with numbers from the March 2000 Current Population Survey.[15]

The increase in the number of private household workers from 1990 to 2000 would tend to confirm Milkman and colleagues' speculation about the possible reversal of the long-term historical decline and coming expansion of employment in domestic service in the United States. As Julia Wrigley notes, by 1991, over 40 percent of parents with family incomes of more than seventy-five thousand dollars hired caregivers to look after their children.[16]

The Bronx-based Domestic Workers United (DWU) estimates that there are about 200,000 domestic workers in New York City (which would be a little under 6 percent of the total population in the labor force, nearly ten times the national figure of 0.7 percent of all employed, as shown in Table 7.1). However, the 1999 New York City Housing and Vacancy Survey gives a figure of 36,715 private household service workers.[17] If we allow for the conceivably large numbers of undocumented and/or unregistered domestic workers in the city, we may come closer to the DWU figure. A recent study by the DWU indicates that most of the domestic workforce is made up of immigrant women of color—95 percent of the survey of over 500 domestic workers—but that the conditions for the growth in domestic work can be attributed to "increasing income disparity," or as we maintain, following Milkman and colleagues, rising class inequality.[18]

Even if the expansion of paid domestic work in New York City and the country as a whole may never approach the dominance of domestic servitude as a social form in Kolkata and elsewhere in the South—or indeed as it once did in the United States in the nineteenth century through World War II—it is undeniable that new generations of employers and domestic workers are negotiating the intricacies of this labor relationship, giving rise to anxieties and tensions that are the focus of increased scholarly and popular attention.[19]

As the form of domestic servitude changes, moving from live-in to live-out work and becoming more contractual in capitalism,[20] what some scholars have deemed "feudal" or "premodern" elements—relations inflected by paternalism, or more correctly, maternalism, and other sorts of "extraeconomic" and intimate ties—remain, or indeed may be part of the very fabric of this labor relation.[21] In both the past and the present, as we have shown, discourses of family and fictive or false kin relationships have been employed to mediate servitude. We have proposed for Kolkata that these are defining features of its culture of servitude and the structure of feeling emanating from the lived experience of this particular labor form and relationship. As the preceding chapters have shown, Kolkata's culture of servitude can be summarized as stemming from three premises: (1) servants are essential to a well-run and well-kept household; (2) servants are "part of the family" and bound to it by ties of affection, loyalty, and dependence; and (3) servants constitute a category with distinctive lifestyles, desires, and habits. These premises particularize and enact a culture of servitude that we have defined as one in which domination/subordination, dependency, and inequality are normalized and permeate both the public and domestic spheres. In our explication of the culture of servitude, domestic servitude inescapably joins the public and domestic spheres and makes domesticity a public phenomenon by its incorporation of structural inequalities and difference—fundamentally those of class, gender, and national origin, but also race/ethnicity, especially in the North. Cultures of servitude, of course, are neither timeless nor placeless; they arise in specific historical circumstances and in relation to other cultural and social forms.

In this chapter, we pursue this line of argument by placing Kolkata's culture of servitude in transnational context: Bengali employers and servants living in twenty-first-century New York. This entails an inquiry into the presence of a culture of servitude in New York; we find the emergence of certain of the same elements that characterize Kolkata's culture of servitude, as well as significant divergences, which are discussed in the concluding section. We first examine the narrative of an upper-middle-class South Asian woman in New York, Ruchira, who employs another South Asian as her nanny. Both are women, immigrants, and people of color and come from the same culture of servitude; what divides them is class and power. The narrative moves back and forth between the relationship with the servant Ruchira grew up with in India and that with the nanny in New York, from the familiarities of an established culture of servitude to the complexities of an emerging one. Ruchira is married to a non-Bengali, a man of European descent, which is interesting in the sense that comparisons and difference naturally arise in the course of daily life, but not unusual. We comment on Ruchira's narrative with evidence from other Bengali and mixed households in New York City.

We then turn to New Yorker Abigail Pogrebin's account of the relationship with her children's caregiver—one of the plethora of nanny tales spun out of that globalized, transnational city—which follows the classic pattern of white, upper-middle-class employer and immigrant nanny of color.[22] The juxtaposition of the two narratives allows us to speculate on the distinctive attributes and structure of feeling of domestic servitude as a labor relation in itself.

Ruchira's Story

Like most of the servant-employing middle and upper-middle class in Kolkata, Ruchira grew up with a family retainer, Chandra, whom Ruchira refers to as a "factotum," or a person employed to do all sorts of work.[23] Chandra came from a peasant family in East Bengal and eventually made her way to Kolkata with a friend to find work.[24] Hired when Ruchira was just a baby, Chandra has now worked and lived with Ruchira's family for over forty years. We have seen that the family retainer is an archetype of Kolkata's culture of servitude and as such, carries the full weight of employer expectation and desire. It is a category based on long duration of service in one home and/or to one family, often over the course of decades, and is necessarily applied to a servant in retrospect. Ruchira echoes the descriptions we have heard of family retainers from Kolkata's employers. To her, Chandra was faithful, loyal, affectionate, dependent and dependable, and always there.

Ruchira's idea of a servant has been inevitably shaped by the experience of growing up with Chandra, whom she also calls her "second mother." Chandra "had rule of the roost." She was the family cook—famously not allowing anyone else into the kitchen—and also brought Ruchira up. Ruchira says that in her family it was unthinkable to be disrespectful to servants. She would never have dreamed of "dissing" them. Her parents left Ruchira and her siblings with the servants when they traveled, and thus the servants became part of Ruchira's "safety net," as she puts it. Chandra provided love but was also a "disciplinarian"—Ruchira feared her temper more than her mother's, who was more easygoing. As an adult, Ruchira wondered about her mother's reaction to the bond of affection between herself and Chandra and once asked her mother whether she felt "displaced," but her mother said she had never felt that threat. Being of a generation immersed in corporate discourses, Ruchira recently approached her mother with a retirement plan for Chandra, but her intervention was rebuffed: "What do you mean by retirement?" Ruchira's mother and Chandra share the idea that Chandra will stay on with the family and supervise other servants who will do the housework, despite Chandra's savings and ownership of a house with land outside Kolkata. Chandra is mentioned in Ruchira's mother's will, for Chandra "embraced" Ruchira's family and has "had no parallel life of her own."

In evoking Chandra's "embrace" of the family, Ruchira's account tallies with the narratives of other employers, young and old, in Kolkata in which the relationship that family retainers have with employing families is privileged: "He

adopted our family as his own"; "They were not in an employment relationship; they were in a family relationship"; "We knew he had a wife and children
somewhere but only went to see them once a year, and never extended his visit,
and never brought them to Kolkata"; "We should treat them as members of
the family and love them because they have given up everything"; or "[They
became] a part of you." And less overwhelmingly so on the side of servants: "We
are happy here because they [the employers] maintain the house well and give
everybody love"; or "When my mother died, I thought to myself, I will make
these my own people."

The power of the rhetoric of love in that culture of servitude is such that
even having lived away from home and outside India for over twenty years,
Ruchira continues to represent the relationship with Chandra as a family one.
Chandra visited Ruchira in New York the year her father died, and both want
to repeat the visit. When Ruchira goes back to India, she goes back to her
mother—and Chandra.

Yet as an adult, newly married, and living in New York City, Ruchira and
her husband, Justin, "did not think it was philosophically correct to have servants or even weekly cleaners." Ruchira tells us with a laugh: "He said, 'I'm
perfectly fine cleaning the kitchen and the bathroom'—Of course he never did
it!" In part the decision had to do with Justin's influence as someone who had
not grown up with servants and could not conceive of others doing his dirty
work—except, of course, his wife—but also with the deliberate adoption of
a "modern and progressive" outlook that associates domestic servitude with
the feudal past and unacceptable relations of domination and servility. In this
sense, Ruchira did break with Kolkata's culture of servitude. Among her contemporaries back home, there has not been a rejection of domestic servitude
per se. Rather, we have noted a desire for modern, more impersonal contractual relations instead of feudal family-retainer relations with their emblematic rhetoric of love, and a concomitant move away from live-in servants who
could be considered "part of the family" to part-time domestic workers who
have homes of their own. But the institution of domestic servitude remains
firmly in place.

People like Ruchira and Justin and their contemporaries in their thirties
and forties in New York, who may or may not have grown up with servants, are
increasingly acquiring paid domestic labor in a way that the previous generation in the city did not. For some, such as senior insurance company executive Shankar, recalling the early stages of his career twenty years ago, hiring a

weekly cleaning woman was a "sign of progress on the success ladder" in corporate Manhattan. This was to be followed upon promotion and marriage to real estate broker Christine by, in addition to the cleaner, the full-time, live-in nanny, part-time babysitters in the afternoons and weekends, and part-time cook whom they employ today. Hiring a nanny was an automatic gesture upon the birth of their first child: "There was no question about it; we didn't even discuss it; it was the thing to do."[25] Shankar, having grown up with a household staff in Kolkata, had always expected to have the same once he joined the corporate sector, as his father did before him. The cook was found through Shankar's mother, who lives in Kolkata, perhaps an indication of a servant-hiring network extending from West Bengal to New York City.

In the particular case of Ruchira and Justin, the decision to give up their resistance to keeping a servant came not with the first pregnancy, as might have been expected from a couple where both partners had careers, but a move to South Asia. Justin's firm sent him to South Asia, but Ruchira did not accompany him during the initial period. As is often the case for expatriates who would never have had servants at home but do so when living in countries with an abundant supply of cheap labor, he went along with the custom. For the first time he had to hire and manage servants—a male chowkidar and a female part-time cook. Ruchira recalls that she would say to him in response to his stories: " 'It's so clear that you don't have the experience!' They would rip him off, but they were generally so nice and gentle," she explains. When Ruchira joined her husband, she took over the practical arrangements involving servants. There was now, as she puts it, a "memsahib in the house," and the servant had an interlocutor who understood the rules of the game.[26] Justin's lack of immersion in a culture of servitude had not equipped him to deal with the particularities of the employer–domestic worker relationship.

Sameera and Pratap also learned how to keep servants when they moved from New York City to Kolkata for a few years. Both are Bengalis, she an academic, and he an import-export businessman, but have spent their adult lives in New York. Like Ruchira and Justin, it did not occur to them to hire and live with domestic workers until setting up housekeeping in India (even though they, like all the other Bengali employers interviewed, had grown up with a household staff in Kolkata). Sameera's mother sent a couple who had worked for the family for years to take care of Sameera and Pratap's household; thus, as Sameera recalls, she "didn't have to deal with the house at all." Upon their return to New York, Sameera decided to mitigate Pratap's readjustment after "having lived in the lap of luxury" by hiring a part-time Indian cook, Anita, who would cater to Pratap's wishes, for example, "when he wanted to eat kebab."

By the time Ruchira and Justin came back to New York City, Ruchira was pregnant, and they took advantage of the possibility of legally bringing back one domestic worker as a nanny. Ruchira wanted someone who shared the same culture, a common desire among South Asian employers in New York City. Other employers we interviewed in New York who are originally from India expressed a strong preference for hiring South Asian domestic workers. This is, in fact, a version of the strategy used by white employers that Wrigley calls "choosing similarity." While Wrigley's employers seek European au pairs and nannies to impart certain kinds of cultural capital to their children, South Asian employers who choose similarity seek domestic workers who will cook familiar food and nannies who will impart specific manners, customs, and above all, language, to their children.[27] In the case of Shankar and Christine, however, the nanny and babysitters are all Spanish speaking, so the children have grown up speaking English and Spanish rather than Bengali. As Christine pointed out, "The language would have been important had Shankar spoken Bengali to the kids to begin with" (rather than English, which is the lingua franca of the globalized Indians). She went on to remark that "the advantage of Latin American help is that they all have a full-service mentality, and especially that they are very good with kids."[28]

Immigrant South Asian women report that it is easier to find jobs as domestic workers in the South Asian community when they first arrive in New York because of language, access, and cultural familiarity, especially since most have never worked as paid domestics before. Said Tahira, a domestic worker from Bangladesh, "If I stay with an American family, they won't know that I need to eat rice three times a day." Another important factor, according to domestic workers, is that South Asian employers tend not to ask for immigration papers, work permits, and legal status, whereas "Americans" almost always do. However, they have decidedly mixed opinions on whether they prefer working for South Asians over "white Americans" because, they claim, South Asian employers pay less, take advantage, and are more abusive.[29] Sheba, an Indian domestic worker who has worked in several different Manhattan apartment households, both Indian and North American, as a cook and cleaner, told us that she would work for South Asians only under exceptional circumstances if they proved themselves to be good employers.[30]

Justin suggested finding a South Asian nanny already living in New York, but Ruchira preferred asking their cook, Kanchan, who now worked full-time, to consider moving back with them. Justin was opposed to taking her because she had two children of her own whom she would effectively abandon to the care of their father, and it was discomfiting to think that "she'll be taking care of mine." Implicit here is the moral dilemma that Kanchan would be taking love and care away from her own children and transferring it to Justin's, an emotional transference that has been referred to as the transnational "care drain."[31] We would submit, however, that this extraction of love and care from the third world to benefit the first is a recent if extreme form of the ancient contradiction of some women being obliged to care for other's children in lieu of or in addition to their own, be they domesticated workers, indentured servants, or wet nurses—mothers separated from their children in the slaveholding or Jim Crow southern United States, between villages and cities in Bengal, or between boroughs in New York City.[32]

Ruchira argued that they knew Kanchan; she was tried and tested, had proven herself to be soft and gentle with children, read and wrote some English (she married before finishing school), had her own recipe books written out in longhand (she was a "recipe queen"), and was spotlessly clean like Chandra. Ruchira also justified the proposal as having the potential to improve Kanchan's life—she would be able to earn more money for her family, have the opportunity to live abroad, and do something new. She suggested that they propose a trial for one year after discussing the possibility with Kanchan's family and giving her a realistic picture of what her life would be like in New York. Looking back on those conversations, Ruchira considers that Kanchan heard selectively what she wanted to hear and decided to come with them.

Kanchan has taken care of Ruchira's daughter since shortly after her birth. When they first returned to New York, Kanchan lived with them in their two-bedroom Manhattan apartment and had her own room. Although she offered to sleep in the living room as a servant might typically do back home, Ruchira and Justin thought such practices were unacceptable. In contrast, another Indian employer in Manhattan told us that one of the reasons she preferred South Asian live-in nannies is that "they don't make a fuss about sleeping on the floor in my son's room." Ruchira and Justin set up things differently, they believe, from the way their friends and colleagues in New York (and for that matter, in South Asia) have done. They never asked Kanchan to look after the baby at night; they would get up themselves. They pay her a salary higher than the U.S. minimum wage; she works a forty-hour week, has two weeks paid vacation, and ✂

is covered by medical insurance.[33] Kanchan also makes a trip every year to see her family, which usually coincides with Ruchira's visit home to Kolkata.

As Ruchira recounted the move back to New York, it became apparent that she was consumed by the story she wanted to tell. It was a story about friendship and betrayal, and the articulation of the rhetoric of love, with its attributes of mutuality based on affection, dependency, and loyalty, in two different cultures of servitude. Although Kanchan was never described as "part of the family" in the Chandra family-retainer mold—after all, Ruchira and Justin consider themselves to be modern, enlightened employers, and they and Kanchan, all of whom are in their thirties and early forties, belong to a new generation that has presumably left such feudal trappings behind—another sort of intimate relationship was at hand.

An affective bond between Ruchira and Kanchan had existed before they arrived in New York, based on the experience of Ruchira seeing Kanchan through a series of personal crises. Ruchira not only paid the considerable expenses involved but also advised Kanchan on the different options available, introducing her, as Ruchira recalls, to "the concept of a second expert opinion." Thus, Ruchira believed, there was an understanding between them as women, one that arose from Ruchira serving as a guide for Kanchan to the intricacies of modern institutions. While it is not unusual for employers to assist servants in this way in Kolkata and elsewhere, this shared experience served to propel what Ruchira would later call her attempts to "empower" Kanchan and Kanchan's newfound awareness of her choices and rights.

After Ruchira's family moved to a single-family home in Park Slope (Brooklyn), Kanchan continued to have her own bedroom, and now her own bath and television. The house is within walking distance of the subway into Manhattan, and Kanchan, who loves the city, took full advantage of her time off on weekends. Kanchan also enjoyed taking her charge for long walks in Prospect Park where she frequently met friends, many of whom were nannies or other domestic workers in the neighborhood. Kanchan's English began to improve, and she also picked up some Spanish from her peers who hailed from Latin America.

Then things began to change. As Kanchan began to learn the rules of the game for domestic employment in New York, she decided to ask to not work on weekends at all, and she turned to Justin rather than Ruchira to make this request. Justin had always been more easygoing and, having never completely overcome his qualms about having domestic help, he agreed without consulting Ruchira. For Ruchira this signaled the deterioration of the relationship with

Kanchan: "This has become a big bone of contention. I am not going to pay extra for her to look after my daughter [on the weekend]. A movie costs ten dollars and the babysitting thirty dollars. And we raise her salary every year!" In the same vein, during Ruchira's second pregnancy, Kanchan made two other changes. First, she told Ruchira that she wanted to stop working on weekdays at 5:00 P.M. so that she could enroll in night classes to get her GED. And second, she said that she would cook only two days a week and suggested that they hire a cleaning person. In other words, she was increasing her task specialization so that her work corresponded more specifically to that of a nanny, not a general domestic worker. Ruchira responded, "How can you expect to work *less* when we're going to have a second child?"

Ruchira's frustration with the incursion of contractual roles and responsibilities is echoed in Shankar and Christine's assessment that "the worst setups are the American households where the employers feel compelled to abide by a more rigid contract and feel they ought to share in the domestic tasks, and the servants also limit what they will do and not. So the burden falls on the woman of the household." Nevertheless, Christine and Shankar differ in their approach to the help. Christine assumes that she should abide by the original (verbal) contract; anything outside that should be posed as a request. She explains that the reason is that she is more typically North American and believes that it is the fair thing to do. Shankar is, according to Christine, more imperious. His attitude is to "just tell her—this is her job." Shankar himself does not think that this is a bad attitude. In fact, they both agree that if we interviewed their household help, the workers would say that Shankar has the better attitude (which perhaps reflects their appreciation for his clarity, as well as his absence). The vagaries of the contract in contemporary New York are encapsulated in the findings of the DWU study:

> In most low-wage work, wages are calculated hourly. In domestic work, the standard practice is for employers to pay a flat rate per week for unpredictable and sometimes unlimited hours of work. Live-in workers may be expected to be on call 24 hours per day, 5 to 6 days per week. This practice is a unique feature of the domestic work industry; it is both a manifestation and a cause of exploitation of the workforce. It points to the legacy of servitude from which this sector emerges and a lack of respect for the work itself.[34]

Ruchira then decided that she and Kanchan would sit down and have a serious talk to try to resolve matters. "I have learned how not to do things. It is too clichéd to say that you can't treat servants a certain way because they will then take advantage of you. But it is a question of parameters, and Justin doesn't understand, and she manipulates this."[35] Since Ruchira comes from a tradition of hiring servants, she believes that she understands the complexities of the relationship in a way that Justin, raised in a middle-class family without servants, simply cannot. The management of the relationship thus falls to Ruchira, both because it is usually delegated to women as the "natural" housekeepers and because Ruchira believes experience made her more competent and capable of dealing with such issues. Sameera, rather than Pratap, also negotiates the relationship with their cook, Anita, even though she considers herself not at all the housewife or micromanager type but has taken on the role, it could be said, by gender default. In their case as well, it is a question of "parameters" in the context of an "easygoing" relationship in which Sameera and Anita have tea together and sometimes the three eat together, and Anita has benefits such as Social Security and the confidence to ask for and obtain sizable loans. But as Sameera puts it, "Recently we have had discussions about my feeling that she was taking advantage of me and taking me for granted." The confusion that arises from the competing desires for intimacy and professionalism in contemporary employer-domestic relationships in New York is expressed in the following extract from an employer interview conducted by the DWU:

> The first time I heard "Christie," our son's caregiver, refer to me as her boss, I was taken aback. The word seemed too formal. I had hopes for the kind of intimacy I'd known other parents and nannies to experience and wanted "Christie" to relate to me as someone other than her employer. I've now come to see that whether an employer hopes to replicate the mistress-servant dynamic or tries to negate the power relationship altogether, both attitudes can undermine the rights of a domestic worker. Without workplace standards, which kind of employer she ends up with is wholly arbitrary. "Christie" ended up with me; my resistance to seeing myself as an employer meant that it took too long for "Christie" to be treated like an employee; rather than signing a contract and agreeing to the terms of work on day one, we talked about benefits casually, after she'd already started work. I would not have tolerated such lack of professionalism in my own job.[36]

When Kanchan began to redefine her work conditions, she felt that she could not adequately express herself to Ruchira verbally, telling her: "I can't explain myself, so I'm going to put it in writing." Ruchira says, "She wrote me the most offensive e-mail saying that we had made her suffer for so many years. It was hurtful and accusatory, and one for the lawyers. I wrote back asking her why she had tolerated this for so many years—she was not indentured. We thought it was a mutually beneficial relationship." The use of e-mail enraged Ruchira in particular because she had taught Kanchan how to use the Internet to communicate with her children, who were, after all, so far away from her. Thus, it seemed to Ruchira that her attempts to educate and empower Kanchan were continually backfiring. Kanchan's singular recourse to the written word and to electronic communication as a means of distancing herself from the exigencies of an intimate and private relationship is indeed striking. Would conversations tête-à-tête have kept Kanchan within the confines of the rhetoric of love?[37]

Kanchan's insinuation of being somehow bound and subservient to them stunned Ruchira, even as she chafed against the demands for more freedom that Kanchan made. The "mutually beneficial relationship" was unraveling and revealing the possibility that it had actually been something quite different. Within the terms of the inherited culture of servitude, Ruchira's mother reached this conclusion: "You have spoiled her. You have taken her needs first over your own," an assessment with which Ruchira has come to agree. That the servant is essential is the primary premise of Kolkata's culture of servitude, but that essentiality is, in turn, predicated on the (dependent) labor that the servant performs for the employer, not on the ideology of mutual benefit often associated with more contractual relations.

We asked Ruchira why Kanchan was still with them given that tensions had escalated to such an extent. "I keep her because she is very loving with the children. My son used to fly to her after preschool, but they're a bit less close now. She won't call me Didi anymore—I don't know why. I would have sacked her, that is, not brought her back this year [after the annual holiday in India], but my husband is a bit zamindari and takes the easy way out." In other words, Justin would have rather muddled along than confront the unpleasantness of firing Kanchan. Eventually, after Ruchira and Justin told Kanchan what they now needed and expected from her, she decided that this would be her last year with them. According to Ruchira,

> Kanchan wanted to remake herself in the U.S. If anything stings, it is that I set out very consciously to empower her and now that empowerment is biting me. My husband says that she is like a rebellious teenager. If I say something in anger, I have to remember that there is an inherent power relationship, and that I can be nasty to her but she can't be nasty to me. It's not that I want her

to be subservient, docile, or submissive, but she has manipulated us. . . . It was especially bad when I was seven or eight months pregnant and it should have been easy sailing—I will never forgive her. Maybe she will be a better person, have a better life, and I contributed to that. But what I mind most is the betrayal of the friendship.

Ruchira's narrative makes clear that Kanchan is consistently distancing herself from the older culture of servitude by refusing to use familial terms with Ruchira, by placing limits around her workday, and setting out arguments in favor of her rights. It is significant that she continues to be a good and loving child-care worker. The betrayal that Ruchira speaks of does not then refer to the actual work performed by Kanchan, but to her friendship. Perceptions of betrayal following attempts to empower, educate, or befriend domestic workers emerge in several narratives both in New York and Kolkata, particularly among liberal or progressive women employers. Let us turn now to Abigail Pogrebin's emblematic narrative of betrayal that appeared in the popular weekly magazine *New York*.

Pogrebin's Story

> Half of me wanted to implore her, "How can you do this?"
> The other half wanted to threaten her: "I'm not the fool you take me for."
> **Abigail Pogrebin, "Nanny Scam"**

Vanity Fair columnist Leslie Bennetts dedicates her recent book *The Feminine Mistake*, a critique of the infamous opt-out debate about highly successful professional women who drop out from the workforce to be with their children, "To my babysitter, Norma." Men, says Bennetts, are unreliable. They lose their jobs, they run off with other women, they squander money—in short, they are unsafe investments. Better to invest in oneself, keep your career, and depend upon Norma, who picks up the slack "with unfailing love."[38]

Although we are no fans of the opt-out revolution, we find ourselves returning time and again to the question of Norma's unfailing love, to interrogate, cross-culturally, this particular and peculiar relationship of employment. The faltering of a Norma's love and loyalty occasions much anxiety, as can be seen in Abigail Pogrebin's article titled "Nanny Scam," in which the following text invites us to identify with an employing mother: "What would you do if your trusted caregiver, someone you consider family, turned out to be stealing from you? Here is what one mother did."[39]

The words *trust* and *family* immediately invite a comparison to Ruchira's narrative. Abigail Pogrebin and her husband are one of many dual-career middle- or upper-middle-class couples with children in New York who turn to cheap and available child care provided by immigrant women. Maria, the nanny in the story, was thought to be perfect because she "cared lovingly and tirelessly" for the couple's children. We do not know whether, unlike Ruchira and Justin, they had hired domestic workers before they had children, but we do know that Maria was the fourth nanny—someone, unlike the previous three, who seemed to have Mary Poppins–like qualities. Yet—they discovered to their dismay—Maria had been stealing from them. How did Maria get the opportunity to steal? Apparently, Pogrebin was so trusting (and so unwilling to go to the bank herself) that she frequently sent Maria to the bank with her ATM card. Maria, Pogrebin discovered, had been withdrawing money for herself at the same time that she had withdrawn money for her employer.

Pogrebin's primary emotion appears to be the shocked realization that "maybe she's never been a friend in the first place" and that "the relationship was probably too imbalanced to be authentic." She describes her relationship with Maria as laced with guilt because she was so aware of the "economic gap" between them. Thus, she compensated by buying Maria gifts, giving her bonuses, and not treating her as a subordinate. She and Maria shared lunch, "modeled bargain purchases from . . . Filene's basement for one another and on one occasion, even got our nails done side by side." Given the attendant inequalities of this occupation, the reader might be expected to be pleasantly surprised by the idea of the employer and nanny sitting side by side in a salon. The two, after all, embody the latest iteration of a complexly racialized relationship that has developed over the past two centuries in the United States.

Pogrebin's dilemmas are echoed in the interviews with employers conducted during the DWU study. As one Manhattan woman employer agonized:

> I don't know what the solutions are because it is slavery. I think it's slavery, and it's horrible, and on one level I hated participating in it. . . . She had dental problems, and I helped. She has been struggling with her rent, and I am throwing her an extra $100 per month. Her money problems are very different from mine. I have no idea [how to improve domestic work]. My brain isn't big enough for that. It's a horribly racist world. People take advantage, and it's a mess.[40]

When Pogrebin and her husband realized that Maria had been stealing from them, a part of their world began to unravel. The story of Maria's theft opened the door to a torrent of "confessions" on the part of Pogrebin's friends about being similarly betrayed by their maids and nannies.[41] Pogrebin and her husband immediately dismissed Maria and then worried about how to break the news of Maria's sudden departure to their children, aged four and six. While the children cried at the news at first, Pogrebin was "surprised at how easily Maria drifted out of their lives; despite the intimacy, her disappearance wasn't a major upheaval. . . . The strange thing though, was that *I* missed her."

Pogrebin's narrative reveals immense hurt and a powerful sense of betrayal—"I lurched from incredulity to rage to heartache"—but then the structural inequalities begin to assert themselves. Maria frequently called and left tearful messages on her former employer's answering machine, and Pogrebin's now angry reaction was to tape them in case they were needed as proof. She reported Maria to the local police and then, worried that Maria would not know how to protect herself, urged Maria to get a lawyer from Legal Aid. Finally, in an ultimate act of what can only be thought of as revenge, Pogrebin tracked down Maria's former references and told them what she had done, in effect making it next to impossible for Maria to find another job in the city. Yet Pogrebin ends her account on a note that resists the advice that "[a]n employee in your home will always on some level resent you," even as she knows she will never fully trust a nanny again.

Reactions to this article were numerous and similarly passionate. Some letters to the editor scorned Pogrebin's naïveté, others excoriated her vengeful righteousness, some urged her to "get over" her liberal guilt, while yet others reminded her that she had crossed the line by asking her nanny to go the bank for her. The letters reveal, however, an awareness that this is a class relation of great power and that to deny it by putting a "liberal" face on it is disingenuous.[42]

What can we make of these tales of betrayal, and these loss-of-innocence narratives on the part of the employers in New York? They do not stem from the same source and yet, taken together, perhaps hint at one of the enduring attributes of cultures of servitude. Ruchira was raised within Kolkata's culture of servitude infused with the rhetoric of love, where the servant was bound to the employer by ties of loyalty and dependency. Once in New York, like Abigail Pogrebin, Ruchira deliberately participated in a new culture of servitude based on the assumption of workers' rights and empowerment. In this culture of servitude, different from Kolkata's, Kanchan had set hours, paid vacation, and a room of her own and lived as a contractual worker. Both Ruchira and Pogrebin believed that they were creating the space for an alternative culture of servitude based on a liberal capitalist notion of mutual benefit.

What were the ties that bound the domestic workers to their employers? Both Ruchira and Pogrebin claimed friendship—which can arise only among equals—with their nannies, even as they were aware that they were not equals. The tenor of the employers' discussion of these friendships—teaching their maids about their rights, helping them make their way in the world, fretting about sexual affairs that they could be having—all suggest a relationship of maternalism, not friendship. And when that maternalism is thwarted, the friendship or loyalty seen to be betrayed, then comes the dismissal or the vengeance, or both in the case of Pogrebin.[43] But why claim friendship at all in a market relationship? One argument for the claims of friendship could be that it makes a service relationship more palatable. But another, we suggest, goes to the heart of the contradiction of this work, done for a wage, within the privatized confines of a home. The home is not an emotionally neutral site—it is the site of love, trauma, and feeling. The claims of friendship, then, are an "egalitarian" version of the rhetoric of love—to bind the worker to the family in a recognition precisely, as one elderly Kolkata employer eloquently told us, of preventing the market from "winning." Thus, claims of friendship not only make employers feel better about this unequal relationship but also trump the market calls for domestic workers to seek better lives and opportunities.

Global Cultures of Servitude

> In our left-wing, middle-class Bengali family, servants have always been treated with consideration. They are paid well, and their health and retirement costs are covered. We refer to those who are older than us with the respectfully affectionate honorifics di and da, meaning older sister and older brother. And yet the line is clearly drawn between their world and ours. They eat the same food, but only after we've finished our meal. They sleep in the same house, but on harder beds, with more patches on their mosquito nets. They share in our family dramas but are relegated to the role of bit players.
> **Indrani Sen, "Are You Being Served?"**

Reflecting on the unease she feels being waited upon by elderly servants, young journalist Indrani Sen acknowledges that the inequality she observes in her grandmother's house—which we have posited is inherent in Kolkata's culture of servitude and, for that matter, in all cultures of servitude—is no worse than that which she lives with daily back at home in New York. It is an inequality mediated by the rhetoric of love, for as Sen's grandmother explains to her, "Sometimes I scold them, but they love me. . . . [The servants] are truly my family. When I die, my children will cry, my grandchildren will cry, but then you will go on with your lives. The servants, though, will really miss me."[44] This inequality is intimate and tangible as opposed to quotidian inequality in New York, which is at once globalized and less visible, in Sen's view, and perhaps easier to ignore or overlook.

Yet both cultures of servitude, although worlds apart, eerily echo one another. Many aspects of the constitutive elements of Kolkata's culture of servitude—the essential servant, the servant as "part of the family," and the servant as distinctive in taste and comportment—and their accompanying contradictions are found among employers and domestic workers, Bengali or not, in New York, as evidenced both by popular and scholarly writing and activist documents such as the DWU study. As in Kolkata, employers in New York struggle with relationships with servants, with the consequences of having domestic workers in the private space of the home; and servants grapple with the challenges of class and cultural distinction, of a relationship of domination, dependency, and inequality that is often channeled through the discourses of mutual benefit and friendship.

Certainly there are differences. All Kolkata households that can afford to do so, even those in the lower middle class, have at least one part-time domestic worker who daily comes to clean or wash dishes. Indeed, as various employer and servant narratives and the historiography have shown, keeping a servant as a sign of the attainment of middle-class status has been a constant in Kolkata since the late nineteenth century. In New York, even though a weekly cleaner may be commonplace, and having a daily or live-in housekeeper and/or nanny is becoming more so, keeping a servant has yet to become (once again?) a marker of the middle class, even if it is clearly a matter of status. In this sense, it may be more reasonable to say that in New York, servants may not yet be considered essential or indispensable for a well-kept middle-class home, but they are certainly desirable and seen to be increasingly affordable.[45]

In New York, the search is for an elusive horizontality; in Kolkata, the question of horizontality does not arise since the affective and emotional bonds with servants, old family retainers in particular, are expressed through familial discourses rooted in distinctions of power and status. Both Ruchira and Abigail Pogrebin tried to practice a liberal discourse of rights and women's empowerment with their servants, even though this attempt at horizontality ultimately ended in mutual unintelligibility. Once matters came to a head, these employers were left with the rage of betrayal and the regret of the loss of friendship—one-sided it must be said, since there is little indication that Kanchan and Maria viewed their working relationships as anything other than that of employer and domestic worker, intrinsically unequal.

To be sure, some younger employers in Kolkata have also tried to enact a relationship based on ideas of a capitalist contract, essaying the elision of what they consider some of the more onerous demands and unpleasant characteristics of an older culture of servitude rooted in a feudal past, while others attempt to inculcate neoliberal ideals of self-help—prevalent in both state and civil society—in their servants. However, servants continue to make claims based on conceptions of rights that are decidedly not part of the language of liberalism. They are instead appeals for the employer's care and resources in recognition of the essential inequality and incommensurability of the relationship. Employers, it is felt, have the obligation to provide and respond because of their greater power and resources even while both parties are well aware that the very fact of power and wealth makes it likely that the obligation may not be met. Similarly, in the stories of friendship and betrayal, the assumption of rights and mutual benefit can be seen to dissolve in New York's culture of servitude. We may conclude, then, that these narratives suggest that the *site* in which domestic labor is performed and the labor relation itself entail a culture of servitude, in both the global North and South, in which domination/subordination, dependency, and inequality are articulated and *re*articulated.

8 Conclusion

THIS BOOK has been a sustained argument for the consideration of domestic space and domestic labor in understanding class. In taking the ideologies and practices of paid domestic work seriously, we have pointed to the home as a site infused with class relations, arguing that classes come into being not only through relations of production and consumption outside the household but critically through quotidian labor and intimate practices within the home. And in so doing, we have highlighted the role of affect and structures of feeling in the everyday production and reproduction of class.

In establishing the concept of a culture of servitude arising from labor relations within the home, we have shown how relations of domination/subordination, dependency, and inequality are normalized through the practices of everyday life. We have also argued that cultures of servitude are shaped by particular historical configurations of structural economic/gender/spatial and often race/caste inequalities, and that these configurations produce particular structures of feeling, in Williams's sense of "meanings and values as they are actively lived and felt."[1] Through the examination of Kolkata's culture of servitude, located in the interstices of the social imaginaries of feudalism and capitalist modernity, we have traced the constitution and reproduction of the employing middle classes in dialectical relation to the serving classes, and we have shown further that cultures of servitude travel and may be transformed.

In this concluding chapter, we return to the question of the nature of household labor and the role it has played in feminist analysis. We also reflect on the trajectories of cultures of servitude and end with a consideration of the politics of paid domestic labor.

Of Morality, Feminism, and Domesticity

Is paid housework morally special?   l̶i̶k̶e̶ ̶S̶W̶
> **Gabrielle Meagher, "Is It Wrong to Pay for Housework?"**

From the very beginning of our study it became obvious that it is difficult to avoid issues of morality and moralism in discussions of domestic servitude. Indeed, the middle- and upper-middle-class academic audiences in the United States and India—often employers of domestic workers themselves—to whom we have presented our findings in the course of our research and writing react in interesting and revealing ways. On occasion, colleagues have exhibited resentment or defensiveness, as if the mere act of social analysis were a judgment, and moreover a judgment of their particular domestic practices. On other occasions, the audience has offered us their confessionals and servant stories—stories of love and betrayal—and these stories, too, seem to ask for vindication. For the most part, however, the substance of our analysis tends to be deflected so that it is assumed to refer to other employers in other places, and thus the charged issues of class, gender, patriarchy, and servility may be readily engaged without any personal allusion.

The sheer volume of popular and scholarly writing on this topic attests to, on the one hand, the unease many feel about keeping servants, especially in the West, and on the other, to the very nature of domestic work, which is either not recognized as labor or is considered fundamentally different from all other labor. Perhaps more accurately put, the intangibility of the product makes the labor appear invisible or immaterial.[2] Moreover, this labor is essentially inscribed as women's work and thereby devalued as such by most, and in Marxist terms, for its nature as reproductive, rather than productive, labor that may be "entirely neglected" analytically.[3] Similarly, it is degraded, or as we have argued, boundary-maintaining, work that no one would want to do unless obliged, labor essentially constituted as the prescribed tasks of the women of the household and enforced by patriarchal ideologies. As such it is the source of ideological battles over whether women can and should abandon the domestic sphere in favor of work outside the home, notwithstanding that most women who work outside the home do so out of economic necessity. The "servant problem," or the "nanny wars" are, after all, never about domestic workers taking over the household responsibilities of men.[4]

It is salutary to take a step aside, as we did in Chapter 5, and consider the situation of domestic workers who are likewise subject to patriarchal ideologies about the domestic sphere but obliged to work as servants outside the home to support their families. They perform work that is at once a necessary constant yet not considered real labor, degraded by its categorization as women's work, and avoided as work that no one would want to do. The response to the desire of many women servants to be able to stay at home and do this work for their own husbands and families, as in fact dictated by patriarchal ideologies, can be ambivalent. The appeal of normalized domestic life with husband, wife, and children inhabiting ordained roles—somehow denying the very real vicissitudes of extreme poverty, family abandonment, and patriarchal domination that led to becoming servants in the first instance—seems simultaneously reasonable and rather extraordinary. Paid work has undeniably afforded women the economic and social means to begin to break with class and gender domination. Thus, a desire on the part of women servants for domestic worker organization and solidarity, to which we turn later in the discussion, would be for many feminists far more satisfactory. In our view, as feminists engaged in this ethnographic work, the question of what women want and why—and the epistemological, ideological, and political ramifications of this query—remains open. Turning to men as both agents and victims of dominant patriarchal ideology, male servants are in some cases able to effect a transformation of stigmatized domestic work—at least in their own eyes—into labor like any other labor because of their gender privilege (which given their precarious circumstances is perhaps more of a burden than a privilege). As long as men servants are able to minimally comply with patriarchal duty, they can access the possibility of turning servitude into ordinary labor.

Stepping back to our consideration of women's work in general, Barbara Ehrenreich and others have argued persuasively that the theoretical and practical tasks begun by feminists in the 1960s and 1970s regarding the politics of housework—to recognize housework as work, to understand housework as a power relation, to advocate initially for wages for housework and subsequently for an equal division of labor between women and men in the household— have been eclipsed in the United States by the class polarization and racial inequality that have led to greater numbers of domestic workers; greater numbers of middle-class professional women, including feminists, who employ them; and greater numbers of men who benefit from their labors:

> Among my middle-class, professional women friends and acquaintances, including some who made important contributions to the early feminist analysis

of housework, the employment of a maid is now nearly universal. . . . Strangely, or perhaps not so strangely at all, no one talks about the "politics of housework" anymore. The demand for "wages for housework" has sunk to the status of a curio, along with the consciousness-raising groups in which women once rallied support in their struggles with messy men. In the academy, according to the feminist sociologists I interviewed, housework has lost much of its former cachet— in part, I suspect, because fewer sociologists actually do it. . . . Fifteen years after the apparent cessation of hostilities, it is probably not too soon to announce the score: in the "chore wars" of the Seventies and Eighties, women gained a little ground, but overall, and after a few strategic concessions, men won.[5]

Joan Tronto accentuates this feminist quandary: "[T]he use of nannies allows upper middle-class women and men to benefit from feminist changes without having to surrender the privilege of the traditional patriarchal family." It is, to her, simultaneously a political, moral, and ethical concern: "[W]hen the wealthiest members of society use domestic servants to meet their child care needs, the result is unjust for individuals and society as a whole."[6]

Of course, the politics of housework as "gender war" has not necessarily been on feminist agendas elsewhere in the world—admittedly, this could also be an artifact of the prevalence of domestic servitude—and women's movements globally have given priority to other pressing political, economic, and cultural concerns. Nor has it been a demand of many feminists of color in the North itself, who have long challenged the racial and class assumptions embedded in this struggle. In the North, the so-called stalled revolution has been resolved in periods of heightened inequality when middle-class and elite women have been able to hire poor women to ease their domestic burden. In India, such a revolution was postponed, perhaps indefinitely, in the presence of entrenched class (and caste) inequality, such that middle-class families could always rely on poorer (and inferior) others to do this work.[7] We would insist, however, that domestic servitude is a moral issue insofar as it is a class and labor relation of great inequality: Such inequality is always unacceptable whatever the nature of the labor. And if it is impossible to escape under present circumstances, the reason is the intense degree of class inequality coupled with the resilience of gender boundaries around the domestic.

Indrani Sen's family, referenced in Chapter 7, is similar to many households we encountered in the course of field research and have analyzed in this book in its mix of both "modern" (good wages, medical and retirement benefits) and "feudal" (respect, loyalty, deference, long service) and its enunciation of family ties and care that are perennially second class. From one angle, this sort of assessment appears to be rather moralistic; from another, an angle we have found more productive, such households are making the best of an inherently unequal and dependent relationship of domination (given the prevailing social imaginaries of feudal and modern and hegemonic family discourses and ideologies).

Joan Tronto takes exception to the counterargument to the moral and ethical concerns about domestic servitude that it is "no different from purchasing services and goods on the market." She emphasizes that since domestic service produces care, it also means developing and sustaining "care relationships" that may approximate family relationships.[8] In contraposition, Ehrenreich argues that cleaning services such as Merry Maids or The Maids International (for which she worked) "at least from an abstract, historical perspective . . . are finally transforming the home into a fully capitalist-style workplace, and in ways that the old wages-for-housework advocates could never have imagined . . . [through] the intense Taylorization imposed by the companies."[9] Ehrenreich describes the choreographed routines the cleaning companies require of their low-paid, largely immigrant crews for the mechanical production of the simulacra of cleanliness and orderliness on a weekly basis in (white) middle-class homes. Workers must be inured to the gaze of the employer or child who might be present to maintain the robotic anonymity of this job that obviates the need for personal exchange.

We would emphasize the engulfing inequalities of daily life in a city like New York—the working-class and immigrant labor that produces what we have outsourced from the home (not to mention all the products and services that do not emerge from the domestic sphere)—that are erased in these discussions. However, that domestic servitude inhabits the private, intimate space of the home and domestic life does make it fundamentally different from the market, as many older Kolkata employers would concur. A classic capital/labor relationship cannot arise because of the intimacy of the site of labor. Put another way, even if a perfect contract with perfect working conditions could be effected for domestic service, the power relations, hierarchies, and domination/dependency, which are as much idealist hallmarks of the home and family as love and loyalty, would not disappear. The arrangements that Kanchan was able to achieve in Ruchira and Justin's home in New York (Chapter 7), although clearly imperfect as glimpsed through Ruchira's narrative, come perhaps the closest to an adequate setup yet were fraught with tension and conflict because of the structure of feeling of the home as a site of labor. Mrinalini's unusual household in Kolkata (Chapter 6), where servants both clean bathrooms and act as financial advisers while challenging the politics of sitting by moving up off the floor, is nonetheless configured according to the emotional registers and hierarchies of the joint family.[10] Progressive younger employers like Viji (Chapter 6) try to inculcate liberal democratic values and behaviors in their children but are foiled by the class, caste, gender, and generational inequalities that family members express and reproduce in the home. (Here, too, we must recall that the casteist and patriarchal class culture of the older generation, as we have shown in Chapter 4, may actually share a nonliberal language of rights with some servants.)

There are indeed conditions under which the intimate inequalities we have here analyzed are significantly diminished, for example, the weekly cleaner who has little or no interaction with her employer, who comes in to clean on assigned days to an empty home with a check left for wages. Gabrielle Meagher argues that such formalization of domestic work minimizes interpersonal subordination and thus makes it virtually indistinguishable from other forms of blue-collar labor.[11] Weekly cleaners and cleaning crews, certainly significant in the global capitalist economy,[12] thus may be on a continuum with the domestic workers and servants discussed in this book, but are of a different order. In other words, to the extent to which the personal is removed from the relations of domestic work, it may then come to resemble the more simple exploitation of a capitalist economy. Despite the structured and anonymous exchange upon which companies such as Merry Maids are predicated, however, we suspect that the home may never be a "fully capitalist-style workplace." Jennifer Mendez has demonstrated that cleaning services in fact rely on notions of "caring for clients" and a "work culture of care and service" to manage and retain workers and mask poor pay and working conditions. Workers, in turn, deploy "strategic personalism" to withstand and negotiate with managers, clients, and adverse working conditions. The impersonal and bureaucratized organization of domestic work by cleaning services, Mendez argues, may in fact militate against worker autonomy, and individual domestic workers—rather than cleaning crews—may be able to negotiate better working conditions in the space of the home precisely because of the personal contact between worker and employer.[13] Our work has also shown that replacing personalism and affective ties with the contract in relations of domestic work is insufficient to ameliorate the status and working conditions of domestics.

Trajectories of Servitude

The historical trajectory of domestic servitude may not move inexorably in the direction of the capitalist work regime that Ehrenreich and Meagher evoke. We have cautioned throughout this book against developmentalist or teleological assumptions about domestic servitude, or presuppositions that under capitalism, domestic servitude would only exist in liberal, contractual forms.[14] Recall that the prophesied obsolescence of domestic service through the twin processes of modernization and technological innovation in the domestic sphere has not come to pass; indeed, there are increasing numbers of domestic workers. If we have noted that elements of domestic servitude occur both in contemporary and colonial Kolkata, or in contemporary Kolkata and Victorian England or eighteenth-century France or New York today, this means that these are common to cultures of servitude, not that one place or another is caught in a developmental time warp. For the same reasons we have declined to draw a line between "domestic worker" and "servant"; although the categories of servants and domestic servitude may not be thought to apply in capitalist modernities and make many in the West uncomfortable, the institution and relations of servitude endure or are rearticulated, whether the person involved is called a "domestic worker," "nanny," "housekeeper," or "babysitter." Just like the part-time domestic workers living in their own homes in Kolkata who may have more relative autonomy than their live-in peers, these workers, too, may suffer from a "lifetime of bondage."[15]

The task at hand, then, is to delineate both the universality and the particularity of cultures of servitude. Through our examination of the premises of Kolkata's culture of servitude—the servant essentiality in the middle-class home, binding ties of affection and dependency between employer and servant, servant class and cultural distinctiveness—we find that they coincide to a certain extent with the observations of much of the literature on domestic servitude, be it in Asia, Africa, or the Americas. It is beyond the scope of this study to undertake an exploration of cultures of servitude in comparative perspective, aside from what we have indicated throughout this book, but we can make certain judgments about the premises in practice. With the first premise laid out in Chapter 2, that servants are essential to a well-run and well-kept household, there is widespread agreement among the middle classes in Kolkata and India—and we would speculate, elsewhere in the global South and increasingly in the global North, as we have noted in Chapter 7. Rubbo and Taussig stated twenty-five years ago that it would be an exaggeration to refer to "servant-based societies" in the South, but nonetheless roughly categorized Colombian households as those that supply servants and those that employ servants.[16] Employers in Kolkata today struggle to come to terms with the consequences of the move from the big house to the flat, and the replacement of long-time, live-in servants with mobile part-timers, while embracing the idea of modernity. Even so, the discourse of servant indispensability persists. In New York, servant indispensability is being rearticulated in an emerging culture of servitude, couched in terms of the needs of busy dual-career families.

Regarding the second premise, that servants are "part of the family" and bound to it by ties of affection, loyalty, and dependence, scholarship from around the world has revealed that "part of the family" is an almost automatic refrain about servants in many cultures of servitude. Kolkata's specificity, we have argued in Chapter 4, emerges in the deployment of the "rhetoric of love" and related employer and servant claims and practices arising from a feudal imaginary. Yet skepticism, sarcasm, or strategic use of familial rhetoric reveals fissures in the armature of cultures of servitude, as seen in Alice Childress's brilliant satire *Like One of the Family: Conversations from a Domestic's Life*, narrated by an African American domestic in New York's postwar culture of servitude of the 1950s. Similarly, Bonnie Thornton Dill recalls an African American domestic refusing to be called "my girl."[17] Romero comments on the steadfast distinction Chicana domestic workers make between "professionalism" on the job and the "work of love" that is exclusively reserved for their own families.[18] Rhacel Parreñas shows that Filipina maids are cynical about claims of familial bonds on the part of their employers.[19] In our study, young women employers in Kolkata, similarly to those described by Hondagneu-Sotelo in Los Angeles,[20] deliberately resist familial rhetoric and maternalism, though for most older employers it is the most comfortable way to maintain relationships with servants. Younger female servants encourage maternalism to secure protection and aid, while older male servants analyze the odds of whether the familial bargain will hold when they are no longer able to work (Chapter 3). Familial discourses are employed to mitigate the complicated unease stemming from the intersection of the worlds of work and intimacy in the home, and perhaps even more so when claims of family or friendship are revealed as fictions.

The third premise, that servants constitute a class with distinctive lifestyles, desires, and habits, is undermined by greater servant access to rights and autonomy, even with the accelerating class and spatial inequality in Kolkata. In Kolkata's culture of servitude, servants and employers are still configured as embodying distinctive class characteristics. If servants were once perceived as loyal, affectionate, and dependent, a class that would put the employers' lives before their own, they are now often viewed as untrustworthy, instrumental, and threateningly aware of their own rights. The ascription of specific traits to domestics appears to be quite common across cultures of servitude. In Pei-Chia Lan's study of foreign maids in Taiwan, she finds that Taiwanese labor brokers attribute national characteristics to maids: Filipinas are well educated, smart, sensitive to employers' moods, and conscious of labor rights, whereas Indonesian maids are considered obedient, simple-minded, accommodating, but slow.[21] In both instances, the objectifying maneuver serves above all to differentiate maids as a class from employers. Wrigley documents New York employers' contradictory preference for child minders who may share their child-rearing values and can function independently, and at the same are cheap, biddable, and reliable. In most cases, employers hire less-educated, immigrant nannies of color, and the racial, cultural, and class gulf gives employers greater control and the ability to extract more labor and places the worker in a subservient position.[22] The significance of these classification techniques for maintaining distinction cannot be underestimated, for they have both symbolic and material effects. As analyzed in Chapter 6, the politics of quotidian space, leisure, hygiene, and the body simultaneously corrodes and rearticulates class and caste distinction.

It is, nonetheless, the premise of fundamental distinction that is most unambiguously rejected by Kolkata's servants, as this book has shown, particularly by part-timers and other servants who live out and thus can escape the employers' purview. Indeed, living out gives servants the ability to constitute a social world beyond the reach of employers; moreover, the city's politicized worker culture does provide a publicly accessible language of rights and the promise of solidarity. Yet in the context of Kolkata's political field, the dearth of domestic worker organization and mobilization, whether by the ruling CPI(M) or women's organizations, is surprising.[23]

Organization and Absence

Precisely because of the often contradictory and certainly ambiguous site and nature of their labor, domestic workers have a relatively short and uneven history of being organized. In this section, we consider some efforts to organize domestic workers, contemplate the reasons for Kolkata's failure to do so, and reflect on the possibilities that new models of politics may serve domestic workers better than the union model.

Even though several countries have enacted laws on the rights of domestic workers, most have not, with some countries explicitly writing domestic workers out of labor legislation. South Africa has emerged as a leader in this field, with new legislation providing retirement and unemployment benefits. But even here, as Shireen Ally's remarkable study shows, South African domestic workers feel that not only has recent legislation endowed the state with too much control over them but that by treating them as "vulnerable workers" who are unable to bargain for themselves, the state has actually disempowered workers relative to their employers.[24] In Latin America, various countries have legislated for domestic workers, usually in the form of a chapter or "special section" in their civil codes, and some of this legislation is discriminatory, for example, allowing employers to pay domestic workers less than the official minimum wage. Bolivia's domestic worker law (2003) grants servants all of the rights under the national General Labor Law; sets a maximum ten-hour workday for live-in workers and eight hours for those who live out; and provides for holidays, days off, and schooling. However, only a small proportion of Bolivian domestic workers are unionized, which is usually the path to accessing the rights provided by law. In Asia, legislation to protect the rights of domestic workers is closest to fruition, perhaps not surprisingly, in the Philippines.[25] The evidence overall suggests that the formation of domestic worker organizations that are able to demand rights, set wages, and maintain standards is as important as the attainment of legal provisions.

In India the National Domestic Workers' Movement (NDWM), a worker rights organization with offices in twenty-three states and over two million members, is fighting for the recognition of domestic workers and improved working conditions. No national legislation covering domestic workers yet exists. Individual Indian states such as Kerala and Karnataka do have minimum wage legislation for domestics, several other states are considering such legislation, and Maharashtra has adopted a minimal social security scheme. The movement of domestic workers is most dynamic in cities such as Pune (where it started) and Mumbai (building on the wealth of women's, slum, neighborhood, and union organizations) but is virtually absent in Kolkata, although there are occasional glimmerings of incipient organizing drives.[26] In other major cities, such as New Delhi and Bangalore, domestic work may be regulated in different ways, whether by household help or charitable agencies setting the terms of services when servants are recruited, or collective standards created and applied by domestic workers themselves, although these modes apply to only some servants.

The relative lack of domestic worker organizing in Kolkata—despite its long history of industrial unions, active women's movement, and mobilized political culture—poses a conundrum. Various resolutions can be offered. As we have mentioned, some Communist and NGO workers stress the difficulties in approaching domestic servants because of their isolation (in the homes of their employers), lack of time for meetings, and skepticism about the possibilities of change. Moreover, organizing domestic workers does not really appear to be on the agenda of either political parties or women's organizations in the city, perhaps because of the particular feudal and patriarchal undergirding of Kolkata's culture of servitude that renders servants invisible as workers. Although the presence of a strong trade union as a partner may be an asset for organizing domestic workers, this has not been the case in Kolkata, where the hegemony of industrial unions and the mode of factory organizing are more dominant than in many other cities, making the political field less permeable to alternative forms of organizing.

The collective, where members can meet and exchange views and try to set better terms for their work, may be a viable alternative to unions.[27] Parichiti, an NGO in Kolkata, seeks to "facilitate the process of creating autonomous collectives of domestic workers who will fight for their own rights."[28] As a first step, it has been collecting information about workers and their needs at nodal railway stations used by part-timers in their daily commute. The organization has also established a drop-in center for domestic workers at the Dhakuria station, which is intended precisely to ameliorate two crucial issues that arose in our interviews—the isolation of working in private homes and the absence of a public place to rest. Recall that in Chapter 3, part-time workers wished they had somewhere to take a break between jobs but that the cityscape offered no place for them. In addition, part-time workers are not necessarily as isolated as live-in workers might be, but the drop-in center gives workers a space to compare notes and share grievances. Even though ideas of worker autonomy and politics are largely derived from the factory as the ideal-typical workplace, unions may not be the most appropriate vehicles for worker empowerment when the site of labor is the home. Nonetheless, this question remains a pressing one for future inquiry and analysis.

Cultures of Servitude at Large

We have posited that the domination, dependency, and inequality normalized in cultures of servitude are immanent in both the domestic and public spheres.

We have examined the enactment of relations of domination and subordination and class, caste, gender, and generational inequality in the home as a site of labor, but such relations are certainly not limited to the home. We now reflect in closing upon the wider societal implications of cultures of servitude.

Rubbo and Taussig's insight that "the existence of the servant ensures that the household microcosm more fully approximates the macrocosm of wider society" is an important one.[29] However, we have argued that the existence of both servant and employer in the household, and the lived experience and practice of the dialectics of class and power relations and their reproduction in the domestic sphere, may fundamentally shape the social formation. The household does not simply mirror the inequalities of society at large but is a constitutive part of it, both reflecting and re-creating those inequalities. In one sense, empirically, children in servant-employing households, whether they are masters or servants, learn class and gender domination and inequality at home and practice them in the world. In another sense, the class inequality, relations of domination, and structure of feeling of domestic servitude normalized in the home set the terms and are reproduced in the social formation. Of course, other hierarchically organized workplaces and institutions (schools, military, prisons, corporations) merit study in this regard, as do other instances of social interaction in the public sphere, such as markets, plazas, and the street. In this book, we have analyzed the quotidian interactions and negotiations of servants with employers that articulate Kolkata's culture of servitude and shown how the Indian middle classes reproduce as normal and inevitable unequal social relations by which lower classes naturally serve the higher classes at home and in the world.

Notes

Chapter 1

1. The 1956 film was based on the novel *Aparajito* (1931) by Bibhuti Bhushan Bandopadhyay.

2. "Mukhujje-ginni: Do you have anyone where you come from?

"Sarbajaya: I have no one.

"Mukhujje-ginni: Then there is no problem, you may as well come with us."

Satyajit Ray, The Apu Trilogy, 76.

3. Ibid.

4. Sarkar, *Hindu Wife, Hindu Nation*; Davidoff, *Worlds Between*.

5. We emphasize here that this claim is not restricted to India but encompasses societies in which keeping servants has been significant over the longue durée. Indeed, as Carolyn Steedman shows, the great legal scholars of late eighteenth- and nineteenth-century England were well aware that the relationship between master and servant was of central importance. Steedman quotes Sir William Blackstone as asserting that the contract between employer and servant embodied the first of the three great relations of private life—the other two being between wife and husband and between parent and child. Most important, he claimed that the other two relationships were founded on this primary one. See Steedman, "Servant's Labour," 8. On the importance of the institution of domestic servitude for understanding the logic of European household formation, see Laslett, *World We Have Lost*, and Laslett and Wall, *Household and Family*.

6. As scholarship on servants in early modern Europe and colonial India indicates, servanthood could be considered an occupation, a stage in the life cycle, and a social condition; moreover, Raffaella Sarti notes that "the history of domestic service is (partially) intertwined with the history of slavery," making definitions of servants,

service, and servitude difficult but nonetheless vital for understanding those societies. See note 5 and Sarti, "Introduction to Forum"; Fairchilds, *Domestic Enemies*; and Chatterjee, *Gender, Slavery*.

7. See Hochschild, *Managed Heart*; and Sayer, *Moral Significance of Class*.

8. Williams, *Marxism and Literature*, 110. On the ways in which culture is socially constituted and socially constituting, see Williams, "Base and Superstructure.

9. Williams, *Marxism*, 110. As Aijaz Ahmad has elaborated, a "materialist conception . . . looks at culture not as spiritual or religious heritage but as a set of material practices through which people live and produce the meanings of their lives. . . . It is a field, rather, of contention and conflict, among classes and among other social forces that struggle for dominance." Ahmad, "Politics of Culture," 65–66.

10. "Servitude" recalls the myriad sorts of unfree labor that existed historically in colonial and precolonial India. See Chatterjee, *Gender, Slavery*. In New York City, a recent study by the Domestic Workers United (DWU) refers to a "lifetime of bondage," and the results of a survey of over five hundred domestic workers show that they "stay in the industry, often with the same employer, for significant periods of their lives." Domestic Workers United, *Home Is Where*.

11. Bourdieu, *Distinction*, 170.

12. "And we do not yet know whether cultural life can survive the disappearance of domestic servants." Alain Besançon, *Être russe au XIXe siècle*, cited in Bourdieu, *Distinction*, 11.

13. Williams, *Marxism and Literature*, 132; and Williams, *Politics and Letters*, 156–74.

14. Rubbo and Taussig, "Up off Their Knees," 6.

15. Hegel, *Phenomenology of Spirit*, 111–19.

16. As Kojève puts it: "The relation between Master and Slave, therefore, is not recognition properly so-called. . . . The Master is not the only one to consider himself Master. The Slave, also, considers him as such. Hence, he is recognized in his human reality and dignity. But this recognition is one-sided, for he does not recognize in turn the Slave's human reality and dignity. Hence, he is recognized by someone whom he does not recognize. And this is what is insufficient—what is tragic—in his situation. . . . For he can be satisfied only by recognition from one whom he recognizes as worthy of recognizing him." Kojève, *Introduction to the Reading of Hegel*, 19.

17. "I hope I have shown that here the master differs basically from the master described by Hegel. For Hegel there is reciprocity; here the master laughs at the consciousness of the slave. What he wants from the slave is not recognition but work." Fanon, *Black Skin, White Masks*, 220–21.

18. Taylor, *Modern Social Imaginaries*, 23.

19. Ibid., 25.

20. See Coser, "Servants," 31–40; and Stigler, *Domestic Servants*. Stigler reported

falling demand for servants in the 1930s due to smaller family size and greater reliance on household appliances.

21. "Despite such low pay and harsh conditions, though, cleaners are situated at an important nexus of the global economy, for they are essential to ensuring that the spaces of production, consumption, and social reproduction which define the social architecture of the contemporary global economy remain sanitary and functional." Herod and Aguiar, "Introduction: Cleaners," 427.

22. See Hondagneu-Sotelo, *Doméstica*; Romero, *Maid in the U.S.A.*; Anderson, *Doing the Dirty Work?*; Constable, *Maid to Order*; Chin, *In Service and Servitude*; Ehrenreich and Hochschild, *Global Woman*; Parreñas, *Servants of Globalization*; Glenn, *Issei, Nisei, War Bride*; Zimmerman, Litt, and Bose, *Global Dimensions*; Sassen, *Global Networks, Linked Cities*; Chang, *Disposable Domestics*; and Cheng, *Serving the Household*.

23. See Rollins, *Between Women*; Wrigley, *Other People's Children*; Gregson and Lowe, *Servicing the Middle Classes*; and Uttal, *Making Care Work*.

24. Anderson, "Doing the Dirty Work?" 231.

25. See Zelizer, *Purchase of Intimacy*.

26. The labor-force participation statistic comes from Government of India, *Census of India 2001*. Note that this figure is likely to be an undercount. There is a more or less unbroken historical record of domestic servants (and slaves) in India, from Kautilya's *Arthashastra* (fourth century BCE) through medieval Mughal narratives to the present, which makes the paucity of serious study of the institution even more surprising. For servants who were also slaves, see Chatterjee, *Gender, Slavery*.

27. "A crucial determinant of the extent of employment in paid domestic labor in a given location is the degree of economic inequality there." Milkman, Reese, and Roth, "Macrosociology," 486.

28. Cf. Rachel Sherman's illuminating study of guests and workers in U.S. luxury hotels, which demonstrates how luxury service is produced and consumed, and through it, class inequality. Sherman, *Class Acts*.

29. On construction of boundaries, see Lamont, *Dignity of Working Men*.

30. Dickey, "Mutual Exclusions."

31. See, for example, Chaney and Garcia Castro, *Muchachas No More*; and Gill, *Precarious Dependencies*. For within-country migration in another region, see Ozyegin, *Untidy Gender*. See also, for apartheid South Africa, Cock, *Maids and Madams*.

32. Indian Social Institute, *Tribal Domestic Worker*; and Mehta, *Domestic Servant Class*. Mehta does not, as Patricia Uberoi reminds us, actually address the issue of migration, but all the servants Mehta interviewed were migrants to Bombay. Uberoi, "Introduction," 5.

33. An interesting contrast is provided by a recent study of maids in China, which argues that the older women domestics of the 1950s who were employed by elite Communist families have now been replaced with "young, mobile" maids of village origin

who "expect to return one day to their home village and thus are anxious to maximize the benefits of their temporary migration." Davin, "Domestic Service in Contemporary China," 45.

34. See the work cited in notes 22 and 23. Indeed, despite the fact that their own data show that there are many thousands of male domestic servants in India, a study sponsored by the Catholic Bishops Conference of India declares that "[i]n Indian tradition, females are most often involved in domestic chores" and claims that in most cases employers prefer female servants because of the idea that women are more "submissive, polite and loyal." Catholic Bishop's Conference, *National Socio-economic Survey*, 31.

35. Hansen, *Distant Companions*. Swapna Banerjee's book *Men, Women and Domestics* is another exception since it directly addresses the question of male servants in colonial India.

36. See Government of India, *Census of India 1971*, *Census of India 1981*, and *Census of India 1991*. This will be discussed further in Chapter 2.

37. Tomic, Trumper, and Hidalgo Dattwyler, "Manufacturing Modernity," 512.

38. Romero, *Maid in the U.S.A.*, 123.

39. Ibid., 60. Thus, in Romero's categorization of employers (such as bosses, utopian feminists, and maternalists) contractors are the best because they recognize that they are employers and are willing to negotiate wages by the job (195–200). Cf. "maternalism" as a mechanism of employer exploitation in Rollins, *Between Women*.

40. Banerjee, *Women Workers*, 14. Frøystad, "Master-Servant Relations," 88–89, synthesizes the critiques as well as pointing to the utility of the jajmani or patronage models for understanding servitude.

41. Bayly, *Caste, Society*, 314. See also Raghuram, "Caste and Gender."

42. See, for example, Banerjee, *Women Workers*; and Roy, *City Requiem*.

43. Hondagneu-Sotelo thus advocates neither maternalism nor contractor-type employers but personalism—a two-way relationship that involves "the employer's recognition of the employee as a particular person." Hondagneu-Sotelo, *Doméstica*, 208.

44. Hansen, *Distant Companions*; and Banerjee, *Men, Women and Domestics*.

45. "Many of us feel awkward hiring domestic help, especially if we didn't grow up with any," write Susan Carlton and Coco Meyer in *The Nanny Book*, 33.

46. Two recent additions are Auerbach, *And Nanny Makes Three*, and Kaylin, *The Perfect Stranger*.

47. See, for colonial India, Steel and Gardiner, *Complete Indian Housekeeper*, and Gordon, *Anglo-Indian Cuisine (Khana Kitab) and Domestic Economy*; for Victorian England, the classic was Beeton, *Book of Household Management*; for the late nineteenth-century United States, Beecher and Stowe, *American Woman's Home*.

48. Birkett, "Why Nanny Is No Longer a Dirty Word."

49. During our research in Kolkata, we encountered only one solidly middle-class household without servants, the elder male member of which had a well-articulated and long-standing position against keeping servants.

50. Mazzarella, "Middle Class," 1.

51. Ibid., 7.

52. One such was the ultimately ill-fated "India Shining" campaign of the Hindu nationalist Bharatiya Janata Party (BJP) during the 2004 national elections, after five years of a BJP-led coalition national government (1999–2004) marked by increasing economic liberalization and policies designed to respond to the consumer and investment demands of the affluent middle classes, amid growing class inequality and sociocultural conflict. "India Shining" celebrated economic prosperity and growth but failed because it captured the reality only of an elite, urban portion of the country's vast and poor population.

53. Fernandes and Heller, "Hegemonic Aspirations." As one observer commented, "India is one of the world's most unequal societies. An emerging and increasingly confident middle class is fueling a consumer boom while millions remain mired in unemployment and appalling living conditions. The rich have markets, the poor have bureaucrats." Deb, "The Rich Have Markets."

54. See, for example, Sridharan, "Growth and Sectoral Composition of India's Middle Class."

55. Deshpande, *Contemporary India*, 136–38.

56. Ibid., 139.

57. John Harriss, "Political Participation"; Fernandes and Heller, "Hegemonic Aspirations"; Fernandes, *India's New Middle Class*.

58. Baviskar, "Politics of the City."

59. Kumar, "The Scholar and Her Servants." For a fascinating account of the creation of national elites through schooling, see Srivastava, *Constructing Post-colonial India*.

60. Fernandes and Heller, "Hegemonic Aspirations," 502.

61. Chakrabarty, *Provincializing Europe*, 9–10. See also Rofel, *Other Modernities*, 3.

62. Kaviraj, "Modernity and Politics," 137.

63. In the debates around modernity, scholars such as S. N. Eisenstadt, Sudipta Kaviraj, and Dipesh Chakrabarty have argued that Marx, Weber, and Durkheim assumed that modernity arose from one principle—for Marx, capitalist commodity production; for Weber, rationalization; for Durkheim, individual reason—first in the West and then spread gradually to those parts of the world that came to approximate the West. Eisenstadt, "Multiple Modernities"; Kaviraj, "Modernity and Politics"; Chakrabarty, *Provincializing Europe*. As Aijaz Ahmad has noted, in Marx we find "the essential multiplicity of contradictions that gives to the historicity of the modern its

special, unique character of unequal and combined development." Ahmad, "Communist Manifesto and 'World Literature,'" 8.

64. A recent example is the debate around ayurvedic medicine and yoga being carried out in the Indian media, with particular reference to the argument between a leader of the Communist Party of India (Marxist), Brinda Karat, and popular guru Baba Ramdev on the cancer-curing properties of yoga. Asserting that yoga can indeed cure AIDS, Baba Ramdev has called for scientific research on the subject. "Yoga Can Cure AIDS."

65. In her intriguing article on the institution of home science in the Madras presidency, Mary Hancock writes, "Home Science treated the home as a laboratory where family and society could be physically and morally improved, but it also furnished a conceptual laboratory where Indian women, influenced by Gandhian notions of self-help as well as by Eurowestern feminisms, sought to create a discourse of both nationalist autonomy and gender equality." Hancock, "Home Science," 872. For a discussion of the dialectics of domesticity, modernity, and colonialism—"homemade hegemony"—in South Africa, see Comaroff and Comaroff, *Ethnography*.

66. For instance, Davidoff in *Worlds Between* argues that social divisions in Victorian England were most clearly revealed in the reproductive sphere, and thus the household should constitute a primary unit of analysis.

67. See Rosaldo and Lamphere, *Women, Culture, and Society*; Tilly and Scott, *Women, Work, and Family*; Barrett, *Women's Oppression Today*; Barrett and McIntosh, *Anti-social Family*; and Hochschild and Machung, *Second Shift*.

68. As Di Leonardo has remarked, "For domestic servants, the largest group of employed women in Victorian Britain and the United States, household and workplace were profoundly interpenetrating institutions." We would hold this to be the case in all societies in which the institution of domestic servitude has flourished. Di Leonardo, "Gender, Culture and Political Economy," 16.

69. "Since the household is a space for the daily production and recreation of social inequality not only on gender but also on class and caste lines, the cross-cutting class relations *inside* households would themselves severally mediate the ideological translations of labour." Sangari, *Politics of the Possible*, 292.

70. Sarkar, *Hindu Wife, Hindu Nation*, 38; and Chatterjee, *The Nation*.

71. Banerjee, *Men, Women and Domestics*, 3, 205. Borthwick also argues that class status for the late nineteenth-century middle class was predicated on keeping servants. Borthwick, *Changing Role of Women*. Hobsbawm makes a similar observation for England in the second half of the nineteenth century: "Sociologically the difference between working and middle classes was that between servant-keepers and potential servants." Hobsbawm, *Age of Capital*, 238.

72. Sangari, *Politics of the Possible*, 301. See also Sen, *Women and Labour*; and Standing, *Dependence and Autonomy*.

73. Douglas, *Purity and Danger*, 114–28.

74. Davidoff, *Worlds Between*, 75.

75. "Western patterns of modernity are not the only 'authentic' modernities, though they enjoy historical precedence and continue to be a basic reference point for others." Eisenstadt, "Multiple Modernities," 3.

76. The survey was carried out by Bela Bandopadhyay and her team.

77. In case of nonresponse the survey team went to the next house in the sampling frame.

Chapter 2

1. Berman, *All That Is Solid*, 5.

2. As will be discussed, employers of servants range from the lower-middle class to the political and economic elite.

3. Harvey, *Condition of Postmodernity*, 240. Harvey has famously argued for a "time-space compression" as a defining concept for our times. The history of capitalism has so speeded up the pace of life that spatial barriers have collapsed—through global telecommunications and transportation capabilities, for example—and people face an overwhelming sense of compression of time (to the present) and space.

4. Massey, *Space, Place, and Gender*, 161–71.

5. Ibid., 154.

6. Chakravorty, "From Colonial City," 57.

7. Mukherjee, *Calcutta*, 89.

8. Guha, *Rule of Property*, xv.

9. Sinha, *Calcutta in Urban History*; Chakravorty, "From Colonial City"; and Sarkar, *Writing Social History*.

10. However, we would agree with Swati Chattopadhyay in questioning the model of dual colonial cities, split strictly into black/indigenous and white/British areas. Chattopadhyay, "Blurring Boundaries."

11. Ray, *Calcutta*.

12. Nilsson, *European Architecture in India*, 67.

13. Data on Calcutta's expansion is drawn from Ghosh, Dutta, and Ray, *Calcutta*, 54; and *Census of India 1951*, vol. VI, pt. III.

14. Between 1822 and 1827, six thousand huts disappeared and more than three thousand new brick buildings were erected. Mukherjee, *Calcutta*, 36.

15. In the thika system large landowners rented plots of land to tenants, known as thika tenants, who in turn built numerous huts on their plots to sublet to workers and migrants to the city. The thika tenant rented the land but owned the buildings on it. See Ramaswamy and Chakravarti, "Falahak, Inshallah."

16. Nilsson, *European Architecture*, 69.

17. The name *Kolkata* was derived from *Kalikata*, one of the three villages in the area before the arrival of the British.

18. Population data are drawn from Population Division, *World Population Prospects* and *World Urbanization Prospects*.

19. Banerjee, *Women Workers*, 20.

20. Government of India, *Census of India 1991*.

21. The population density in parts of Kolkata ranges between eight hundred and one thousand people per hectare as compared with seventy or fewer in most North American cities. World Resources Institute et al., *World Resources 1996–97*.

22. Chaudhuri, "Traffic and Transport in Calcutta," 154.

23. Chaudhuri, "Refugees in West Bengal," 20.

24. Chakraborty, "Growth of Calcutta," 5; and Chatterjee, "Midnight's Unwanted Children."

25. Martin, *Changing Face of Calcutta*, 43.

26. De Haan, "Unsettled Settlers."

27. Bardhan and Mookherjee, "Political Economy."

28. Roy, *City Requiem*. There is debate on the true extent of land reforms in West Bengal, but the general consensus is that the reforms have most benefited middle peasants. Although this is certainly better than the lack of reform, as many observers have noted, the middle peasantry now constitute the new elite in rural Bengal. See Echeverri-Gent, "Popular Participation and Poverty Alleviation"; and Mallick, *Development Policy*.

29. Chakraborty, "Growth of Calcutta," 11.

30. Ibid., 4–5.

31. Ghosh, "Demography of Calcutta," 56–57.

32. Eighty percent of the slum population earn rupees (Rs) 500–1,700 per month ($11–$37, calculated when $1 = Rs 45), and only 10 percent earn Rs 1,500–5,000 ($33–$110). Kundu, "Case of Kolkata, India."

33. Chatterjee, "Town Planning in Calcutta."

34. Dasgupta, "Evictions in Calcutta."

35. Dasgupta notes that the natural slope of city land is eastward, away from the Hooghly River, and that since colonial times the city has developed on relatively high land from north to south, whereas the east—salt lakes, marshes, and wetlands—was the natural outlet for drainage and sewage carried by a network of canals to the Bay of Bengal. Ibid., 36.

36. Ibid., 35. The CMDA was established as the overarching planning and development agency in 1970–71 and eventually incorporated the CIT.

37. Chakraborty, "Growth of Calcutta," 64.

38. Ibid.

39. Dasgupta, "From Colonial City," 42.

40. Chakravorty, "From Colonial City," 76n21.

41. Dasgupta, "Evictions in Calcutta," 35.

42. Ibid., 35, 42–43. See also Roy, *City Requiem*.

43. Todi, "Up, and Rising."

44. Dasgupta, "Evictions in Calcutta," 38.

45. Todi, "Up, and Rising."

46. Deb, "Basic Instinct." The minister gave the example of a flat that would cost Rs 84,000 and another flat in the same project with a price tag of Rs 210,000, and opined that Kolkata needs another ninety thousand dwelling units by 2025.

47. Todi, "Up, and Rising."

48. Interview, January 26, 2004.

49. All names and certain characteristics have been changed to protect subjects' identities.

50. For a fascinating account of this particular form of sociability in Kolkata, see the chapter "Adda: A History of Sociality" in Chakrabarty, *Provincializing Europe*, 180–213. Swati Chattopadhyay examines the evolution of the *ro'ak*, a space for male sociability, from a platform constructed in a courtyard of a domestic residence to its placement outside facing the street, between the eighteenth century and the early twentieth century. Chattopadhyay, *Representing Calcutta*, 156, 183.

51. Broomfield defines the bhadralok as "a socially privileged and consciously superior group, economically dependent upon landed rents and professional and clerical employment; keeping its distance from the masses by its acceptance of high-caste prescriptions and its command of education; sharing a pride in its language, in its literate culture, and its history; and maintaining its communal integration through a fairly complex institutional structure that it had proved remarkably ready to adapt and augment to extend its social power and economic opportunities." Broomfield, *Elite Conflict*, 12–13.

52. Sarkar, *Swadeshi Movement*, 509.

53. Sarkar, *Writing Social History*, 168–69. *Dewans* (revenue administrators) and *banians* (trading intermediaries) were the indispensable agents and intermediaries associated with the East India and other British companies who also made fortunes in their own right in finance, trade, and land.

54. S. N. Mukherjee notes that bhadralok status was not ascriptive and had to be acquired and that membership was open to all groups, but that "the majority of Brahmins and kayasthas did not belong to this class, as they were poor, uneducated and did not share this 'middle class' lifestyle." Mukherjee, *Calcutta*, 65.

55. Bhattacharya, *Sentinels of Culture*, 52.

56. Mukherjee, *Calcutta*, 63–64.

57. Banerjee, *Parlour and the Streets*, 54.

58. Sarkar, *Hindu Wife*, 9.

59. Ibid., 10–11.

60. Ray, *Social Conflict*, 35.

61. Bandopadhyay, *From Plassey to Partition*, 142.

62. Ibid., 151.

63. Chakrabarty, *Provincializing Europe*, 4.

64. In Sumit Sarkar's apt summary, the bundle of issues such as women's education, widow immolation, polygamy, age of consent, child marriage, and seclusion of
women came to be seen in the 1860s and 1870s as *stri-swadhinata*, or the emancipa-
tion of women. Sarkar, *Beyond Nationalist Frames*.

65. See Sinha, *Colonial Masculinity*.

66. From the early nineteenth-century newspaper *Sambad Prabhakar*, quoted in
Ray, *Sekaler Narishiksha*, 24.

67. Sarkar, *Writing Social History*.

68. From the late nineteenth-century journal *Bamabodhini Patrika*, BS [Bengali
calendar] 1310 (1903), cited in Ray, *Sekaler Narishiksha*, 253.

69. Sarkar, *Hindu Wife*, 34.

70. Ibid., 38.

71. Borthwick, *Changing Role*.

72. Banerjee, *Men, Women and Domestics*. See also Bandopadhyay, *Ma o Chele*;
Basu, *Stridiger Prati Upadesh*; Majumdar, *Stri*. Mitra, *Strir Prati Swamir Upadesh*, a
Brahmo text, is emblematic of this sort of didactic literature. Cf. Walsh, *Domesticity
in Colonial India* and *How to Be the Goddess of Your Home*.

73. Sangari, *Politics of the Possible*, 327.

74. Borthwick, *Changing Role*, 14.

75. Chatterjee, "Nationalist Resolution."

76. Banerjee, "Attired in Virtue," 81.

77. See ibid.; Sen, *Women and Labour*; and Chatterjee, "Prostitution in Nineteenth Century Bengal," 159–72.

78. Sangari, *Politics of the Possible*, 307.

79. As Fernandes has shown in her book on jute workers, *Producing Workers*,
women workers also faced the consequences of this consensus, since as women, they
were not considered workers and were thus denied the protection of labor laws.

80. The household and grounds of a yet older generation of this type of employer
are described in the following:

A long drive, flanked on one side by a row of servant go downs discreetly hidden behind
a hedge, and on the other by an enormous coach-house, led up to the house, with its
huge portico and imposing marble entrance hall and beautiful wooden staircase (with
80 steps?) built with galleries on each floor. On the ground floor was a large state dining room in the centre, to the east of which was a suite of three rooms, ante room, study
and bedroom, and a bathroom; to the west was a lesser dining room and a still smaller

children's dining room beyond it; and to the west of this, a second suite of three rooms similar to the first. These rooms all led to a deep south verandah, with steps down to the garden. [And in this house, there were servants] who stayed on till they died or were pensioned off. Among these were Lakshmi Ayah . . . the Sudder Bearer, Ramjan Coachman, the old Kamsamah, and Kumur ud-din Kitmitgar, some of whom used to come and see us after we were married and demand buksis on the strength of having carried us about when we were small.

From Majumdar's "Family History," a description of her home in Park Street in 1885, quoted in Burton, "House/Daughter/Nation," 931.

81. *Jhuta* or *ato* refers to pollution. Once someone has eaten from a plate, it becomes polluted and hence the reluctance of the Brahmin servant to touch it. This will be discussed further in Chapter 3.

82. In a telling conversation between a newly middle-class husband and wife from the 1982 film *Kharij*, director Mrinal Sen shows a husband asking his wife what she would like, given that they were now doing well at last. The wife refuses a car, clothes, a refrigerator, and a radio and says, "What I really need now is a servant." Sen, *Absence Trilogy*, 63.

83. See Sunil Gangopadhyay's evocative novel *Those Days* for a description of the domestic arrangements of landed gentry in nineteenth- and early twentieth-century Calcutta.

84. In Janet Bujra's study of Tanzania, only two out of the sixty employers interviewed thought women were better servants. See Bujra, "Men at Work." Hansen, *African Encounters with Domesticity*, reports a similar dynamic in Zambia.

85. See the *Census of India* for 1971, 1981, and 1991. However, this is a vastly undercounted number since the census includes only maids and other house cleaners (531) but not cooks, ayahs, or any other category of domestic worker. In addition to men and women, this class comprises thousands of children, both girls and boys, who work as domestic servants, whom the census leaves out. According to a study commissioned by the Catholic Bishops' Conference of India, 16.65 percent of the domestic servants interviewed were under the age of fifteen. See Catholic Bishops' Conference, *National Socio-economic Survey*, 36. However, accurate statistics on child labor in private homes are next to impossible to procure.

86. Banerjee, *Women Workers*; and Bela Bandopadhyay, pers. comm., January 1998.

87. Gautam Bhadra, pers. comm., January 1998.

88. A friend reported an exchange she had with a real estate agent while searching for an apartment in Kolkata in 2001. When she expressed surprise at being shown a "servant's room" that was six feet wide and seven feet long, the real estate agent responded that his company had undertaken a study that determined that no servants in Kolkata were more than five feet six inches in height.

89. Bhagat Singh was a legendary Indian freedom fighter and martyr. This particular interview subject asked to be referred to as Bhagat Singh when we told him that we would pick a name for him in order to protect his anonymity.

90. Sen, *Absence Trilogy*, 107.

91. Lefebvre, *Production of Space*.

Chapter 3

1. In this chapter, we use Gitanjali "resident," "apartment dweller," and "employer" interchangeably.

2. Mauss, *The Gift*, especially 78–83.

3. The *American Heritage Dictionary* (4th ed., 2000) defines *freelancer* as "a person who sells services to employers without a long-term commitment to any of them." In our study, the lack of commitment is by no means unidirectional.

4. Whereas 47 percent of the workers in the survey had worked for a particular household for one to five years, 36 percent had worked for the same household for five to ten years or more.

5. Popular accounts of early twentieth-century Calcutta indicate that many servants came from specific regions of Bengal, such as Medinipur (Midnapore) and Burdwan. See Mahendranath Datta (1929) as cited in Banerjee, "Down Memory Lane," 688; and Map 2 on page 29 of this book.

6. On the East Bengali refugees and resettlement, see Chatterjee, "Midnight's Unwanted Children."

7. That 50 percent of the servants in our survey report no land at all indicates that indeed the most economically vulnerable migrants are the ones who become servants in Kolkata.

8. Wages in Kolkata are distinctly lower than in the other major cities of India, where part-time workers may well receive Rs 1,000 from each of five houses in which they work. According to Amit Kundu, the West Bengal government recommended in 2007 that the minimum daily wage in West Bengal be Rs 64.22 per day. Kundu, "Conditions of Work." Assuming that part-time workers work a six-day week, their minimum wage should be at least Rs 1,605 per month. Thus, part-time workers in Kolkata earn substantially less than the recommended minimum wage.

9. See Sarti, "Domestic Service."

10. The list of chores given here is similar to the list presented to Hondagneu-Sotelo in Los Angeles, although those tasks are presumably given once a week to the visiting housecleaner. This list is fascinating not only because of the detail provided about how the worker is expected to perform the task but also because it delineates the exact products the worker is expected to use (Old English Polish, Dust Wax, etc.), thus placing this routine in a more highly commodified culture where each surface has its own associated cleaning product. See Hondagneu-Sotelo, *Doméstica*, 166–67.

11. Mukherjee, *Calcutta*, 31–32.

12. Banerjee, *Men, Women and Domestics*, 113. She also reports a fascinating exchange between social reformer Ramtanu Lahiri and Pandit Iswarchandra Vidyasagar when Lahiri, despite discarding many outward signs of his Brahmin caste, asked Vidyasagar to find him a Brahmin cook (116).

13. Scheduled castes correspond to the British colonial "schedule" of the many caste groupings that fall below the four main castes of the Hindu system: Brahmin, Kshatriya, Vaisya, Sudra. The term was adopted by the Indian constitution and in compensatory legislation intended to rectify historic discrimination and exclusion, along with "scheduled tribes" (a list of indigenous tribal populations) and "other backward classes" (Sudras whose ritual rank and occupational status are above "untouchables" but who themselves remain socially and economically depressed). The derogatory epithet "untouchable" to refer to persons imputed with low caste is no longer acceptable. Members of scheduled castes have adopted the political identity of *dalit*—literally "broken," but which signifies oppressed, downtrodden, and socially exploited.

14. As one of the younger employers we interviewed puts it, "The jamadar comes and cleans the loos because nobody else cleans the loos." When we asked why that was the case, he responded: "A loo is supposed to be out of bounds for anyone else, including the person who cleans the floors that people walk on with their bare feet, because the same swab should not be used for the loo. . . . In certain homes in earlier days you had a separate entrance for the sweeper straight to the loo so he wouldn't even go through the main rooms and the main doors—the sweeper was very low class and low caste, and he did the menial job of cleaning the shit house, so he wouldn't even be allowed to walk in. I'm talking about even in the grandparents' generation, so they would have a separate spiral staircase leading to the loo, so the jamadar would come and clean and exit, and he wouldn't even come in the house. But it wasn't so stringent when we were kids."

15. Domestic servants are considered to be notoriously difficult to mobilize because there is no factory floor or common site of production or work where workers congregate. The fact that almost all domestic workers are isolated in individual households makes the task of union organizing very difficult, as does the almost complete absence of free time and mobility to attend union meetings. Moreover, because of the peculiar nature of domestic service, most employers, not to mention most governments, do not consider servants to be "workers" with rights under labor legislation.

16. Haldar, *A Life Less Ordinary*, 130.

17. This may also gesture to domestic servitude's lineage and possible origins in domestic slavery in Bengal. See Chatterjee, *Gender, Slavery*.

18. Hondagneu-Sotelo, *Doméstica*.

19. Recall the definition of *slavery* used by the editors of *Slavery and South Asian History*: "the condition of uprooted outsiders, impoverished insiders—or the descendants of either—serving persons or institutions on which they are wholly dependent." Chatterjee and Eaton, *Slavery and South Asian History*, 2.

20. Thompson, "Time, Work-Discipline."

21. De Certeau, *Practice of Everyday Life*, 97.

22. Roy, *City Requiem*, 81, 84.

Chapter 4

1. Ann Stoler similarly describes the "lush sentimentality" of Dutch colonial narratives about Indonesian servants, in contrast to the flat and disaffected narratives of the servants themselves. See Stoler, *Carnal Knowledge*, 165.

2. Banerjee argues that in early twentieth-century writings about servants in Bengal, the emphasis on dependence, sharing, and love deliberately suppresses the issues of subordination and treatment of workers in order to establish hegemony over the lower classes. Banerjee, *Men, Women and Domestics*, 162.

3. The nature of "modern" reflections on the past is such that the past is idealized. Writing in the early twentieth century, observers of the domestic world rued that "in the good old days, servants were treated as members of the family. . . . [T]he servants did not hesitate to lay their lives down for their master." From the Bengali journal *Bamabodhini Patrika* (1920), cited in Ray, *Nari o Paribar*, 146.

4. Cf. Orlando Patterson's argument that the slaveholder, who was himself parasitically dependent on the slave, deployed a countervailing ideological strategy of defining the slave as dependent. Patterson, *Slavery and Social Death*.

5. The "rhetoric of love" in various guises has been deployed in many cultures of servitude. See, for example, Constable, *Maid to Order*, for jokes told by Filipina domestic workers about being considered a member of the family.

6. Middle-class Bengalis generally eat varieties of *atap* (sun-dried rice), whereas servants and others of the working classes eat parboiled rice.

7. Stoler, *Carnal Knowledge*, 168. See Nishtha Jain's perceptive and moving documentary film *Lakshmi and Me* (2008), set in Mumbai, for a textured portrait of the relationship with her maid.

8. See, for example, Young, "Myth of Being 'Like a Daughter.'" See also Pei-Chan Lan for the argument that migrant workers who may be disdained and thought of as alien are not so easily incorporated into the family. Lan, *Global Cinderellas*, 207.

9. In Bengali, *barir loker moton chhilo*—literally, "was like one of the members of our house."

10. We refer here to the family as discourse and ideology. For excellent work that interrogates the idealized notions of the family, see Thorne and Yalom, *Rethinking the Family*; and Chatterjee, *Gender, Slavery*. Chatterjee, in *Unfamiliar Relations*, makes

clear the multiple forms of labor, kinship, and relationships that mark Indian families historically.

11. Rollins, *Between Women.*

12. "It helps to be reminded," as Bruce Robbins writes, "that the word 'family' derives from the Latin *famulus* or 'servant.'" Before the middle of the eighteenth century in England, indicates Robbins, citing Raymond Williams, family meant the household, that is, the blood relations plus servants. Robbins, *Servant's Hand,* 111. In the Indian context, households consisting of blood relations, servants, and other dependents persisted well into the twentieth century, and many of the older generation of employers and servants in this study were brought up with such domestic arrangements.

13. Shah, "Service or Servitude?"

14. Anandachandra Sen Gupa, *Grihinir Kartavyar,* translated by and quoted in Banerjee, *Men, Women and Domestics,* 116. Other examples of domestic manuals include Mitra, *Strir Prati Swamir Upadesh*; Roy Chowdhury, *Grihalakshmi*; Mitra, *Ramanir Kartavya*; Basu, *Sridiger Prati Upadesh*; Basu, *Nari Niti*; Mukhopadhyay, "Paribarik Prasanga"; and Mitra, "Grihakatha, Strishiksha." See also Walsh, *Domesticity in Colonial India.*

15. It is also the subject of articles in the popular press throughout India. To cite just one example, the Chandigarh-based *Tribune* carried a series of articles in 2001 on employer–domestic servant relationships, one of which, "A Time-Tested Trustworthy Bond," was about those families who still had old faithful servants. Here is an excerpt:

> Bahadur came to the Dhillons in July 1982 and is at present well ensconced in the annexe of their house along with his wife and two sons. "I believe that a portion of this type fetches a rent of Rs 3000–4000, but we feel that Bahadur deserves it the most because of his unfailing loyalty to our family," says Brig K. S. Dhillon, "We'd installed Bahadur in this portion of the house when it was under litigation. . . . [W]e'd been trying to have it vacated for years. Many times Bahadur was threatened and abused and even beaten up by the other party in a bid to make him vacate but he held on nonetheless." (Sekhon, "Time-Tested Trustworthy Bond")

16. Bardhan, "Dasdasi o amra," 15–18.

17. On domestics' desire to be treated like human beings in this "historically degraded occupation," see the pathbreaking study by Rollins, *Between Women,* 132.

18. Dickey, "Mutual Exclusions," also notes these desires for more than a wage in her study of servants and employers in Madurai.

19. Bourdieu, *Outline,* 196.

20. In her study of a nineteenth-century zamindari, Pamela Price suggests that maidservants had intimate knowledge of their mistresses that rendered their mistresses dependent on them. Indeed, family fortunes could rise and fall with the trading of this knowledge. See Price, *Kingship and Political Practice.* See also Vikram Chandra's short story "Shakti," in which a maid gives information about one household in

which she works to another employer, thus enabling that employer to exact revenge upon the first. Chandra, *Love and Longing.*

21. As Saubhagya Shah astutely notes: "Straddling the intersection of various discourses, people tend to selectively employ aspects of kinship, modernization, or leftist rhetoric to engage the labor and the identity of their subordinates. Masters too draw from the same fluidity to 'craft' their self-identities as benevolent patrons, civilizers, mentors, or the facilitators of modern education." Shah, "Service or Servitude?" 108.

22. One employer tells the story of his father's driver who sold the tires on the family's car, but the driver was not fired, and his son was even taken on—all because the driver, even though a thief, was a good and loyal servant.

23. Servants are, however, not scarce—particularly in West Bengal. Indeed, in an increasingly tight labor market, they try to hold on to the jobs they have, fearing competition from the ever-ready supply of migrants and commuters. For servants, good jobs with good employers are scarce. See also Kundu, "Conditions of Work and Rights," 19, who suggests that due to the "huge supply of domestic workers from near-by South 24 Parganas district in the southern part of Kolkata, the bargaining power of the employer is much higher than the northern part of Kolkata where the supply of domestic workers is comparatively less."

24. Kolkata newspapers carry news items about servant thievery and murders quite frequently. See, for example, from the *Telegraph*, "Servant Held for Murder" (August 17, 2004) or "Servant Trapped with Widow's Wealth" (December 7, 2005). In an article titled "Insure at Your Own Risk" (May 12, 2005), the author warns that though most burglaries are committed by servants, most insurance companies do not insure goods against theft by employees, a fact that employers need to be cognizant of when choosing an insurance company.

25. In our survey, 68 percent of the servants found their present job through local servant networks, whereas only 11 percent were recruited via employer networks.

26. "There have been a few reported incidents in the past when current or former domestic servants have kidnapped children of families for whom they have worked and held them for ransom. Such incidents can possibly be avoided through proper screening measures. Two separate kidnapping incidents were reported in Calcutta in late April 2002; at least one of the incidents has been attributed to the cooperation of household staff." U.S. State Department warning cited in Qayum and Ray, "Grappling with Modernity," 536.

27. Cf. discussions of the contest over traditional and capitalist rights in eighteenth-century England. Thompson, *Whigs and Hunters.*

28. Cf. "maternalism" as a mechanism of employer exploitation in Rollins, *Between Women*; Glenn, *Issei, Nisei, War Bride*; and Hondagneu-Sotelo, *Doméstica.* For Rollins, in particular, maternalism was the core dynamic around which the employer–domestic worker relationship revolved (*Between Women*, 178).

29. Dickey, "Mutual Exclusions," 35.

30. Critics of microfinance and other self-help programs for the poor, such as the efforts of the much-lauded Grameen Bank, note that these efforts do little to address the structural causes of poverty and simply affirm neoliberalism by encouraging individual women to work harder, save more money, and have fewer children. See, for example, Feiner and Barker, "Microcredit and Women's Poverty," 10–11.

31. Hondagneu-Sotelo, *Doméstica*, 11.

32. As one young executive explained his stance toward servants, "You do your job and then you go, you're paid, we're taking care of you, you take care of us—it's very clinical."

33. These sentiments have echoes elsewhere in the Indian subcontinent. Cf. the words of a domestic worker from Tamil Nadu: "This is the difference between rich and poor people. Only if we work can we have *kanji* [rice water]. But they could eat meat and rice even if they stay at home for two to ten days. . . . If we don't have work, we couldn't even have *kanji* to drink. That's the difference between rich and poor people." Dickey, "Mutual Exclusions," 47.

34. These young, professional women employers are comfortable neither with Romero's "professionalism" (*Maid in the U.S.A.*, 10, 187) nor with Hondagneu-Sotelo's "personalism" (*Doméstica*, 207–9).

35. "When couples struggle, it is seldom simply over who does what. Far more often, it is over giving and receiving of gratitude." Hochschild and Machung, *The Second Shift*, 19.

Chapter 5

Portions of this chapter previously appeared in Qayum and Ray, "Grappling with Modernity"; and Ray, "Masculinity, Femininity, and Servitude."

1. Song of a lament of a woman searching for domestic work sung by Runa Laila, one of Bangladesh's most popular folksingers.

2. Fanon, *Black Skin, White Masks*, 218.

3. "The facile assumption that the history of public life, a political arena of broad import populated mainly by male historical actors, is sharply demarcated from the history of private life, a social arena of narrower concerns populated mainly by women, family, and male losers, begins to look like an artifice whose foundations require critical reexamination." Stern, *Secret History of Gender*, 9.

4. Our approach is consistent with that of Stuart Hall, who, inspired by Gramsci, has called for "the need of new conceptualizations at . . . the levels of the analysis of specific historical conjunctures, or of the political and ideological aspects," that is, "[of] the culturally specific quality of class formations in any historically specific society." Hall, "Gramsci's Relevance," 415, 436. Irene Silverblatt has further explicated this approach as "conjunctural analysis—the analysis of what can

only be grasped as it is produced in history." Silverblatt, "Interpreting Women in States," 158.

5. Cf. feminist scholars such as Carmen Diana Deere, who may initially reject "patriarchy" in favor of looking at "gender relations as an arena of potential conflict and struggle," but whose analysis is predicated on something called "patriarchy." Deere, *Household and Class Relations*, 18.

6. Harris, "Households as Natural Units," 138.

7. See, for example, Fernandes, *Producing Workers*.

8. Government of India, *Census of India 2001*.

9. Standing, *Dependence and Autonomy*, 69.

10. From the journal *Antahpur* (May/June 1899), cited in Standing, *Dependence and Autonomy*, 63.

11. Ibid., 76. The other aspect of bhadralok masculine practice is to disengage from the domestic and engage in the public sphere through intricately organized and ongoing political, cultural, and intellectual conversation, about which see the discussion of *adda* in Chakraborty, *Provincializing Europe*, 180–213.

12. Basu, "Chakure Meyer Sonar Patharbati."

13. Standing, *Dependence and Autonomy*, 72.

14. Ibid., 163–65.

15. Stern, *Secret History of Gender*, 305.

16. This is also echoed in Roy, *City Requiem*, 193: "Our husbands are useless so they might as well be dead."

17. Kumar, *History of Doing*, 125.

18. Blair-Loy, *Competing Devotions*.

19. To give some sense of the relative value of this wage, a driver (always male), who has more status than a servant, will typically earn at least Rs 3,000 a month, without overtime. Mira, then, works essentially a twenty-four-hour day to earn as much as a driver does in a ten-hour day.

20. In discussions of transnational migrants, for example, Parreñas and Hochschild have noted the use of "nanny chains"—poorer women whom Filipinas working as nannies in Los Angeles may hire to look after the children they have left behind. In turn, the children of the nanny for the children of the transnational nanny may rely on their older siblings to look after them. Hochschild, "Love and Gold"; Parreñas, *Servants of Globalization*.

21. Salt Lake was conceived as a residential development that would not be pockmarked by unsightly slums, as are the older residential neighborhoods of Kolkata. See Chakravorty, "From Colonial City."

22. Stoler, *Carnal Knowledge*, 180.

23. Black feminists in the United States have critiqued mainstream white feminism for assuming that liberation means "going out to work" and earning a living in

order to be (more) independent of men and patriarchal relations. See, for example, hooks, *Feminist Theory*.

24. If women are provided with education and livelihoods, the following benefits are said to accrue: poverty alleviation; healthier, school-attending children (reduction in infant and child mortality and malnutrition); empowerment (to better deal with their [patriarchal or abusive] husbands and fathers); increased decision-making power and, concomitantly, greater control over reproduction (population control and environmental mitigation); and deployment of citizenship rights (better governance). See, among others, Young, *Women and Economic Development*; Moser, "Gender Planning," 1799–1825; Kabeer, *Reversed Realities*; Marchand and Parpart, *Feminism/Postmodernism/Development*; and John and Nair, *A Question of Silence?*

25. Roy, *City Requiem*, 104.

26. Rubin, "The Traffic in Women."

27. Hiring after-school tutors to help children study and prepare for exams is a common practice in India in those families that can afford it, from lower middle class to upper class.

28. Rubbo and Taussig, "Up off Their Knees."

29. See also Hansen, *African Encounters with Domesticity*. In fact, although most servants in Kolkata today are women, the past preference for male servants as a sign of status persists, and affluent employers, like their parents before them, continue to employ male servants. Male servants are not considered to pose as much of a threat or source of shame as would an ordinary, unrelated man in the home. The ongoing preference for male cooks may be attributed to a variety of factors, including ritual concerns about female contamination compounded by fear of female servant sexuality.

30. *Pukka* (brick construction) is understood in contrast to *kuchha* (mud and plaster construction).

31. In India, "service" refers to working in the civil service or government bureaucracy or in the offices of private companies and institutions.

32. Sennett and Cobb, *Hidden Injuries of Class*, 125.

33. "What gift do you think a good servant has that marks them apart from the rest? It is the gift of anticipation. And I am a good servant. I am better than good, I am the best, the *perfect* servant." Fellowes, *Gosford Park*, scene 139.

34. As discussed in Chapter 2, real estate developers, architects, and urban planners agreed that with a salary less than Rs 10,000 per month (US$250)—compared to the Indian average income of Rs 2,066 per month (US$52, based on figures available at www .worldbank.org)—a family of four cannot afford to live in twenty-first-century Kolkata and must settle for outlying areas. Thus Raja, for example, who makes well below Rs 5,000, could obtain a house only in South 24 Parganas district outside the city proper.

35. "It is surely because the project of fully subjecting women to the control of men is so contradictory that an ideological definition of the domestic in terms of a

natural finality has remained so powerful and persuasive." Harris, "Households as Natural Units," 153.

36. For example, see "Domestic Workers Go on Strike," which reports a strike by ten thousand domestic workers on Domestic Workers' Day in Mumbai, who demanded that they be included in the Unorganised Labour Bill and that the Domestic Workers Bill, 1998, be passed. No such day was commemorated in Kolkata despite its Communist government, a contradiction that is explored in the next chapter.

Chapter 6

1. It is noteworthy that consciousness in each century of the modern age, whether in Russia in the nineteenth century, France in the twentieth, or the United States or India in the twenty-first, seems to be plagued by the servant question.

2. When the term "contract" or "contractual" is used here and in previous chapters, it should be clarified that with virtually no exceptions in our study and survey, there are informal, verbal agreements rather than formal, written contracts between servants and employers.

3. Stigler, "Domestic Servants"; Coser, "Servants."

4. In writing about the making of the respectable middle class of Bengal, Borthwick notes that from the 1880s on, the ability to keep a servant became a mark of bhadralok status. Although the numbers and types of servants are no longer the same as in the nineteenth century, the inability to hire at least one servant may still be seen as the failure to reach bhadralok status. Cf. Sara Dickey on twentieth-century Madurai: "Servants are crucial for maintaining class standing." She quotes a friend who explained, "Everyone decides to have a servant in order to get prestige from commanding someone else's work, not because they need a servant to help them with the work they are incapable of doing." Dickey, "Permeable Homes," 477.

5. In the preface to the English translation of *Distinction*, Bourdieu insists on the comparative value of the explication of distinction beyond the confines of French society and culture: "The model of the relationships between the universe of economic and social conditions and the universe of life-styles which is put forward here, based on an endeavor to rethink Max Weber's opposition between class and *Stand*, seems to me to be valid beyond the particular French case and, no doubt, for every stratified society, even if the system of distinctive features which express or reveal economic and social differences (themselves variable in scale and structure) varies considerably from one period, and one society, to another" (pp. xi–xii).

6. Cf. Dickey, "Permeable Homes," for a fascinating account of the notion that servants bring the pollution of the outside into the safe and pure homes of the middle classes in the southern Indian city of Madurai.

7. Rollins, *Between Women*, 232.

8. This seems to be a common employer complaint in Asia, yet servants in Kol-

kata continue to sit on the floor, whereas they may not elsewhere. In Nepal, a "house-wife reported firing a hardworking servant of six years when she found him sitting on the living room sofa on several occasions." Shah, "Service or Servitude," 104. Cf. the following comment by an employer in Sulawesi, Indonesia: "Back then they wouldn't dare sit on chairs to watch TV—they knew their place was on the floor. Today they are so brazen." Dickey and Adams, "Negotiating Homes," 1.

9. The bed in middle-class Kolkata functions as social space during the day. People use it for informal seating, entertaining, or television watching. Nonetheless, it is an intimate space, restricted to family and close friends.

10. Cf. Bourdieu, *Distinction*, 251: "The nature against which culture is here constructed is nothing other than what is 'popular,' 'low,' 'vulgar,' 'common.' This means that anyone who wants to 'succeed in life' must pay for his accession to everything which defines truly humane humans by a change of nature, a 'social promotion' experienced as an ontological promotion, a process of 'civilization.'"

11. Rachel Tolen also discusses how employers wish to put brakes on servant desires for consumption of luxury goods in Madras. Tolen, "Transfers of Knowledge," 78–79. Although employers may be uncomfortable with the perceived development of shared tastes, they may rest easy. Citing the power of media, Herbert Marcuse warned in 1964 that a convergence in tastes indicated not classlessness but rather the triumph of ideology: "[T]he so-called equalization of class distinction reveals its ideological function. If the worker and his boss enjoy the same television program and visit the same resort places, if the typist is as attractively made up as the daughter of her employer, if the Negro owns a Cadillac, if they all read the same newspaper, then this assimilation indicates not the disappearance of classes, but the extent to which the needs and satisfactions that serve the preservation of the Establishment are shared by the underlying population." Marcuse, *One Dimensional Man*, 8.

12. We would agree with Satish Deshpande's pithy assessment of the vagaries of caste in the twentieth-century nationalist imaginary and its banishment as an atavistic, colonial, and rural-traditional phenomenon: "Caste had no place in modern India, as our nationalist leaders never tired of declaring. As soon as we get rid of the colonial conditions and apparatuses which foster and encourage it, it will soon wither away. We were so committed to this prognosis that we believed it to be fact. . . . Indian sociology was unable to address adequately the forms in which caste was being reinvented as a modern institution, specially its new modes of reproduction and the fresh meanings and functions it was acquiring in urban India." Deshpande, *Contemporary India*, 124.

13. "'Dirtiness' appears always in a constellation of the suspect qualities that, along with sexuality, immorality, laziness, and ignorance, justify social rankings of race, class, and gender." Palmer, *Domesticity and Dirt*, 140.

14. Cf. Thorstein Veblen on "ceremonial uncleanliness attaching to occupations

associated in our habits of thought with menial service." Veblen, *Theory of the Leisure Class*, 37.

15. Rauts, once nomadic cattle herders, are part of the middle-caste Yadavs, and tribals are *adivasis*, the indigenous groups of India.

16. For similar findings among upper castes in the city of Kanpur, see Frøystad, "Master-Servant Relations."

17. The bazaar book is the household accounts, where food and other purchases made at the bazaar or market are recorded and tabulated. When servants do the marketing, they are typically expected to account in the bazaar book for the money spent.

18. "This affirmation of power over a dominated necessity always implies a claim to a legitimate superiority over those who, because they cannot assert the same contempt for contingencies in gratuitous luxury and conspicuous consumption, remain dominated by ordinary interests and urgencies. . . . The most 'classifying' privilege thus has the privilege of appearing to be the most natural one." Bourdieu, *Distinction*, 55.

19. Veblen, *Theory of the Leisure Class*, 60.

20. Bourdieu, *Distinction*, 77.

21. Pranab Bardhan has a telling anecdote about sitting in a woman's living room and listening to her altered voice and speech as she alternately speaks to him in soft tones and loudly and rudely to the young girl dusting the windows of the room. Bardhan, "Dasdasi o amra." Contrast this with G. G. Weix's observation about servant speech in the presence of employers: "They speak softly in melodious tones of high Javanese, in contrast to the rough cackle of low Javanese spoken by family members. Among themselves, servants speak in low Javanese." Weix, "Inside the Home," 145.

22. Kanshi Ram (1934–2006) was the Dalit Sikh founder of the Bahujan Samaj Party (BSP), a political party of the lower castes, including Sudras and Dalits. The party has been a powerful force in India's most populous state, Uttar Pradesh, since the mid-1990s.

23. Roy, *City Requiem*, 107.

Chapter 7

1. One possible exception is the foreign-born Latino colleague Romero discusses in the beginning of *Maid in the U.S.A.*, 31–34, although it is difficult to discern whether his identity would be inscribed as "Latino of color" or "white." Where employers of color do dominate is in the much-publicized cases of abuse and exploitation involving foreign diplomats and international civil servants, often from Asian and African countries and living and working in New York or Washington, D.C., who employ live-in migrant domestic workers under special visa arrangements. For an in-depth investigation, see the June 2001 Human Rights Watch report, *Hidden in the Home*; and Domestic Workers United, *Home Is Where*.

2. Rollins, *Between Women*; Romero, *Maid in the U.S.A.*; Wrigley, *Other People's Children*; Hondagneu-Sotelo, *Doméstica*; and Colen, "'Just a Little Respect.'"

3. Romero, *Maid in the U.S.A.*, 105.

4. Ibid., 57–58.

5. Katzman, *Seven Days a Week*, 53; Dudden, *Serving Women*, 1–4; and Lintelman, "Our Serving Sisters," 91.

6. Milkman, Reese, and Roth, "Macrosociology."

7. As Rollins concluded, "The presence of the 'inferior' domestic . . . supports the idea of unequal human worth: it suggests that there might be categories of people (the lower classes, people of color) who are inherently inferior to others (middle and upper classes, whites). And this idea provides ideological justification for a social system that institutionalizes inequality." Rollins, *Between Women*, 203.

8. See Buckley and Correal, "Domestic Workers Organize"; and "Women's Work."

9. Cf. Rubbo and Taussig's division of Colombian society into servant-supplying and servant-employing households. Rubbo and Taussig, "Up off Their Knees," 12.

10. To be sure, the twenty middle- and upper-middle-class employers whom Judith Rollins interviewed in the Boston area in the early 1980s all had grown up with mothers who had employed domestic help of some sort. However, none of the women under forty had had live-in help. Rollins, *Between Women*, 93–99.

11. "Women's Work."

12. Lutz, "At Your Service Madam!" 91.

13. Gregson and Lowe, *Servicing the Middle Classes*, 17.

14. Milkman, Reese, and Roth, "Macrosociology," 491, 504.

15. According to U.S. Census Bureau Technical Paper #65, there is no longer a separate category for private household workers; they are grouped with workers with similar occupations, such as "maids and housekeeping cleaners" and "child care workers" who may or may not be working in private homes. This change makes comparisons rather difficult with the 1990 census data analyzed in Milkman, Reese, and Roth's 1998 article. However, we did find U.S. Census Bureau data from the March 2000 Current Population Survey that provides information on the number of men and women employed as private household service workers, even though this category is not used in general.

16. Wrigley, *Other People's Children*, ix.

17. This would be an increase from the 27,395 women employed in New York in 1990 cited by Milkman, Reese, and Roth, even given that the 1999 total includes men. The 2002 New York City Housing and Vacancy Survey no longer gives information for this occupational category since its classificatory scheme is based on the U.S. Census. See note 15.

18. Domestic Workers United, *Home Is Where*, 9–10.

19. See, for example, Flanagan, "How Serfdom Saved the Women's Movement"; McLaughlin and Kraus, *Nanny Diaries*; Lee, "Women Raise the City"; Rafkin, *Other People's Dirt*; Ehrenreich, "Maid to Order"; and numerous articles in the *New York Times* and *New York* magazine.

20. See, among other studies, Katzman, *Seven Days a Week*; and Romero, *Maid in the U.S.A.*

21. See, for example, Hondagneu-Sotelo, *Doméstica*; Rollins, *Between Women*; and Glenn, *Issei, Nisei, War Bride*.

22. See Pogrebin, "Nanny Scam." Journalist Pogrebin is a feminist and the daughter of Letty Cottin Pogrebin, a founding editor of *Ms.* magazine.

23. According to the *Oxford English Dictionary*, 2d ed., *factotum* is "a man of all-work; also, a servant who has the entire management of his master's affairs." *Factotum* is from the Latin *fac totum*, "do everything," from *facere*, "to do," and *totus*, "all."

24. Migrants and refugees from East Bengal who settled in squatter camps and refugee settlements in and around Kolkata have historically been a source of domestic labor in the city.

25. As Rollins observed of Boston couples in the 1980s: "Typically, they came to define themselves as needing help around the time of the birth of their first child." Rollins, *Between Women*, 94.

26. A term originally employed to refer to British women in colonial India, "memsahib" refers to the mistress of the household, or female employer.

27. See Wrigley, *Other People's Children*, chap. 3.

28. Employers in New York City, both Indian and North American, are constantly comparing the national and ethnic origin and characteristics of nannies and other household help, even though many would admit that it is a fallacy to speak of national characters or attributes. Several employers we interviewed emphasized the warmth and loving concern demonstrated toward their children by nannies from Bolivia, Guatemala, Peru, and Puerto Rico. "Full-service mentality" refers to the willingness of domestic workers to take on tasks beyond those they were hired to perform, for example, nannies who will do the laundry or cook dinner.

29. Journalist Tracey Middlekauff, in "Maid in America," recounts a not atypical saga of immigration and abusive working conditions in South Asian homes:

> When Marjina, a young Bangladeshi woman working as a live-in housekeeper for an Indian family in Dubai, was invited to accompany the family to live and work in the U.S., she jumped at the opportunity. To her, America meant money and freedom. But soon after she arrived to begin her new life, Marjina says her dreams quickly dissolved. "I thought they would treat me like a family member," she says, speaking in her native Bengali through an interpreter. "But I was lied to." . . . Indeed, Marjina describes a grueling work schedule with little or no compensation: 18-hour days on Monday to Friday, 8-hour days on her "days off" during the weekend. She says she was never allowed to eat until the family was

finished, she was forced to sleep in the basement with no mattress, and she was made to shovel snow in the cold Teaneck, N.J. winter wearing the only shoes she brought with her from Dubai: sandals. During this time, she says "I didn't even know what a U.S. dollar looked like." Marjina found an advocate in one of her employers' friends, who located a Bangladeshi family in need of her services. But according to Marjina, things went from bad to worse. Her new employers forced her to work similar backbreaking hours, Marjina says, and promised to pay her a meager $400 per month, most of which she never received. . . . After three months, Marjina finally demanded payment, upon which she was locked in a basement, then ordered to leave with only $375 cash. . . . Subsequently, Marjina was put in contact with Andolan, a Queens-based South Asian workers' rights group. Last fall Marjina filed a lawsuit against her former employers, who deny all her allegations.

30. See also Bhattacharjee, "Habit of Ex-nomination"; and Samar Collective, "One Big, Happy Community?"

31. See Hochschild, "Love and Gold"; and Parreñas, "Care Crisis in the Philippines." See also Nilita Vachani's film *When Mother Comes Home for Christmas*, the story of Josephine, an illegal child-care worker from Sri Lanka in Greece, who after an absence of eight years, is able to go back home to her children for a month's visit.

32. Mahasweta Devi's story "The Breast-Giver," an excruciating tale of such "surplus extraction," tells of the ultimate betrayal of the wet nurse, Jashoda, who succumbs to breast cancer. Devi, *Breast Stories*.

33. As such, the terms of the arrangement approximated the "creation of a businesslike environment" that Romero advocates for the necessary transformation of paid domestic work in the United States, except, of course, that Kanchan lives with Ruchira and her family. Romero, *Maid in the U.S.A.*, 165–92. Kanchan's benefits are most unusual in New York, where even "progressive" employers of domestic workers balk at vacation leave or pay, not to mention medical and social security.

34. Domestic Workers United, *Home Is Where*, 17.

35. Cf. Pamela Toutant's chats with her housekeeper Maria from Nicaragua: "With each 'discussion' we had about my need to have her follow through on the things I asked her to do, she shared another sad piece of her life with me." Toutant, "Generations of Servitude."

36. Domestic Workers United, *Home Is Where*, 31.

37. Cf. Alice Childress's use of conversational vignettes between an African American domestic worker and her friend—or, rather, monologue, since the reader is privy to only the former's side of the conversation—to convey everyday resistance and revindication in New York's culture of servitude of the 1950s in her satirical collection *Like One of the Family*.

38. Bennetts, *Feminine Mistake*; and the article on it by Goldenberg, "No Surrender!"

39. Pogrebin, "Nanny Scam," 18.

40. Domestic Workers United, *Home Is Where*, 34.

41. Cf. Hondagneu-Sotelo, "Blowups." Also contrast the unrelieved earnestness of Pogrebin's account with Childress's send-up of employer fears about theft in "The Pocketbook Game," in which domestic worker Mildred tells her friend Marge about her employer's propensity to walk around the house with her handbag whenever Mildred was there. One day Mildred was asked to go out on an errand but rushed back to get her *own* pocketbook: "Later, when I was leavin' she says real timid-like, 'Mildred, I hope that you don't think I distrust you because . . .' I cut her off real quick. . . . 'That's all right, Mrs. E . . . , I understand. 'Cause if I paid anybody as little as you pay me, I'd hold my pocketbook too!'" Childress, *Like One of the Family*, 26–27.

42. See "Letters," *New York*, August 16, 2004, 5.

43. Clendinnen, "Disciplining the Indians," 27–48. In this brilliant study of Franciscan violence against Indians, Clendinnen demonstrates how in a culture of paternalism, the flip side of paternal kindness is rage, which may turn into violence when the parent or patron believes that loyalty has been betrayed by the child or dependent.

44. Sen, "Are You Being Served?" 41.

45. Fitzgerald Sherman, in *Cheaper Than a Divorce*, claims: "Hiring household help is not a luxury for the wealthy, but a time-management tool for busy people." These and similar exhortations to turn to servants to solve domestic gender disputes over time, work, child care, and housework unsurprisingly calculate the costs and benefits almost exclusively from the employer's standpoint, while eliding the condition of the prospective domestic worker as, in all likelihood, an immigrant woman of color or of the poor urban working class.

Chapter 8

1. Williams, *Marxism and Literature*, 132.

2. For an interesting discussion of the concepts of immaterial and affective labor, see Akalin, "Commodification of Intimacy," 9–11.

3. See epigraph to Chapter 1. We are mindful of the brilliant tradition of Marxist feminist theory and scholarship that has reversed this neglect.

4. In interviews with 138 men, "most (over three-fourths) of these households relied on paid or unpaid help from an additional caretaker. Involved fathers knew this help was essential for their own well-being, but they tended to view paid baby-sitters, housekeepers, and even relatives as substitutes for their wives (or, in some cases, ex-wives) and not for themselves. Since even the most involved fathers did not consider their responsibilities at work to be negotiable, the wife's decision to remain employed (or her absence from the home altogether) triggered the search for a 'substitute mother.'" Gerson, "A Few Good Men" 78–90.

5. Ehrenreich, "Maid to Order."

6. Tronto, "'Nanny' Question," 47, 35. Tronto's arguments are based on quite pos-

sibly flawed assertions about what she calls the "unintended consequences" of the feminist movement: greater numbers of women professionals leading to greater inequality between households and greater demand for child care.

7. Sonia Faleiro, a novelist, journalist, and blogger who has written about the issue of domestic work in India, maintains that there are some cruel employers and some decent ones, but, testifying to how employers take for granted the prevalence of domestic servitude and its inequalities, "between the two, are the majority of us, who though not unkind are disinterested, or patronizing, viewing domestic workers as a necessary evil." Faleiro, "Riddle of Domestic Work."

8. Tronto, "'Nanny' Question," 37. Consider also this comment:

The irony was that in some ways Jasmine became the closest person to him. As he became more and more disabled, we increasingly relied on her understanding of his needs. During his final hospitalization, she was able to offer a type of sympathy and reassurance that greatly surpassed our own. When a question arose about where our father should spend his last weeks, it became clear that Jasmine was more important than any of his children and that he had to remain where she could see him every day. We could reminisce and try to enact old roles, but she related to him on the basis of the life they shared together. (Abel and Nelson, "Intimate Care for Hire," 26–29)

9. Ehrenreich, "Maid to Order," 66.

10. Mrinalini recently expressed her contentment that her servant Arjun has married and brought a bride home, and soon there will be a child to bring joy to the house.

11. Meagher, "Is It Wrong?" 56.

12. See *Antipode* 38, no. 3 (June 2006), on cleaners, neoliberalism, and globalization.

13. Mendez, "Of Mops and Maids."

14. See, for example, Domestic Workers United, *Home Is Where*, for a catalog of domestic worker testimonies that would dispute this presupposition.

15. See Chapter 1, note 10.

16. Rubbo and Taussig, "Up off Their Knees," 5, 12.

17. Dill, "'Making Your Job Good Yourself.'" In this narration, the domestic worker was clearly rejecting the racialized infantilizing that accompanied the use of familial rhetoric.

18. Romero, *Maid in the U.S.A.*, 187–88.

19. Parreñas, *Servants of Globalization*.

20. Hondagneu-Sotelo, *Doméstica*.

21. Lan, *Global Cinderellas*, 76.

22. Wrigley, *Other People's Children*, passim.

23. On the opportunities and constraints for women's organization and mobilization in the political fields of Kolkata and Mumbai, see Ray, *Fields of Protest*.

24. Ally, "'Maid' with Rights." Interestingly, in New York, where Domestic Workers United is leading the fight for the New York State Domestic Workers' Bill of Rights (which would be the first in the nation), organizer Ai-Jen Poo states, "Collective bargaining is not possible. The power dynamics are different, if you try to negotiate, you're out." Buckley and Correal, "Domestic Workers Organize."

25. Senate S.B. No. 1141, introduced by Senator Aquilino Q. Pimentel Jr., recognizes the dignity and the nobility of the household helper industry. Under this proposed legislation, the rights and interests of household helper are enhanced and protected by ensuring just and equitable terms and conditions of their employment are embodied in their contract with their employers. This includes the payment of at least the minimum wage, 13th month pay, Social Security System (SSS) and Philippine Health Insurance Corporation (Philhealth) coverage, maternity and paternity benefits. Under this proposed law, employers are prohibited from sub-contracting the service of the household helper to any third party or household.

26. See, for example, Dhavse, "Organizing inside the Home," which highlights the activism of domestic workers in Pune; and Sharma, "Invisible Labour," about Mumbai. Domestic worker activism in India is at this point, as part of a larger campaign to eliminate child labor, largely focused on children who do this work.

27. For example, the collective in the San Francisco Bay Area analyzed by Leslie Salzinger, "A Maid by Any Other Name"; or the worker-run cooperative Unity Housekeepers in New York.

28. Letter from Parichiti to the chairperson of the Indian National Commission on Enterprises in the Unorganised Sector, June 30, 2005.

29. Rubbo and Taussig, "Up off Their Knees," 14.

Glossary

abhijat   richer class of bhadralok

adda   conversation and discussion; a particular form of Bengali sociability

adivasis   indigenous groups of India

ajalchal   belonging to lower-caste groups from whom upper-caste Hindus could not accept water

aksham   incapable

asabhya   uncivilized

atap   sun-dried rice

atmar shanti   literally, peace to the soul; to ease their conscience

ayah   nursemaid

babu   clerk or bureaucrat; originally a title like Mr. or Esq.; used by servants to refer to male employers

bagan bari   weekend country home

bandha   bound; dependent

baniya (also *banian*)   trading caste

barir kaaj   housework

basti   slum

bhadra   civilized and respectable

bhadralok   respectable middle and upper classes

bhadramahila   women of the bhadralok

bibi   westernized woman

bidi   indigenous, hand-rolled cigarette

chakor   servant

chakure meye   working women

chhuta   free; independent

chowkidar   watchman and doorman

churi   bangle

dalit   literally, broken; signifies members of scheduled (lower) castes who suffer social exclusion, discrimination, and oppression

dhobi   washerman; laundryman

didi   "older sister" in Bengali and a term of respect used by younger relatives, close friends, and servants

durbal   weak

durwan   gatekeeper

ghenna   disgust

grihadharm   domestic ideology involving women's duty to the household

grihasthya   poorer class of bhadralok

jajmani   model in which particular castes exchange labor and services for agricultural produce and protection from other castes in a village

jalchal   belonging to lower castes from whom upper castes can accept water

jamadar   servant who primarily cleans bathrooms

jhi   maid

jhuta (Hindi)/*ato* (Bengali)   polluted; dirty

kacha (Bengali)/*kuchha* (Hindi)   literally, raw, uncooked; refers to houses made of mud and thatch

kajer lok   person who works; domestic worker

kanji   rice water

karta   head of a household

koshto   to suffer

lajja   shame and modesty

madur   sleeping mat

mora   stool

mukhagni   igniting the body (part of a funeral rite); the privilege and right of the eldest son in Hindu tradition

munsiff   lower-level judge

murkha   stupid; uneducated

panchayat   village council

paradhin   literally, unfree; dependent

paradhinata   unfreedom; lack of freedom

pranam   a ritual gesture of respect to elders that involves touching their feet

puja   prayer; "the pujas" refer to the main Bengali Hindu festival of the goddess Durga

pukka   literally, cooked, solid; refers to houses constructed of brick or other durable material

raat/din   literally, night/day; refers to live-in servants

ro'akey adda   a space for male sociability; originally a platform (*ro'ak*) constructed in the courtyard of a residence, later located outside the home facing the street, where men congregate and converse (*adda*)

sansar   dual meaning: the home and the world

shaukhin   to have desires/fancies

shraddha   Hindu ritual for the dead

sindoor   vermillion on the hair parting that is the sign of Bengali Hindu marriage

sonar patharbati   refers to an impossibility: a stoneware bowl made of gold

stri-swadhinata   independence of women

swadhin   independent

thela   cart

thika   tenancy system in which tenants rented plots from large landowners and built huts on them to sublet to workers and migrants

tiffin   a snack or light meal carried to work or school

zamindar (*zamindari*, adj.)   landholder or landlord during colonial rule

Bibliography

Abel, Emily K., and Margaret K. Nelson. "Intimate Care for Hire." *The American Prospect* 12, no. 9 (May 21, 2001): 26–29.

Ahmad, Aijaz. "The Communist Manifesto and 'World Literature.'" *Social Scientist* 28 (July–August 2000): 3–30.

———. "The Politics of Culture." *Social Scientist* 27 (September–October 1999): 65–69.

Akalin, Ayse. "Commodification of Intimacy: Care for the Elderly in the Migrant Domestic Workers Sector in Turkey." Paper presented at the Waged Domestic Work in the Modern World Conference, University of Warwick, U.K., May 9–11, 2008.

Ally, Shireen. "'Maid' with Rights: The Contradictory Citizenship of Domestic Workers in Post-apartheid South Africa." Ph.D. diss., University of Wisconsin–Madison, 2006.

Anderson, Bridget. *Doing the Dirty Work? The Global Politics of Domestic Labour.* London: Zed Books, 2000.

———. "Doing the Dirty Work? The Global Politics of Domestic Labour." In *Global Dimensions of Gender and Carework,* edited by Mary K. Zimmerman, Jacquelyn S. Litt, and Christine E. Bose, 226–40. Stanford, Calif.: Stanford University Press, 2006.

Auerbach, Jessika. *And Nanny Makes Three: Mothers and Nannies Tell the Truth about Work, Love, Money, and Each Other.* New York: St. Martin's Press, 2007.

Bakhtin, Mikhail. *The Dialogic Imagination: Four Essays.* Edited by Michael Holquist. Austin: University of Texas Press, 1981.

Bandopadhyay, Bibhuti Bhushan. *Aparajito.* 1931.

Bandopadhyay, Chandicharan. *Ma o Chele* [Mother and Son]. Calcutta, 1887.

Bandopadhyay, Sekhar. *From Plassey to Partition.* Delhi: Orient Longman, 2004.

Banerjee, Himani. "Attired in Virtue: The Discourse on Shame (*lajja*) and Clothing of the Bhadramahila in Colonial Bengal." In *From the Seams of History*, edited by Bharati Ray, 67–106. Delhi: Oxford University Press, 1995.

Banerjee, Nirmala. "Modernisation and Marginalisation." *Social Scientist* 13 (October–November 1985): 48–71.

———. *Women Workers in the Unorganized Sector: The Calcutta Experience*. Hyderabad: Sangam Books; distributed in India by Orient Longman, 1985.

Banerjee, Sumanta. *The Parlour and the Streets: Elite and Popular Culture in Nineteenth Century Calcutta*. Calcutta: Seagull Books, 1989.

Banerjee, Swapna. "Down Memory Lane: Representations of Domestic Workers in Middle Class Personal Narratives of Colonial Bengal." *Journal of Social History* 37, no. 3 (2004): 681–708.

———. *Men, Women and Domestics: Articulating Middle Class Identity in Colonial Bengal*. New York: Oxford University Press, 2004.

Bardhan, Pranab. "Dasdasi o amra [Servants and Ourselves]." *Desh*, June 7, 1986, 15–18.

Bardhan, Pranab, and Dilip Mookherjee. "Political Economy of Land Reforms in West Bengal 1978–98." Institute of International Studies, University of California, Berkeley, May 2005. http://globetrotter.berkeley.edu/macarthur/inequality/papers/BardhanPoliticalEconofLandReformsWB.pdf.

Barrett, Michèle. *Women's Oppression Today: Problems in Marxist Feminist Analysis*. London: Verso, 1980.

Barrett, Michèle, and Mary McIntosh. *The Anti-social Family*. London: Verso, 1982.

Basu, Bani. "Chakure Meyer Sonar Patharbati [Working Women Stoneware Bowl Made of Gold]." *Sukhi Grihakon*, November 2001.

Basu, Ishan Chandra. *Nari Niti* [Principles for a Woman]. Calcutta: Gurudas Chattopadhyay, 1884.

———. *Sridiger Prati Upadesh* [Advice to Women]. Calcutta: Victoria Press, 1884.

Baviskar, Amita. "The Politics of the City." *Seminar* 516 (August 2002): 40–42.

Bayly, Susan. *Caste, Society and Politics in India from the Eighteenth Century to the Modern Age*. The New Cambridge History of India. Cambridge: Cambridge University Press, 1999.

Beecher, Catharine E., and Harriet Beecher Stowe. *The American Woman's Home*. Edited and with an introduction by Nicole Tonkovich. Piscataway, N.J.: Rutgers University Press, 2002. (Orig. pub. 1869.)

Beeton, Isabella. *Mrs Beeton's Book of Household Management*. Edited with an introduction and notes by Nicola Humble. New York: Oxford University Press, 2000. (Orig. pub. c. 1860.)

Bennetts, Leslie. *The Feminine Mistake: Are We Giving Up Too Much?* New York: Voice/Hyperion, 2007.

Berman, Marshall. *All That Is Solid Melts into Air*. New York: Penguin, 1988.

Bhattacharjee, Anannya. "The Habit of Ex-nomination: Nation, Woman, and the Indian Immigrant Bourgeoisie." *Public Culture* 5, no. 1 (1992): 19–44.

Bhattacharya, Tithi. "In the Name of Culture." *South Asia Research* 21, no. 1 (2000): 161–87.

———. *The Sentinels of Culture: Class, Education and the Colonial Intellectual in Bengal.* Delhi: Oxford University Press, 2005.

Birkett, Dea. "Why Nanny Is No Longer a Dirty Word." *Guardian*, April 16, 2006.

Blair-Loy, Mary. *Competing Devotions: Career and Family among Women Executives.* Cambridge, Mass.: Harvard University Press, 2003.

Borthwick, Meredith. *The Changing Role of Women in Bengal, 1849–1905.* Princeton: Princeton University Press, 1984.

Bourdieu, Pierre. *Distinction: A Social Critique of the Judgment of Taste.* Translated by Richard Nice. Cambridge, Mass.: Harvard University Press, 1984.

———. *Outline of a Theory of Practice.* Cambridge: Cambridge University Press, 1977.

Broomfield, J. H. *Elite Conflict in a Plural Society: Twentieth Century Bengal.* Berkeley: University of California Press, 1968.

Buckley, Cara, and Annie Correal. "Domestic Workers Organize to End an 'Atmosphere of Violence' on the Job." *New York Times*, June 6, 2008.

Bujra, Janet. "Men at Work in the Tanzanian Home: How Did They Ever Learn?" In *African Encounters with Domesticity*, edited by Karen Hansen, 242–65. New Brunswick, N.J.: Rutgers University Press, 1992.

Carlton, Susan, and Coco Meyer. *The Nanny Book: The Smart Parent's Guide to Hiring, Firing, and Every Sticky Situation In Between.* New York: St. Martin's Griffin, 1999.

Catholic Bishops' Conference of India. *A National Socio-economic Survey of Domestic Workers.* Madras: Catholic Bishops' Conference of India Commission for Labour, 1980.

Chakrabarty, Dipesh. "The Difference-Deferral of a Colonial Modernity: Public Debates on Domesticity in British India." *Subaltern Studies* 8 (1994): 50–88.

———. *Provincializing Europe: Postcolonial Thought and Historical Difference.* Princeton: Princeton University Press, 2000.

Chakraborty, Satyesh C. "The Growth of Calcutta in the Twentieth Century." In *Calcutta: The Living City, Volume II: The Present and Future*, edited by Sukanta Chaudhuri, 1–14. New Delhi: Oxford University Press, 1990.

Chakravorty, Sanjoy. "From Colonial City to Global City?: The Far-from-Complete Spatial Transformation of Calcutta." In *Globalizing Cities: A New Spatial Order?* edited by Peter Marcuse and Ronald van Kempen, 56–77. Oxford: Blackwell, 2000.

Chandra, Vikram. *Love and Longing in Bombay.* Boston: Little, Brown, 1997.

Chaney, Elsa, and Mary Garcia Castro. *Muchachas No More: Household Workers in Latin America and the Caribbean.* Philadelphia: Temple University Press, 1989.

Chang, Grace. *Disposable Domestics: Immigrant Women Workers in the Global Economy.* Cambridge, Mass.: South End Press, 2000.

Chatterjee, Indrani. *Gender, Slavery and Law in Colonial India.* New York: Oxford University Press, 1999.

——, ed. *Unfamiliar Relations: Family and History in South Asia.* New Brunswick, N.J.: Rutgers University Press, 2004.

Chatterjee, Indrani, and Richard Eaton, eds. *Slavery and South Asian History.* Bloomington: Indiana University Press, 2006.

Chatterjee, Monidip. "Town Planning in Calcutta: Past, Present and Future." In *Calcutta: The Living City, Volume II: The Present and Future,* edited by Sukanta Chaudhuri, 133–47. New Delhi: Oxford University Press, 1990.

Chatterjee, Nilanjana. "Midnight's Unwanted Children: East Bengali Refugees and the Politics of Rehabilitation." Ph.D. diss., Brown University, 1992.

Chatterjee, Partha. *The Nation and Its Fragments: Colonial and Postcolonial Histories.* Princeton: Princeton University Press, 1993.

——. "The Nationalist Resolution of the Woman Question." In *Recasting Women: Essays in Indian Colonial History,* edited by Kumkum Sangari and Sudesh Vaid, 233–53. New Brunswick, N.J.: Rutgers University Press, 1990.

Chatterjee, Ratnabali. "Prostitution in Nineteenth Century Bengal: Construction of Class and Gender." *Social Scientist* 21, nos. 9–11 (1993): 159–72.

Chattopadhyay, Swati. "Blurring Boundaries: The Limits of 'White Town' in Colonial Calcutta." *Journal of the Society of Architectural Historians* 59, no. 2 (June 2000): 154–79.

——. *Representing Calcutta: Modernity, Nationalism, and the Colonial Uncanny.* London: Routledge, 2006.

Chaudhuri, Pranati. "Refugees in West Bengal: A Study of the Growth and Distribution of Refugee Settlements within the CMD." Occasional Paper 55. Calcutta: Centre for Studies in Social Sciences, Calcutta (CSSSC), 1983.

Chaudhuri, Sukanta. "Traffic and Transport in Calcutta." In *Calcutta: The Living City, Volume II: The Present and Future,* edited by Sukanta Chaudhuri, 148–59. New Delhi: Oxford University Press, 1990.

Cheng, Shu-Ada. *Serving the Household and the Nation: Filipina Domestics and the Politics of Identity in Taiwan.* Lanham, Md.: Lexington Books, 2006.

Childress, Alice. *Like One of the Family: Conversations from a Domestic's Life.* New York: Independence Publishers, 1956.

Chin, Christine. *In Service and Servitude: Foreign Female Domestic Workers and the Malaysian "Modernity" Project.* New York: Columbia University Press, 1998.

Clendinnen, Inga. "Disciplining the Indians: Franciscan Ideology and Missionary Violence in Sixteenth-Century Yucatán." *Past and Present* 94 (February 1982): 27–48.

Cock, Jacklyn. *Maids and Madams: A Study of the Politics of Exploitation.* Johannesburg: Ravan Press, 1980.

Colen, Shellee. "'Just a Little Respect': West Indian Domestic Workers in New York City." In *Muchachas No More: Household Workers in Latin America and the Carib-*

bean, edited by Elsa Chaney and Mary Garcia Castro, 171–94. Philadelphia: Temple University Press, 1989.

Comaroff, John, and Jean Comaroff. *Ethnography and the Historical Imagination*. Boulder, Colo.: Westview Press, 1992.

Constable, Nicole. *Maid to Order in Hong Kong: Stories of Filipina Workers*. Ithaca, N.Y.: Cornell University Press, 1997.

Coser, Lewis A. "Servants: The Obsolescence of an Occupational Role." *Social Forces* 52, no. 1 (1973): 31–40.

Dasgupta, Keya. "Evictions in Calcutta: Creating the Spaces of 'Modernity.'" *City* 4 (Karachi) (September 2003): 31–43.

Davidoff, Leonore. *Worlds Between: Historical Perspectives on Gender and Class*. New York: Routledge, 1995.

Davin, Delia. "Domestic Service in Contemporary China and the Spread of New Lifestyles to the Rural Areas." In *Gender and the Political Economy of Domestic Service: Comparative Perspectives from India and China*, edited by Patricia Uberoi and Sreemati Chakrabarti. Occasional Studies No. 2. New Delhi: Institute of Chinese Studies, 2004.

De Certeau, Michel. *The Practice of Everyday Life*. Berkeley: University of California Press, 1988.

De Haan, Arjaan. "Unsettled Settlers: Migrant Workers and Industrial Capital in Calcutta." *Modern Asian Studies* 31, no. 4 (1997): 919–49.

Deb, Arkaprabha. "The Rich Have Markets, the Poor Have Bureaucrats." *The Statesman* (Kolkata), October 9, 2006.

Deb, Gautam. "Basic Instinct." *The Times of India* (Kolkata), January 18, 2006.

Deere, Carmen Diana. *Household and Class Relations: Peasants and Landlords in Northern Peru*. Berkeley: University of California Press, 1990.

Deshpande, Satish. *Contemporary India: A Sociological View*. New Delhi: Penguin Books, 2003.

Devi, Mahasweta. *Breast Stories*. Calcutta: Seagull Books, 1997.

Dhavse, Rasika. "Organising inside the Home." April 2004. http://www.indiatogether .org/2004/apr/eco-domestic.htm.

Di Leonardo, Micaela. "Introduction. Gender, Culture and Political Economy: Feminist Anthropology in Historical Perspective." In *Gender at the Crossroads of Knowledge: Feminist Anthropology in the Postmodern Era*, edited by Micaela di Leonardo, 1–50. Berkeley: University of California Press, 1991.

Dickey, Sara. "Mutual Exclusions: Domestic Workers and Employers on Labor, Class and Character in South India." In *Home and Hegemony: Domestic Service and Identity Politics in South and Southeast Asia*, edited by Kathleen Adams and Sara Dickey, 31–62. Ann Arbor: University of Michigan Press, 2000.

———. "Permeable Homes: Domestic Service, Household Space, and the Vulnerability of Class Boundaries in Urban India." *American Ethnologist* 27, no. 2 (2000): 462–89.

Dickey, Sara, and Kathleen M. Adams. "Introduction: Negotiating Homes, Hegemonies, Identities, and Politics." In *Home and Hegemony: Domestic Service and Identity Politics in South and Southeast Asia*, edited by Kathleen Adams and Sara Dickey, 5–29. Ann Arbor: University of Michigan Press, 2000.

Dill, Bonnie Thornton. "'Making Your Job Good Yourself': Domestic Service and the Construction of Personal Dignity." In *Women and the Politics of Empowerment*, edited by Ann Bookman and Sandra Morgen, 33–52. Philadelphia: Temple University Press, 1988.

"Domestic Workers Go on Strike in Mumbai." *The Times of India*, January 9, 2006.

Domestic Workers United. *Home Is Where the Work Is: Inside New York's Domestic Work Industry*. Domestic Workers United and DataCenter, July 2006. http://www .datacenter.org/reports/homeiswheretheworkis.pdf.

Douglas, Mary. *Purity and Danger: An Analysis of the Concepts of Pollution and Taboo*. London: Routledge & Kegan Paul, 1966.

Dudden, Faye. *Serving Women: Household Service in Nineteenth Century America*. Middletown, Conn.: Wesleyan University Press, 1983.

Echeverri-Gent, John. "Popular Participation and Poverty Alleviation: The Experience of Reform Communists in India's West Bengal." *World Development* 20, no. 10 (October 1992): 1401–22.

Ehrenreich, Barbara. "Maid to Order: The Politics of Other Women's Work." *Harper's Magazine*, April 2000, 59–70.

Ehrenreich, Barbara, and Arlie Hochschild, eds. *Global Woman: Nannies, Maids, and Sex Workers in the New Economy*. New York: Henry Holt, 2002.

Eisenstadt, S. N. "Multiple Modernities." *Daedalus* 129, no. 1 (Winter 2000): 1–29.

Fairchilds, Cissie. *Domestic Enemies: Servants and Their Masters in Old Regime France*. Baltimore: Johns Hopkins University Press, 1983.

Faleiro, Sonia. "The Riddle of Domestic Work in India." September 22, 2006. http:// soniafaleiro.blogspot.com/2006/09/riddle-of-domestic-work-in-india.html.

Fanon, Frantz. *Black Skin, White Masks*. Translated by Constance Farrington. New York: Grove Press, 1967.

Feiner, Susan F., and Drucilla K. Barker. "Microcredit and Women's Poverty." *Dollars and Sense* 268 (November–December 2006): 10–11.

Fellowes, Julian. *Gosford Park: The Shooting Script*. New York: Newmarket Press, 2002.

Fernandes, Leela. *India's New Middle Class: Democratic Politics in an Era of Reform*. Minneapolis: University of Minnesota Press, 2006.

———. *Producing Workers: The Politics of Gender, Class and Culture in the Calcutta Jute Mills*. Philadelphia: University of Pennsylvania Press, 1997.

———. "Restructuring the New Middle Class in Liberalizing India." *Comparative Studies of South Asia, Africa and the Middle East* 20, nos. 1–2 (2000): 88–112.

Fernandes, Leela, and Patrick Heller. "Hegemonic Aspirations: New Middle Class Politics and India's Democracy in Comparative Perspective." *Critical Asian Studies* 38, no. 4 (2006): 495–522.

Fitzgerald Sherman, Kathy. *A Housekeeper Is Cheaper Than a Divorce: Why You Can Afford to Hire Help and How to Get It*. Mountain View, Calif.: Life Tools Press, 2000.

Flanagan, Caitlin. "How Serfdom Saved the Women's Movement: Dispatches from the Nanny Wars." *Atlantic Monthly*, March 2004.

Frøystad, Kathinka. "Master-Servant Relations and the Domestic Reproduction of Caste in Northern India." *Ethnos* 68, no. 1 (2003): 73–94.

Gangopadhyay, Sunil. *Those Days*. Delhi: Penguin, 1997.

Gerson, Kathleen. "A Few Good Men." *The American Prospect* 5, no. 16 (December 1994): 78–90.

Ghosh, Ambikaprasad. "Demography of Calcutta." In *Calcutta: The Living City, Volume II: The Present and Future*, edited by Sukanta Chaudhuri, 50–61. New Delhi: Oxford University Press, 1990.

Ghosh, Murari, Alok K. Dutta, and Biswanath Ray. *Calcutta: A Study in Urban Growth Dynamics*. Calcutta: Firma K. L. Mukhopadhyay, 1972.

Gill, Lesley. *Precarious Dependencies: Gender, Class and Domestic Service in Bolivia*. New York: Columbia University Press, 1994.

Glenn, Evelyn Nakano. *Issei, Nisei, War Bride: Three Generations of Japanese American Women in Domestic Service*. Philadelphia: Temple University Press, 1986.

Goldenberg, Suzanne. "No Surrender!" *The Guardian*, April 10, 2007.

Gordon, Constance E. *Anglo-Indian Cuisine (Khana Kitab) and Domestic Economy*. Calcutta: Thacker, Spink, 1913.

Government of India. *Census of India 1951*. New Delhi: Manager of Publications.

———. *Census of India 1971*. New Delhi: Controller of Publications.

———. *Census of India 1981*. New Delhi: Controller of Publications.

———. *Census of India 1991*. New Delhi: Controller of Publications.

———. *Census of India 2001*. New Delhi: Controller of Publications.

Gregson, Nicky, and Michelle Lowe. *Servicing the Middle Classes: Class, Gender and Waged Domestic Labour in Contemporary Britain*. London: Routledge, 1994.

Guha, Ranajit. *A Rule of Property for Bengal: An Essay on the Idea of Permanent Settlement*. Durham, N.C.: Duke University Press, 1996.

Haldar, Baby. *A Life Less Ordinary*. Delhi: Zubaan/Penguin, 2006.

Hall, Stuart. "Gramsci's Relevance for the Study of Race and Ethnicity." In *Stuart Hall: Critical Dialogues in Cultural Studies*, edited by David Morley and Kuan-Hsing Chen, 411–41. London: Routledge, 1996.

Hancock, Mary. "Home Science and the Nationalization of Domesticity in Colonial India." *Modern Asian Studies* 35, no. 4 (2001): 871–903.

Hansen, Karen Tranberg, ed. *African Encounters with Domesticity*. New Brunswick, N.J.: Rutgers University Press, 1992.

————. *Distant Companions: Servants and Employers in Zambia, 1900–1985*. Ithaca, N.Y.: Cornell University Press, 1989.

————. "Domestic Trials: Power and Autonomy in Domestic Service in Zambia." *American Ethnologist* 17, no. 2 (1990): 260–375.

Harris, Olivia. "Households as Natural Units." In *Of Marriage and the Market: Women's Subordination Internationally and Its Lessons*, 2d ed., edited by Kate Young, Carol Wolkowitz, and Roslyn McCullagh, 49–68. London: Routledge & Kegan Paul, 1984.

Harriss, John. "Middle-Class Activism and the Politics of the Informal Working Class: A Perspective on Class Relations and Civil Society in Indian Cities." *Critical Asian Studies* 38, no. 4 (December 2006): 445–66.

————. "Political Participation, Representation and the Urban Poor: Findings from Research in Delhi." *Economic and Political Weekly* 40, no. 11 (2006): 1041–54.

Hartmann, Heidi, and Donald J. Treiman. *Women, Work, and Wages: Equal Pay for Jobs of Equal Value*. Washington, D.C.: National Academy Press, 1981.

Harvey, David. *The Condition of Postmodernity*. Oxford: Blackwell, 1990.

Hegel, G. W. F. *Phenomenology of Spirit*. Translated by A.V. Miller. Oxford: Oxford University Press, 1977.

Herod, Andrew, and Luis L. M. Aguiar. "Introduction: Cleaners and the Dirty Work of Neoliberalism." *Antipode* 38, no. 3 (August 2006): 425–34.

Hobsbawm, Eric. *The Age of Capital*. New York: Vintage Books, 1996.

Hochschild, Arlie Russell. "Love and Gold." In *Global Woman: Nannies, Maids, and Sex Workers in the New Economy*, edited by Barbara Ehrenreich and Arlie Hochschild, 15–31. New York: Henry Holt, 2002.

————. *The Managed Heart: Commercialization of Human Feeling*. Berkeley: University of California Press, 1985.

Hochschild, Arlie, and Anne Machung. *The Second Shift: Working Parents and the Revolution at Home*. New York: Viking, 1989.

Hondagneu-Sotelo, Pierrette. "Blowups and Other Unhappy Endings." In *Global Woman: Nannies, Maids, and Sex Workers in the New Economy*, edited by Barbara Ehrenreich and Arlie Hochschild, 59–69. New York: Henry Holt, 2002.

————. *Doméstica: Immigrant Workers Cleaning and Caring in the Shadows of Affluence*. Berkeley: University of California Press, 2001.

hooks, bell. *Feminist Theory from Margin to Center*. Boston: South End Press, 1984.

Human Rights Watch. *Hidden in the Home: Abuse of Domestic Workers with Special Visas in the United States*. New York: Human Rights Watch, 2001.

Indian Social Institute. *The Tribal Domestic Worker at the Crossroads: A Search for Alternatives*. New Delhi: Indian Social Institute Programme for Women's Development, 1993.

"Insure at Your Own Risk." *The Telegraph* (Kolkata), May 12, 2005.

Jain, Nishtha. *Lakshmi and Me.* DVD. 59 min. Mumbai: Raintree Films, 2008.

John, Mary. "Gender, Development and the Women's Movement." In *Signposts: Gender Issues in Post-independence India,* edited by Rajeswari Sunder Rajan, 101–23. Delhi: Kali for Women, 1999.

John, Mary, and Janaki Nair, eds. *A Question of Silence? The Sexual Economies of Modern India.* New Delhi: Kali for Women, 1998.

Kabeer, Naila. *Reversed Realities: Gender Hierarchies in Development Thought.* London: Verso, 1994.

Katzman, David. *Seven Days a Week: Women and Domestic Service in Industrializing America.* Chicago: University of Illinois Press, 1981.

Kaviraj, Sudipta. "Modernity and Politics in India." *Daedalus* 129, no. 1 (Winter 2000): 137–62.

Kaylin, Lucy. *The Perfect Stranger: The Truth about Mothers and Nannies.* London: Bloomsbury, 2007.

Kelley, Robin D. G. "Introduction." In *Home Is Where the Work Is: Inside New York's Domestic Work Industry.* Domestic Workers United and DataCenter, July 2006. http://www.datacenter.org/reports/homeiswheretheworkis.pdf.

Kojève, Alexandre. *Introduction to the Reading of Hegel: Lectures on the Phenomenology of Spirit.* Ithaca, N.Y.: Cornell University Press, 1969.

Kumar, Nita. "The Scholar and Her Servants: Further Thoughts on Postcolonialism and Education." *India Review* 5, no. 3 (2006): 519–50.

Kumar, Radha. *History of Doing: An Illustrated Account of Movements for Women's Rights and Feminism in India, 1800–1990.* London: Verso, 1993.

Kundu, Amit. "Conditions of Work and Rights of the Female Domestic Workers of Kolkata." *Indian Journal of Labour Economics* 4, no. 50 (2007): 853–66.

Kundu, Nitai. "The Case of Kolkata, India." In *Understanding Slums: Case Studies for the Global Report 2003.* UN–Habitat and Development Planning Institute, University College London. www.ucl.ac.uk/dpu-projects/Global_Report/pdfs/Kolkata_bw.pdf.

Lamont, Michele. *The Dignity of Working Men: Morality and the Boundaries of Race, Class and Immigration.* Cambridge, Mass.: Harvard University Press, 2000.

Lan, Pei-Chan. *Global Cinderellas: Migrant Domestics and Newly Rich Employers in Taiwan.* Durham, N.C.: Duke University Press, 2006.

Laslett, Peter. *The World We Have Lost: Further Explored.* London: Methuen, 1983.

Laslett, Peter, and Richard Wall, eds. *Household and Family in Past Time.* Cambridge: Cambridge University Press, 1972.

Lee, Chisun. "Women Raise the City-Domestic Disturbances: The Help Set Out to Help Themselves." *The Village Voice,* March 12–19, 2002.

Lefebvre, Henri. *The Production of Space.* Translated by Donald Nicholson-Smith. Oxford: Blackwell, 1991.

"Letters." *New York Magazine,* August 16, 2004, 5.

Lintelman, Joy K. "Our Serving Sisters: Swedish American Domestics and Their Ethnic Community." *Social Science History* 15, no. 13 (1991): 381–95.

Lutz, Helma. "At Your Service Madam! The Globalization of Domestic Service." *Feminist Review* 70 (2002): 89–104.

Majumdar, Janaki. "Family History." *Journal of Asian Studies* 56, no. 4 (1997): 921–46.

Majumdar, Pratap Chandra. *Stri Charitra* [Women's Character]. Calcutta: 1898.

Mallick, Ross. *Development Policy of a Communist Government: West Bengal since 1977.* Cambridge: Cambridge University Press, 1993.

Marchand, Marianne, and Jane Parpart, eds. *Feminism/Postmodernism/Development.* New York: Routledge, 1995.

Marcuse, Herbert. *One Dimensional Man.* Boston: Beacon Press, 1991.

Martin, David William. *The Changing Face of Calcutta.* New Delhi: Wikas Publishing House, 1997.

Marx, Karl. *Capital: A Critique of Political Economy.* New York: Vintage, 1977.

Massey, Doreen. *Space, Place, and Gender.* Minneapolis: University of Minnesota Press, 1994.

Mauss, Marcel. *The Gift: The Form and Reason for Exchange in Archaic Societies,* translated by W. D. Halls. New York: W. W. Norton, 1990 [1950].

Mazzarella, William. "Middle Class." In *South Asian Keywords,* edited by Rachel Dwyer. London: University of London, Center of South Asian Studies, 2005. http://www.soas.ac.uk/southasianstudies/keywords/keywords-in-south-asian-studies.html.

McLaughlin, Emma, and Nicola Kraus. *The Nanny Diaries: A Novel.* New York: St. Martin's Press, 2002.

Meagher, Gabrielle. "Is It Wrong to Pay for Housework?" *Hypatia* 17, no. 2 (2002): 52–66.

Mehta, Aban. *The Domestic Servant Class.* Bombay: Popular Book Depot, 1960.

Mendez, Jennifer. "Of Mops and Maids: Contradictions and Continuities in Bureaucratized Domestic Work." *Social Problems* 45, no. 1 (1998): 114–35.

Middlekauff, Tracey. "Maid in America." *Gotham Gazette Magazine* [issue on Immigrant New York], Fall 2002. http://www.gothamgazette.com/commentary/46.middlekauff.shtml.

Milkman, Ruth, Ellen Reese, and Benita Roth. "The Macrosociology of Paid Domestic Labor." *Work and Occupations* 25, no. 4 (November 1998): 483–510.

Mitra, Jay Krishna. *Ramanir Kartavya* [Duties of a Woman]. Calcutta: Giribala Mitra, 1890.

Mitra, Pyari Chand. "Grihakatha, Strishiksha—Gyanakari Bidya" [On the Home, Women's Education—Knowledge]. In *Narir Katha* [On Women], edited by Anisuzzaman and Maleka Begum. Dhaka: Dhaka University Press, 1994.

Mitra, Satyacharan. *Strir Prati Swamir Upadesh* [Advice of a Husband to His Wife]. Calcutta: Victoria Printing Works, 1884.

Moser, Carolyn. "Gender Planning in the Third World: Meeting Practical and Strategic

Gender Needs." *World Development* 17, no. 11 (1989): 1799–1825.

Mukerjee, Samir. "Vignettes of a Vintage Town." *The Telegraph* (Kolkata), December 7, 2001.

Mukherjee, S. N. *Calcutta: Myths and History.* Calcutta: Subarnarekha, 1977.

Mukhopadhyay, Bhudev. "Paribarik Prasanga [Family Matters]." In *Bhudev Rachana Sambhar* [Collected Works of Bhudev], edited by Pramatha Nath Bishi. Calcutta: Mitra & Ghosh, 1962.

New York State AFL-CIO. Legislative Alert. January 26, 2004.

Nilsson, Sten. *European Architecture in India 1750–1850.* London: Faber & Faber, 1969.

Ozyegin, Gul. *Untidy Gender: Domestic Service in Turkey.* Philadelphia: Temple University Press, 2001.

Palmer, Phyllis. *Domesticity and Dirt: Housewives and Domestic Servants in the United States, 1920–1945.* Philadelphia: Temple University Press, 1989.

Parreñas, Rhacel. "The Care Crisis in the Philippines: Children and Transnational Families in the New Global Economy." In *Global Woman: Nannies, Maids, and Sex Workers in the New Economy,* edited by Barbara Ehrenreich and Arlie Hochschild, 39–55. New York: Henry Holt, 2002.

———. *Servants of Globalization: Women, Migration and Domestic Work.* Stanford, Calif.: Stanford University Press, 2001.

Patterson, Orlando. *Slavery and Social Death.* Cambridge, Mass.: Harvard University Press, 1992.

Pogrebin, Abigail. "Nanny Scam." *New York Magazine,* July 26–August 2, 2004.

Population Division of the Department of Economic and Social Affairs of the United Nations Secretariat. *World Population Prospects: The 2004 Revision.* New York: United Nations, 2005.

———. *World Urbanization Prospects: The 2005 Revision.* New York: United Nations, 2006.

Price, Pamela. *Kingship and Political Practice in Colonial India.* Cambridge: Cambridge University Press, 1996.

Qayum, Seemin, and Raka Ray. "Grappling with Modernity: India's Respectable Classes and the Culture of Domestic Servitude." *Ethnography* 4, no. 4 (December 2003): 520–55.

Rafkin, Louise. *Other People's Dirt: A Housecleaner's Curious Adventures.* Chapel Hill, N.C.: Algonquin Books, 1998.

Raghuram, Parvati. "Caste and Gender in the Organization of Paid Domestic Work in India." *Work, Employment, and Society* 15, no. 3 (2001): 607–17.

Ramaswamy, V., and M. Chakravarti. "Falahak, Inshallah [Flowering-God's Will]: The Struggle of the Labouring Poor, and a Vision, Strategy and Programme for Tenant-Led Basti and City Renewal." *Environment and Urbanisation* 9, no. 2 (1997): 63–80.

Ray, Bharati, ed. *Nari o Paribar, Bamabodhini Patrika* [Women and the Family]. Calcutta: Ananda Publishers, 2002.

———. *Sekaler Narishiksha, Bamabodhini Patrika* [Women's Education in the Past]. Calcutta: University of Calcutta Press, 1994.

Ray, Nishith Ranjan. *Calcutta: Profile of a City.* Calcutta: K. P. Bagchi, 1986.

Ray, Rajat Kanta. *Social Conflict and Political Unrest in Bengal, 1875–1927.* Delhi: Oxford University Press, 1984.

Ray, Raka. *Fields of Protest: Women's Movements in India.* Minneapolis: University of Minnesota Press, 1999.

———. "Masculinity, Femininity, and Servitude: Domestic Workers in Calcutta in the Late Twentieth Century." *Feminist Studies* 26, no. 3 (Fall 2000): 691–718.

Ray, Satyajit. *The Apu Trilogy.* Calcutta: Seagull Books, 1985.

Robbins, Bruce. *The Servant's Hand: English Fiction from Below.* Durham, N.C.: Duke University Press, 1993.

Rofel, Lisa. *Other Modernities: Gendered Yearnings in China after Socialism.* Berkeley: University of California Press, 1999.

Rollins, Judith. *Between Women: Domestics and Their Employers.* Philadelphia: Temple University Press, 1985.

Romero, Mary. *Maid in the U.S.A.* 10th anniversary ed. New York: Routledge, 2002.

Rosaldo, Michelle Zimbalist, and Louise Lamphere, eds. *Women, Culture, and Society.* Stanford, Calif.: Stanford University Press, 1974.

Roy, Ananya. *City Requiem, Calcutta: Gender and the Politics of Poverty.* Minneapolis: University of Minnesota Press, 2003.

Roy Chowdhury, Girija Prasanna. *Grihalakshmi* [The Lakshmi of the Home]. Calcutta: Gurudas Chatterjee, 1887.

Rubbo, Anna, and Michael Taussig. "Up off Their Knees: Servanthood in Southwest Colombia." *Latin American Perspectives* 10, no. 4 (Autumn 1983): 5–23.

Rubin, Gayle. "The Traffic in Women: Notes on the Political Economy of Sex." In *Toward an Anthropology of Women,* edited by Rayna Reiter, 157–210. New York: Monthly Review Press, 1975.

Salzinger, Leslie. "A Maid by Any Other Name: The Transformation of 'Dirty Work' by Central American Immigrants." In *Ethnography Unbound,* edited by Michael Burawoy et al., 139–60. Berkeley: University of California Press, 1991.

Samar Collective. "One Big, Happy Community? Class Issues within South Asian Homes." *Samar* 4 (Winter 1994): 10–15.

✗ Sangari, Kumkum. *The Politics of the Possible: Essays on Gender, History, Narratives, Colonial English.* New Delhi: Tulika, 1999.

Sarkar, Sumit. *Beyond Nationalist Frames: Postmodernism, Hindu Fundamentalism, History.* Bloomington: Indiana University Press, 2002.

———. *The Swadeshi Movement in Bengal: 1903–1908*. New Delhi: People's Publishing House, 1973.

———. *Writing Social History*. Delhi: Oxford University Press, 1997.

Sarkar, Tanika. *Hindu Wife, Hindu Nation*. New Delhi: Permanent Black, 2001.

Sarti, Raffaella. "Conclusion: Domestic Service and European Identity." In *The Socioeconomic Role of Domestic Service as a Factor of European Identity*, edited by S. Pasleau, R. Sarti, and I. Schopp. Final Report of the servantproject.com, 2005. http://www.uniurb.it/scipol/drs_servant_project_conclusion.pdf.

———. "Introduction to Forum: Domestic Service since 1750." *Gender and History* 18, no. 2 (2006): 187–96.

Sassen, Saskia, ed. *Global Networks, Linked Cities*. New York: Routledge, 2002.

Sayer, Andrew. *The Moral Significance of Class*. Cambridge: Cambridge University Press, 2005.

Sekhon, Aradhika. "A Time-Tested Trustworthy Bond." *The Tribune*, August 3, 2001.

Sen, Indrani. "Are You Being Served? Everyone Is Family in This Indian Home Kitchen." *Saveur* 95 (September 2006): 39–41.

Sen, Mrinal. *The Absence Trilogy*. Calcutta: Seagull Books, 1999.

Sen, Samita. *Women and Labour in Late Colonial India: The Bengal Jute Industry*. Cambridge: Cambridge University Press, 1999.

Sennett, Richard, and Jonathan Cobb. *The Hidden Injuries of Class*. New York: Vintage, 1972.

"Servant Held for Murder." *The Telegraph* (Kolkata), August 17, 2004.

"Servant Trapped with Widow's Wealth." *The Telegraph* (Kolkata), December 7, 2005.

Shah, Saubhagya. "Service or Servitude? The Domestication of Household Labour in Nepal." In *Home and Hegemony: Domestic Service and Identity Politics in South and Southeast Asia*, edited by Sara Dickey and Kathleen M. Adams, 87–118. Ann Arbor: University of Michigan Press, 2000.

Sharma, Kalpana. "The Invisible Labour." *The Hindu*, June 11, 2004.

Sherman, Rachel. *Class Acts: Service and Inequality in Luxury Hotels*. Berkeley: University of California Press, 2007.

Silverblatt, Irene. "Interpreting Women in States: New Feminist Ethnohistories." In *Gender at the Crossroads of Knowledge: Feminist Anthropology in the Postmodern Era*, edited by Micaela di Leonardi. Berkeley: University of California Press, 1991.

Sinha, Mrinalini. *Colonial Masculinity: The "Manly Englishman" and the "Effeminate Bengali" in the Late Nineteenth Century*. New York: Manchester University Press, 1995.

Sinha, Pradeep. *Calcutta in Urban History*. Calcutta: Firma KLM, 1978.

Sridharan, E. "The Growth and Sectoral Composition of India's Middle Class: Its Impact on the Politics of Economic Liberalization." *India Review* 3, no. 4 (October 2004): 405–28.

Srivastava, Sanjay. *Constructing Post-colonial India: National Character and the Doon School.* London: Routledge, 1998.

Standing, Hilary. *Dependence and Autonomy: Women's Employment and the Family in Calcutta.* London: Routledge, 1991.

Steedman, Carolyn. "The Servant's Labour: The Business of Life, England, 1760–1820." *Social History* 29, no. 1 (February 2004): 1–29.

Steel, Flora A., and G. Gardiner. *The Complete Indian Housekeeper and Cook.* 7th ed. London: William Heinemann, 1909.

Stern, Steve. *The Secret History of Gender: Women, Men, and Power in Late Colonial Mexico.* Chapel Hill: University of North Carolina Press, 1995.

Stigler, George Joseph. *Domestic Servants in the United States, 1900–1940.* New York: National Bureau of Economic Research, 1946.

Stoler, Ann. *Carnal Knowledge and Imperial Power: Race and the Intimate in Colonial Life.* Berkeley: University of California Press, 2002.

Taylor, Charles. *Modern Social Imaginaries.* Durham, N.C.: Duke University Press, 2004.

Tellis-Nayak, V. "Power and Solidarity: Clientage in Domestic Service." *Current Anthropology* 24 (February 1983): 67–79.

Thompson, E. P. "Time, Work-Discipline, and Industrial Capitalism." *Past and Present* 38 (1967): 56–97.

———. *Whigs and Hunters: The Origin of the Black Act.* Harmondsworth, U.K.: Penguin, 1990.

Thorne, Barrie, and Marilyn Yalom, eds. *Rethinking the Family: Some Feminist Questions.* Boston: Northeastern University Press, 1992.

Tilly, Louise, and Joan W. Scott. *Women, Work, and Family.* New York: Holt, Rinehart and Winston, 1978.

Todi, Rahul. "Up, and Rising." *Times of India* (Kolkata), Special Supplement: "Kolkata Rising," January 18, 2006.

Tolen, Rachel. "Transfers of Knowledge and Privileged Spheres of Practice: Servants and Employers in a Madras Railway Colony." In *Home and Hegemony: Domestic Service and Identity Politics in South and Southeast Asia,* edited by Kathleen Adams and Sara Dickey, 63–86. Ann Arbor: University of Michigan Press, 2000.

Tomic, Patricia, Ricardo Trumper, and Rodrigo Hidalgo Dattwyler. "Manufacturing Modernity: Cleaning, Dirt, and Neoliberalism in Chile." *Antipode* 38, no. 3 (June 2006): 508–29.

Toutant, Pamela. "Generations of Servitude." www.salon.com. April 3, 2000. http://archive.salon.com/mwt/feature/2000/04/03/help_wanted/index.html.

Tronto, Joan C. "The 'Nanny' Question in Feminism." *Hypatia* 17, no. 2 (Spring 2002): 34–51.

Uberoi, Patricia. "Introduction: Is Domestic Service a Feminist Issue?" In *Gender and the Political Economy of Domestic Service: Comparative Perspectives from India and*

China, edited by Patricia Uberoi and Sreemati Chakrabarti, 1–29. Occasional Studies No. 2. New Delhi: Institute of Chinese Studies, 2004.

Uberoi, Patricia, and Sreemati Chakrabarti, eds. *Gender and the Political Economy of Domestic Service: Comparative Perspectives from India and China.* Occasional Studies No. 2. New Delhi: Institute of Chinese Studies, 2004.

United States Census Bureau. *Current Population Survey 1990.* Washington, D.C. http://censtats.census.gov/eeo/eeo.shtml.

———. *Current Population Survey March 2000.* Special Populations Branch, Population Division. Washington, D.C., March 2001. http://www.census.gov/population/socdemo/gender/ppl-121/tab12.txt.

———. *The Relationship between the 1990 Census and Census 2000 Industry and Occupation Classification Systems.* Technical Paper #65, prepared by Thomas S. Scopp. Washington, D.C.: U.S. Census Bureau, 2003.

Uttal, Lynet. *Making Care Work: Employed Mothers in the New Childcare Market.* Piscataway, N.J.: Rutgers University Press, 2002.

Vachani, Nilita. *When Mother Comes Home for Christmas.* DVD. 16mm documentary, 109 min. ZDF, the Greek Film Centre and FilmSixteen, 1996.

Veblen, Thorstein. *The Theory of the Leisure Class: An Economic Study of Institutions.* 1899. Reprint, New York: Random House, 1934.

Walsh, Judith. *Domesticity in Colonial India: What Women Learned When Men Gave Them Advice.* Lanham, Md.: Rowman & Littlefield, 2004.

———. *How to Be the Goddess of Your Home: An Anthology of Bengali Domestic Manuals.* New Delhi: Yoda Press, 1995.

Weix, G. G. "Inside the Home and Outside the Family: The Domestic Estrangement of Javanese Servants." In *Home and Hegemony: Domestic Service and Identity Politics in South and Southeast Asia,* edited by Kathleen Adams and Sara Dickey, 137–56. Ann Arbor: University of Michigan Press, 2000.

Williams, Raymond. "Base and Superstructure in Marxist Cultural Theory." *New Left Review* 82 (1973): 3–16.

———. *Marxism and Literature.* Oxford: Oxford University Press, 1977.

———. *Politics and Letters: Interviews with "New Left Review."* London: Verso, 1979.

Willis, Paul. *Learning to Labor: How Working Class Kids Get Working Class Jobs.* New York: Columbia University Press, 1977.

"Women's Work." *New York Times* editorial, June 8, 2008.

World Resources Institute, United Nations Environment Programme, United Nations Development Programme, and the World Bank. *World Resources 1996–97: The Urban Environment Guide to the Global Environment.* Washington, D.C.: World Resources Institute, 1996.

Wrigley, Julia. *Other People's Children.* New York: Basic Books, 1995.

"Yoga Can Cure AIDS: Ramdev." *The Times of India,* December 20, 2006.

Young, Grace Esther. "The Myth of Being 'Like a Daughter.'" *Latin American Perspectives* 14, no. 3 (Summer 1987): 365–80.

Young, Kate, ed. *Women and Economic Development: Local, Regional, and National Planning Strategies.* New York: Berg/UNESCO, 1988.

Zelizer, Viviana. *The Purchase of Intimacy.* Princeton: Princeton University Press, 2005.

Zimmerman, Mary K., Jacquelyn S. Litt, and Christine E. Bose, eds. *Global Dimensions of Gender and Carework.* Stanford, Calif.: Stanford University Press, 2006.

Index

Note: Italic page numbers indicate figures, maps, or tables.